Fibrils

The Rules of the Game, Volume 3

MICHEL LEIRIS

TRANSLATED FROM THE FRENCH BY LYDIA DAVIS

YALE UNIVERSITY PRESS ■ NEW HAVEN & LONDON

A MARGELLOS
WORLD REPUBLIC OF LETTERS BOOK

The Margellos World Republic of Letters is dedicated to making literary works from around the globe available in English through translation. It brings to the English-speaking world the work of leading poets, novelists, essayists, philosophers, and playwrights from Europe, Latin America, Africa, Asia, and the Middle East to stimulate international discourse and creative exchange.

English translation copyright © 2017 by Lydia Davis.

Originally published in French as *La Règle du jeu III: Fibrilles,* copyright © Editions GALLIMARD, Paris, 1966.

All rights reserved. This book may not be reproduced, in whole or in part, including illustrations, in any form (beyond that copying permitted by Sections 107 and 108 of the U.S. Copyright Law and except by reviewers for the public press), without written permission from the publishers.

Yale University Press books may be purchased in quantity for educational, business, or promotional use. For information, please e-mail sales.press@yale.edu (U.S. office) or sales@yaleup.co.uk (U.K. office).

Set in Electra and Nobel type by Tseng Information Systems, Inc. Printed in the United States of America.

Library of Congress Control Number: 2016944312
ISBN 978-0-300-21239-6 (hardcover : alk. paper)

A catalogue record for this book is available from the British Library.

This paper meets the requirements of ANSI/NISO Z39.48-1992 (Permanence of Paper).

10 9 8 7 6 5 4 3 2 1

CONTENTS

Translator's Note   vii

La Fière, la fière . . .

I   1
II   83
III   155
IV   213

TRANSLATOR'S NOTE

1.

In his massive, four-volume autobiographical project, *La Règle du jeu* (*The Rules of the Game*), Michel Leiris anticipated certain works very much of the moment in our twenty-first century: this is a writer's multivolume, ruthlessly honest examination of himself that admits into its arena the banal and quotidian as well as the dramatic and rare. But beyond the fact that Leiris's work was begun some seventy-five years ago, there are a couple of other important critical considerations: Leiris, by the time he began *La Règle*, had rejected fiction and embraced realism—he called what he was doing not a "novel" but an "autobiographical essay." And second, the project extended over thirty-five years—begun when he was barely forty and completed when he was in his seventies—so that it had the scope and endurance to contain his reflections and objectives as they changed over time: we are fully brought into his mind, and we accompany his thinking as it matures.

As he was writing volume one, Leiris evidently foresaw a second volume, but not more. Similarly, in *Fibrilles* (*Fibrils*), the third volume, published in 1966, he appears, from the tone of his conclusion, not to have anticipated volume four. But after that one, was the work finished? Not quite, since the fourth was followed by separate but related work in 1981. *Le Ruban au cou d'Olympia* (*The Ribbon around Olympia's Neck*)—which takes its title, and one of its recurring subjects, from Manet's painting of a recumbent prostitute clothed only in a black ribbon—centers upon the expressive power of fetishism in a broader, not merely erotic, sense. (It includes, for example, a brief text on the act of writing as hurling a lasso, and another about the urgent desire to smoke when one is already smoking.)

In addition, extending the scope of the project backward in time, the four volumes of *La Règle* were in fact preceded not by a trial run but by a first exploration by Leiris into the territory of himself, this one concentrating specifically on his sexuality: *L'Age d'homme* (1939). Published in English, in Richard Howard's translation, as *Manhood* in 1968, it depicts the full range of sexual obsessions of a man—or this man, in any case—as he grows into manhood: daydream, masturbation, impotence, celibacy, homosexuality, prostitution, marriage.

2.

Michel Leiris was born in 1901, within a comfortable bourgeois family in Paris. He was educated at the Lycée Janson de Sailly (in philosophy), the Sorbonne, and the Ecole pratique des hautes études. After a tentative sortie into the study of chemistry, he cast his lot with the world of writing and art, with the ambition of becoming a poet, as he describes in the present volume. When he was not yet twenty, he met Max Jacob and through him became involved in a circle of Dadaists and Surrealists, identifying himself as a Surrealist until he broke with the group in 1929. A somewhat emotional decision in 1931 to take part, as secretary-archivist, in a two-year ethnographic expedition across sub-Saharan Africa led, after extensive further coursework, to a career as professional ethnographer. He continued that career, occupying a post at one division of Paris's natural history museum, the Musée de l'Homme, until late in his working life, pairing it with his equally full career as writer.

Throughout his long life, prolific and productive until close to his death at age eighty-nine, Leiris wrote a variety of works in different genres: essays on jazz, the theater, literature, and art; volumes of poetry and poetic prose; the vast, rich journal that resulted from his African expedition, *L'Afrique fantôme* (*Phantom Africa*); an eccentric dictionary of personal definitions evolving from wordplay and private associations called *Glossaire: J'y serre mes gloses*; the surrealist novel *Aurora*; a collection of his dreams and his dreamlike waking experiences, *Nuits sans nuit et quelques jours sans jour* (translated by Richard Sieburth into English under the title *Nights as Day, Days as Night*); essays and book-length studies in the field of ethnography; prefaces and catalogue texts, book reviews, political texts; and most regularly appreciations of artists and writers, particularly within the wide circle of those he knew personally—among them André Masson, Miró, Raymond Roussel, Francis Bacon, Raymond Queneau, Picasso, Michel Butor, Sartre, Duchamp, Giacometti.

It was in the midst of this other writing activity, in the early 1940s, that Leiris embarked upon what was to be his masterwork, the work on which his enduring literary reputation would rest: the autobiographical essay—as he later described it—called *The Rules of the Game*. Most of the first volume was written during the German occupation of France; the final volume was completed in 1975. He was henceforth to divide his life among his continuing autobiographical project; his multifarious other writing; his editorial activities; his political activities; his family and friendships; his travels; and his ethnographic work.

3.

With *Biffures* (*Scratches*), volume one of *La Règle*, Leiris began his extended project, the objectives of which fully emerge only over the successive volumes—to write in order to see more clearly into himself, to work out his personal identity, at the same time to unite the two tendencies in himself between which he felt divided: on the one hand, poetry, the attraction to the *over-there*, to myth, to timelessness; and on the other, morality, knowledge, the *right-here*, lived reality; and to formulate a definitive "golden rule," the rule that, he hoped, would both govern his *ars poetica*—his poetics—and be a rule for living, a *savoir-vivre*, an ethics, the code by which he would live.

He opens the book with one of his continuing central preoccupations, language in all its aspects: language as the raw material of poetry; the mysteries of language; the sounds of words, taken in themselves; the elusive and personal meanings of these sounds and of words themselves; private language versus shared language; language as connection to others; the discoveries possible through language; the failure of language. Cataloguing, or inventorying, his memories from various periods of his life, but especially from his childhood, he begins the book with the mystery he found in language when he was a child, in his misunderstandings of names, songs, scraps of speech—misunderstandings that created for him an alternate universe of things, people, customs, emotions. In this volume, he comes to define the literary use of speech as a way of sharpening one's consciousness "in order to be more—and in a better way—alive." The relationship, then, is reciprocal: the writer lives in order to write, but also writes in order to be more fully alive.

The next volume, *Fourbis* (*Scraps*), continues the inventory, though its preoccupations have inevitably shifted a little with the passing years. Its main themes and subjects of inquiry, as described by Leiris, are now "to trim the claws of death, to behave like a man, to break one's own walls"—in other words, to tame death, to take action, to break through the circle of the self. This volume begins to reflect the attraction exerted on him by external, historical events, including political activism. It also tells of his continuing preoccupation with the erotic, specifically detailing the story of his liaison with an Algerian prostitute, Khadidja, when he was a soldier stationed near Beni-Ounif during World War II, describing what he saw as her moral as well as physical beauty. In this volume, as in the first, he brings to his method of composition his training as ethnographer, working from slips of paper on which he had previously made notations—of facts, memories, ideas—which he then takes as starting points for his explorations.

In the third and present volume, *Fibrilles* (*Fibrils*), though Leiris worries that his objective itself has shifted over the years, the problem becomes clearer: how to reconcile literary commitment and social commitment. Here he looks in particular to the example of his close friend the poet Aimé Césaire, who combines both without compromising either. Having opened the book with an account of his participation in a delegation to China, his attraction to that country, and his hopes for its future, Leiris continues with an exploration, again, of contrasts: his perception of China (representing morality, constraint, reason) as one of two poles between which he is divided, the other represented by the large market town of Kumasi, in Ashanti country (symbolizing sentiment, dilection, imagination), and the thronged Easter service Leiris attended there in its (ugly, he calls it) cathedral. The heart of *Fibrils*, however, the story that dominates this volume, is that of an emotional dilemma and its consequences: his division of loyalties between the woman with whom he has been having an affair, and his wife, called only "Z." He describes his impossible situation—being frank and honorable with either woman would betray the other—and his resultant suicide attempt, as well as its aftermath and the ramifications of both. The associative explorations in this book delve deep into several significant dreams, including some he had while half-awake in his hospital room in the days following his suicide attempt, but his discussion of these dreams always circles out to include other narratives from his past, accounts of travels, or of friendships. (Leiris's preoccupation with his erotic life and, more broadly, love, as well as his suicidal tendencies and his avowed cowardice in the face of his own "annihilation," began early, showing up, for instance, in *L'Afrique fantôme*, when he was barely thirty and already married to Louise "Zette" Godon.)

We realize, in the course of this volume, that the subject here is not only Leiris himself, and his actions, feelings, and thoughts, but also Leiris in the act of writing, and the writing of this essay itself. He talks about this book in the act of writing it. He describes the slips of paper, he quotes from them, allowing each to lead by association to more "data" for his explorations. He hopes to establish between them connecting threads, the "fibrils" of the title. In this volume, he fears that he will nearly die of the effort it costs him, even before fate finishes him off. Whereas he had hoped by writing to escape time, he is nevertheless subject to time—the past of his life, his present life in the changing world, and the time of the writing itself. Perhaps, he also realizes, the rules he seeks will be directives implied by the game itself. Perhaps he should settle for a "professional morality" as opposed to a more universal Morality.

In the last volume, *Frêle Bruit*, more ample, at four hundred pages, than the previous, Leiris again defines the purpose of the whole of *The Rules of the Game* as to "expose as thoroughly as possible the sample of humanity that he is." He describes this volume not as a logical or chronological sequel to the other volumes, but as a peninsula or constellation; it is not a rational construction, but a "florilegium" drawn from all periods of his life. The form of the final book, therefore, is unlike that of the other volumes of The Rules: whereas they are continuous, with only a few breaks into separate parts, the last volume includes many very brief sections, some less than a page, as though Leiris were bringing his last, disconnected thoughts together into one place. It contains, for instance, stories, chants, curses, poems, meditations, lists of titles, scraps of memory, and bits of his journal. But there could be no "last thoughts"; the ongoing autobiographical project, which included several more shorter works even after Le Ruban au cou d'Olympia, would not be so much ended as finally interrupted by death. And after his death, his vast, self-reflective and self-critical journal was published, at his instruction—more than eight hundred pages.

In the pages of Frêle Bruit, Leiris is all the more acutely conscious of the passage of time, even more relentlessly haunted than in the other volumes by the fear of his own death; because by now, as he concludes the book, he is, in fact, in his mid-seventies—an old man. But he has also managed, over the course of the four volumes, to clarify certain things for himself: he has recognized in himself, he says in this volume, a need "to merge the *yes* and the *no*," a need that sometimes seems to denote "a perverse inclination to find enjoyment only in ambiguity and paradox . . . sometimes . . . sanctified by the idea that a marriage of contraries is the highest summit one can metaphysically attain."

4.

Both Manhood and The Rules of the Game were preoccupied with the horror of the author's own mortality, the specter of his own death. It is possible to imagine Leiris, even more than most chroniclers of their own lives, as wanting to complete the work that can never be completed, by writing about his death. But as the writer can't find a vantage point from which to look upon his death except one that precedes it in time, it seems that Leiris's whole endeavor, in this work, was somehow to get around that difficulty, somehow to comprehend, embrace death beforehand in such a way as to have documented as completely as possible what he might also have liked to document as it was happening or after it had happened. The voice that said this, so lucidly and so frankly, has been silenced by Leiris's actual death in 1990, and in a way that is not yet clear, this changes the voice one hears in the pages of his work. This voice both does and does not come to us from beyond the grave.

On the other hand, it is also possible that Leiris wished to write in precisely the situation in which he did write: documenting his life in the shadow of his death. For a kind of completeness is certainly achieved here in *The Rules of the Game* through the avoidance of closure, changing the terms of the work so that the motion is infinite insight inward, infinitely continuing investigation. No event is "closed," no thought, no datum. Progress is inward, and circular, rather than forward, involving the close examination of all sides of things: not only people and events but motives, effects, interpretations, and the nuances thereof. And digression, as well as expansion outward, is a natural part of this close examination.

Amplification away from the main narrative track throws light on what is being described, fills in the picture, at least, of how Leiris himself reacted to what went on. Amplification can be infinite, of course, and even infinitely justified. It not only illuminates but also works dramatically to suspend the action, to delay satisfaction. It gives the event, which may be quite banal in itself, an added richness and depth; it may extend its meaning from personal to public. Amplification strays from the point but it also particularizes and nuances the subject.

In fact, Leiris's close attention to documenting the ordinary elevates it into something so particular that it becomes strange. As he came to distrust the exotic, he found otherness in the familiar, foreignness in the domestic.

Although his main subject is himself writing these works, part of the activity of his exploration is to bring the world into the discussion: it is through oneself that one gains knowledge of the "other" and of the world. His examination of himself is not exclusive but inclusive. He does not reject politics, history, or culture as part of his own self-portrait. Throughout his life, he was fully involved, literarily and politically, in the world outside himself—particularly with his fellow artists and as an activist against the "flagrant" injustices of society and "our Western arrogance," as he put it—and he includes his political activities and his friendships in his account of himself, as well as the non-Western cultures he studies as an ethnographer.

What is our sense of the narrator himself? It is curiously paradoxical: his constant elaboration and qualification, his ruthless honesty, his stated doubts express or imply a certain modesty, self-recrimination, apology—yet at the same time he effectively and relentlessly commands our steady attention by involving us in his thoughts as they unfold. The play of opposites is in effect here, too, as it is throughout *The Rules of the Game* and in Leiris's work in general: the pendulum swings between reticence and self-display, private and public, inside and outside, self and other.

5.

Leiris is rarely brief, rarely plain, in *Fibrils*, since every thought seems to produce a possible counterthought that should be included. One problem for the translator is, of course, that Leiris's amplifications and qualifications enter into the structure of the sentence itself. Extended pyramidal constructions are common; the work is an accumulation of syntactical architectures, sometimes very long and complex. For the translator, then, one constant exercise of wits involves syntactic acrobatics: most specifically, or most often, to be sure a given phrase or clause ends with the key word from which the next clause must hang.

Leiris's attempt at extreme precision, as he tracks his thoughts and his reactions to events, can produce a heavy weight of material within one sentence, paragraph, or sequence of pages, and an impression almost of excess. The sentences are most often graceful, but they can be close to unwieldy, given their burdens of qualifying subordinate clauses. With a certain pleasure in the challenge, however, I have reproduced them as closely as I could, avoiding any simplification and retaining Leiris's formality both in structure and word choice. I have rarely changed the order in which information was presented—only *in extremis*, when I could not otherwise make the sentence hang together—because that order reflects the order in which Leiris's thought unfolds. I have also respected his punctuation as far as the difference between the languages permits; he took great care with it. The reader may want to read some sentences more than once in order to gather up all their meaning.

Wordplay was an essential part of Leiris's relationship to language. His punning and associative pairing are never arbitrary, but constitute so many knots where some of the multiple threads of Leiris's remembrances and ideas come together. His was a life lived in the French language, so even a translation of his work into English must retain some of his French, must be tied back to the original text with these same knots. For this reason, I have occasionally included the French word that Leiris is discussing, alongside its English equivalent, or have inserted a few words of explanation in brackets. I have also italicized, when it seemed necessary, a word or phrase that Leiris wrote originally in English.

6.

Leiris maintained a separation between his work as writer and his work as ethnographer. He constructed his days themselves as alternations between work at home, as writer (in the mornings), and work at his office, as ethnographer (in the afternoons), the two spaces "stirring up different ideas," as he said: he was rarely an ethnologist when at home and rarely a writer when at the museum.

The two spaces were connected, physically, by the familiar, daily reiterated path of the number 63 bus.

It was in this office, a small room below ground level at the Musée de l'Homme, that I met Leiris for the only time, on a day probably in the mid-1980s that I can no longer pinpoint. To judge only from appearances, his preoccupation with the erotic, his periodic love affairs at home in Paris, and, even more, his liaison with the Algerian Khadidja, would seem quite incongruous for this cloistered scholar, this awkward, reserved man, in tailored clothing so correct and elegant, with his skin so pale, bony skull so naked, expression so tense and haunted, eyes so fearful: this was how he appeared to me that day. The museum, next to the Trocadéro Gardens and across the Pont d'Iéna from the Eiffel Tower, was surrounded by tourists milling about in the morning sun and by African vendors flying uncannily lifelike mechanical birds. Leiris's voice trembled when he greeted me outside the elevator in the basement corridor. He was shy, as I had been warned, and he fell into silence often. He was deaf in one ear—forewarned of this, too, I probably spoke too loudly. The single window, above some radiator pipes, was now and then filled with the faces of curious tourists shading their eyes to see in. They would have seen a woman sitting nervously erect on her chair across from a thin old man, his bald head slightly bowed.

Khadidja herself had at first mistaken him for a monk. But the opposition between external appearance (tailored, spotless, sumptuous) and internal being (emotionally chaotic, uncertain, vulnerable) is inherent to Leiris's central preoccupation, well explored in *Fibrils*, and this apparent contradiction is a part of Leiris's more general complexity, a complexity he was at such pains to try to understand and demonstrate in *The Rules of the Game*.

Leiris wrote me a postcard early in the final year of his life, nearly three decades ago (on this, there is a date), signed in shaky, spidery black script. In it, he offered, most graciously, and with a typical qualification, typically inserted with syntactical elegance into the sentence—*dans la mesure du possible*, "insofar as possible"—to give me whatever assistance I might need with my translation of his work. I was then completing a translation of his collected occasional writings, *Brisées: Broken Branches* (which includes, among other colorful and beguiling offerings, a brief piece on metaphor, one on human saliva, and a decoding of the captivating, to him, Fred Astaire). I never asked him for help, in the end, but there are a few points in *Fibrils* I would not mind checking with him, now that it is too late. But it is too late.

Fibrils

La Fière, la fière . . .

I

November 1955.
I am back from another trip whose theater, this time, was the Far East, behind what the bourgeoisifying newspapers of our countries still call the "iron curtain." Of all the trips I have taken, this is certainly the one that has made me the happiest. But if it pleased me so, why is this also the one that, now that I am back, has probably left me the most confounded?

Five weeks of roaming around in China, which, because of its antiquity as much as its vast size, is for us a sort of older sister. Five weeks of contact with people who at full gallop are carrying out a project of taming the forces of nature and rationalizing society which I would call *promethean* if that reference to one of the central themes of our mythology did not summon up, even more than the heroic image of the acquisition of fire, that of a defeat penalized by an endless torture. Five weeks of close conversation with communism as it transforms Asia, and of such euphoria that I was led to think that, had I been younger and in sole charge of what I did, I would conceivably have tried to settle in the People's Republic of China, which had invited me, along with numerous other delegates from the East and the West, to judge both the extent of its effort and the reality of the progress it had made.

Well, now that those five weeks have passed, and a few more have elapsed since my return, I am still convinced that in just a few years China will be the foremost—instead of merely the oldest—of all the great nations; but I notice that after thinking I was almost on the threshold of a new life (and not having refrained, by any means, from telling my hosts this in the form of toasts, each of which I would have wished to be, without its seeming to be anything much, a perfect work of art, in the manner of a Chinese poem) I find myself once again perceptibly at the point where I was earlier; and that, my trip becoming more questionable as it recedes in time and increases the already considerable separation it derived from mere distance, a brief period (during which I have breathed the air of Paris while my lungs were still quite impregnated with that of Peking) has sufficed for its charm to be broken. How could something that had appeared to me rock-solid be capable of disintegrating so quickly? How can those five weeks of plenitude, after the short vacillation I mentioned, have so emptied

1

themselves of their substance that I would be inclined to wonder whether I had not dreamed them? I will drop everything else and examine this question, even if the plan I had drawn up, for organizing how I would approach my "rules of the game," is disrupted by this or even if—with regard to other questions raised unexpectedly—this plan appears to me to embrace only an ineffectual mass of trifles, so that I would have to admit I was constrained to recast it if not to abandon it, though I would lose face. For it is quite possible that in tackling this problem I am directly (or almost) touching the crux of my research and that I would thus see proof (which would cut short all literature) of the uselessness of continuing on a path that I had perhaps conceived to be so long, and burdened with so many ramifications, only out of perversity, coquetry, or reticence toward myself, if not out of an artistic concern for a sort of symphonic composition.

Without lingering too much over all my "pre-China" before coming to China itself, and without yielding more than halfway to this mania I still have for tackling obliquely—most often after many detours—a question I consider important, I will confide here some chinoiseries drawn from my recent or distant past and almost all noted down (as though the enunciation of what I have to say demanded this preamble) when the trip to China was already behind me, while before me was a new stage of the nonlocalized trip I am taking with my work table as flying carpet.

Seizing first a compact and well-balanced object, I will describe a trinket that is scarcely old at all and not of much calculable value, but which I would rather have received than any other of the family relics that may be passed down to me: a ceramic depicting a recumbent fighter, on a pedestal-bed whose color I have not forgotten, of a dull green tinged with brown, with white and black for the figure, as well as with a purplish-blue tone, one of those Chinese tones (vermilion, currant, indigo, turquoise, olive) which are enticing because of their tiny discrepancy in relation to the apparently purer tones we are used to. At the time of his trip around the world, during which he paid serious attention only to the panorama that was unfolding inside himself, Raymond Roussel, a very marginal representative of our intellectual mandarins, brought this souvenir back from Peking to give to my mother, and for a long time I saw it in her home, placed on a console or some other small piece of furniture, before it disappeared when the Germans occupied the house she lived in for a time at Meudon during the last war. Very slightly concave, the four sides of the pedestal-bed, from which moldings jutted out, were similar to the roofs curved in at their corners which, it seems, are the features of Chinese buildings that the eye seizes most immediately. But more than its typical form or its place of origin, what attached me to this object was the personality of the man who had given it, whom I had admired once I was grown up after having known him when I was a small child: the author of the bizarre and extravagant *Impressions of Africa*, the man who was referred to in my home by the name of "Ramuntcho" (a name lifted by him from Loti, whose stories, with their exotic settings, he much admired), the misunderstood soul who was to end his life tragically in a grand hotel in Palermo, a life that was one of the best endowed by the fairies, but also one of the unhappiest because he could not resign himself to being famous only in his own eyes, the richest of men, elegant and of a princely affability, who for years came almost every week to play music at the house. Accompanying himself at the piano and making marvelous use of a thin voice, he would sometimes sing *Le Roi des Aulnes*, sometimes fragments from operas (the death of Isolde, for instance, or some tune from the *Tales of Hoffmann*) which he would couple, in his programs, with *Tout autour de la tour Saint-Jacques* or some other sentimental romance, along with folk songs arranged by Jaques-Dalcroze like *Sur la route de Nyon* or:

*Les fillettes d'Estavayer
Beau château feuillé, beau château feuillé . . .*

Little girls from Estavayer
Lovely castle in the trees, lovely castle in the trees . . .

one of the ones I liked best, quoted here only approximately, since it lies far back in the time that I have passed by.

A knickknack or rather a toy—of almost no value, since its price could not have exceeded a fraction of a dollar—was the jointed wooden snake I brought back from New York as I was returning from my first trip to the Antilles. I had bought it in a small shop in Chinatown, from a friendly shopkeeper whose very glossy black hair, straw-colored complexion, mongoloid eyes, and perhaps the exquisiteness of her apparently unaffected smile proclaimed her to be the rather particular American she was. I had just dined Chinese-style with a French friend and two New York friends, a man and a woman: he, a sort of sylph, small and round as a tobacco pot and a real Kleinzach-like drinker, but one whose batrachian face was illuminated by the softest eyes, of the most richly layered depths, that one could imagine (as though he were already experiencing his end, which was premature); she, much taller, whose image has remained with me as that of a beautiful Valkyrie without armor, and, of course, uncorseted, who would walk next to you holding your hand in order to protect you from all danger. During the party that had followed the dinner (a party given for me by that European New York–transplant who is now no more than a handful of ashes in a northern Italian cemetery, and who left all his companions the memory of a most intelligently zealous friend and a man with the most refined taste behind his dissipated appearance) we had indulged in—as the jargon of the writers of newspaper fillers would put it—abundant libations, and it was perhaps for that reason that we soon managed to break the thin and supple thread on which were strung the pieces of painted wood representing the rings of the snake, which I had to take back to Paris hastily repaired but henceforth forever lacking the almost disquieting mobility it had originally had. I was sorry I could not have preserved intact that fragile souvenir of the thirty-six hours I spent in New York in 1948, a visit that I would have liked to extend but that a mistrustful decision of the San Juan immigration office in Puerto Rico (where I had gotten off the airplane with a communist from Martinique reencountered at the embarkation by pure chance) reduced to proportions I have always deplored because of the extraordinary beauty of the Atlantic city, less stifled in its stony heights than one might believe.

Either a knickknack or a toy (but this time in the figurative sense, for it has no materiality beyond the piece of paper on which I described it the day after its intrusion into my sleep), here is a dream I had in May last year, when I did not yet know that shortly afterward I would be going to China: I am being received by the philosopher Confucius, a sort of glabrous old Anglo-Saxon, precious and pederastic, who has apparently dressed up as a mandarin with glasses and a long robe for some masked ball; as is suitable with Confucius, the interview—which takes place in a disused drawing room with a vaguely oriental decor—is all about courtesy. I had this dream in Cannes, where my wife and I had gone to spend a few days with Picasso, whose new house (a large villa with exaggerated moldings) we did not yet know. In the afternoon I had had, with him, who, as far as I knew, had not drawn any Chinese figures but that of one of the tumblers in the ballet *Parade*, and who, in his *Massacres in Korea*, had painted only the massacre without for a moment thinking about local color, a rambling conversation touching on very diverse subjects none of which, however, I'm quite sure, had any direct relation to Asia. Still, we talked for a good while about the drugs (opium, hashish) which he had on occasion used in his youth at gatherings of artists and poets. We had had lunch in a very southern manner in a restaurant in Antibes, where our little group included notably Paulo—the painter's son—with his two children; in the course of the lunch, Paulo's little boy had given the ceremonious appellation of "Monsieur Yan" to Picasso's boxer, whose name *Yan* one might easily think was chosen for its Asiatic sound whereas it is actually a Breton name, dictated, quite simply, to those who decided upon it by the obligatory protocol concerning pedigreed dogs. A canine treated like a respectable Chinese gentleman (which, after all, suited his old gentleman's face with its wrinkled forehead and chops), remarks about maunderings due to opium and hashish, the overloaded masonry, and the comically elaborate windows, are obviously not unrelated to the dream I had that night, an anecdote fabricated from the immediate past and not a confused premonition having to do with the trip that would soon be proposed to me by the Association des Amitiés Franco-Chinoises.

Connected to an event that will be outstanding in the history of our theater—the visit which, at the beginning of last summer, the foremost troupe of the Peking Opera made to Paris, where it taught a large audience what immense joy one can derive from a *total* spectacle—is the following scene, at which I was present, during the reception given by the artists of the troupe in the rooms adjoining the Théâtre des Ambassadeurs, for a fashionable Paris crowd mingling all social classes and all intellectual viewpoints. In addition to an endless succession of solid and liquid foods (among them rice wine, a wine the color of dead leaves whose savor is enhanced by its slight bitterness, a beverage related to the Spanish manzanilla with its completely flamenca dryness and one that I would rediscover with pleasure in China, where ordinarily it is served tepid or warm in porcelain cups from teapots), a concert was performed for the guests, and a Chinese singer opened it by singing, and very prettily too, the great aria from *Madame Butterfly*. Several of us experienced a sort of vertigo: a Chinese woman singing for a French audience an aria from an Italian opera set in Japan which associates the American colors with the white flag and its red circle—clearly picturing to oneself such a cascade of multiple layers, it was difficult not to feel one was about to faint! But for our hosts, it was evidently a most normal form of homage by the East to the West.

Speaking of coincidences (which we enjoy seeking out because the encounter of two events whose only connection is analogy or similitude suggests the poetic idea of destiny), I will note that shortly before my departure I was afflicted with a benign but exasperating malady of which I'm afraid I have not yet succeeded in definitively ridding myself: the mycosis commonly called athlete's foot, because it is often caught from walking barefoot on the wet and infected boards of pools, an ailment that in numerous cases (as I have learned to my cost) proves very tenacious and that, widespread in warm and humid regions, is known in southern Asia by the name of Hong Kong foot, as I was told by the dermatologist I consulted. Of course, this Hong Kong foot that I picked up I don't know where (but certainly not in China, nor at a pool) left me completely in peace when I was in the country to which it owes the more picturesque of the names bestowed on it.

Will I go clear back to Ali Baba, abductor of children, that brigand of whom a foxtrot fashionable at the end of the war of 1914, *Chu Chin Chow*, invited us in its refrain to beware, if I am incapable of approaching China—and what I think now that I am back from China—without yet again resorting to one of those anecdotal and personal handholds that allow me not so much to evade an open conflict with the real subject as to explore the ground in some way and not commence that conflict except after making a connection between what has for so long been my customary world and the heretofore rather rebellious thing which I would like to talk about? To seek out, from my years before China, all that could be closely or distantly related to that country—this is what I at first embarked upon, as though by doing so I were finding a way of incorporating it, and as though this sort of greedy thrusting of tentacles were a preliminary stage that I could not avoid. But I understood very soon that by proceeding this way I would scarcely manage to do more than bring together elements that had no real relation to me or to my subject: padding or ornaments, whose effect would be more or less happy, but which would show up my efforts to justify them, however hard I tried to disguise those efforts. I will therefore give it up, and I will not extract from this file, henceforth closed, more than two pieces of information the rejection of which seems to me inopportune, not only because, once they were noted, they acquired for me the value of *facts* (which, after that promotion, it would pain me to discard, as though I were demoting myself) but because by means of them I make my way along two paths that are equally direct, though opposite in direction, into China, instead of first gaining entry, by slipping timidly through some hidden gate, into a backyard of the palace to which I covet access.

Lao Tzu's *Tao Te Ching*, which I read in a French translation when I was twenty-some years old, corresponded for a long time to what was my first requirement with regard to books of philosophy: that the system proposed should be formulated in sibylline maxims, apparently simple and based on our everyday experience, but at the same time curling in on themselves and endowed with strange extensions, as though the laws thus enunciated came from very far away, laden with a truth too ancient and too elementary not to be incontestable, but also with a mystery equal, in this case, to that of the ideograms that served to set it down and, like them, impossible to decipher for anyone not armed with a good dose of patience and sagacity; maxims, then, with the authority of dicta and with a structure perfectly clear and balanced, but concealing as much as they reveal and rich with a content so profound that it cannot be brought to light without a hard effort of decortication. It was at the time of the beginnings of surrealism that I read the *Tao Te Ching*, when, like my companions, I was looking toward Asia as symbol of knowledge plunging back into the night of time, just as Black Africa and Oceania would soon seem to me symbols of a primitiveness also calculated to ruin Western logic, a logic that had succeeded in engendering only coercion and machines. Tibet, with its high-perched monasteries and its living Buddhas, was truly the "roof of the world" (if one means by that the high place par excellence), and I would be, a little later, amazed by the meditation exercises in which, I learned, its ascetics were trained: to dismantle piece by piece and reconstruct in the same way the image of a garden which one has sufficiently observed to see it mentally in all its details, to repeat the operation going more and more quickly but always detail by detail, until this oscillation between luxuriance and the complete absence of terrestrial support brings one to a physical comprehension of emptiness; to stare at a point of light shining in the dark room in which one is enclosed, to transfer oneself mentally into this point, which is now *I* and *I-who-look-at-myself*, to move back and forth many times in succession faster and faster so that at the end of this gymnastics the gulf between subject and object has been abolished. I was thinking very precisely of what the testimony of a European visitor to Lhasa, Mme Alexandra David-Neel, had taught me, certain or tentative, about Tibetan mysticism when I noted, in May 1929, on the subject of the, strictly speaking, Chinese puzzle which is the problem of poetic technique: *To become used to a certain multiplication of consciousness, and to confront one's heart as one ordinarily confronts a tree or a house. I have the impression, in my case, of a kind of revolution taking place in me—a turning movement in which my mind seems to describe a half-circle and thus stands face to face with itself. It is then that words, instead of combining mechanically (parrotlike), take on weight and color: they move even me, and no longer count as words.*

From the bizarre and perverse China of my childhood—the one associated with porcelain pagodas, convicts carrying cane, skulls with long pigtails, and Mirbeau's *The Torture Garden*, a work of which I knew by hearsay a few of the cruelties it contains—I passed, almost without transition, to the metaphysical China in which *yin* and *yang* confront each other and unite, then to the China of war and revolution as it figures in two of the most celebrated novels by my contemporary Malraux. In order to discover a China with a sunnier face, it was necessary for me to round, in my body, the cape of fifty years, hardly very cheering, and for China in turn—as though by an inverse movement—to become, by undertaking the development of its enormous, henceforth divided garden, the habitat of a less unhappy people.

In 1952—during some cold, gray days—I was present at the Peace Congress that brought together in Vienna people of all countries and all colors coming as delegates, guests, or observers; but when, separate from the sessions, a documentary on a meeting of the same sort, held in Peking for Asia and the Pacific, was shown courtesy of the Chinese delegation (which included many men whose heads were crenelated with beautiful fur caps like those the Tartars must have worn at the time of the invasions), it was the exuberance, the good-natured jollity of the whole crowd that one saw in this film, and the tribute it paid to laughter, that amazed me this time.

There were country dances performed by a host of young Chinese women and men; a host of bouquets waved during endless ovations; the sky tumbled by that nondetonating firecracker—the sudden flight of a host of doves; the lengthy handshakes, with a profusion of deliveries of a profusion of gifts: badges, scarves, necklaces of flowers, and sometimes even clothes. There were rounds of applause, almost simultaneously reciprocal in accordance with the ritual prevailing in the countries of the East, for whom (if one trusts in the letter of protocol) the joy shown by a single one of the parties present as he beat his palms together, if it did not immediately provoke a response and thus become the first term of an exchange between equals, could only be taken for a joy that stopped in midcareer. Throughout this film—shot, of course, for purposes of edification, but too unreserved for one to be able to perceive its instructional aspect—there was one long explosion of merriment. Cordiality, laughter, health in hearts and bodies, and even those burlesque interludes that it did not disdain to show in quite a long sequence: the "numbers" that were performed for one another outside the Congress by members of the various delegations during quiet social gatherings. Naturally, a Japanese who, coiffed in a Mexican sombrero, tries his skill at dancing the bolero does not display a very highly inventive humor; but it must be said, after all, that a revolutionary such as Lenin was probably also quite lacking in humor when—according to Trotsky's work on him which, thirty years ago, disclosed to me a few features of Marxist thought at the very moment when a writer of my generation revealed to me a demummified China—he was overcome by a fit of crazy laughter in the presence of the comrades at the end of a heavy work session. The most essential thing, here, is that there should be not a piquant flash of comedy but rather a plunge into comedy, and that as one emerges from serious occupations one step down from one's pedestal in order to relax in the most banal fashion, when necessary, rather than assume the guise of the pedant whose bearing reflects the too superior opinion he has of his person and seems to strain desperately to make one take everything very seriously. For a long time I, in fact, have thought that scarcely anything, of any kind, can be done without at least a touch of buffoonery. It is not immaterial that Mozart qualified his *Don Juan* as a *dramma giocoso* (in other words, a merry tragedy) and that the Romantics had (even if it was sarcastic) their "irony."

That simple style which Lenin, sworn enemy of grandiloquence, practiced like a master, and of which the documentary on the Peace Congress of the peoples of Asia and the Pacific had furnished me an illustration that seemed to demonstrate that Mao Tse-tung's China could—on this point at least—teach us something, was one I came across again and again in the course of the trip I took. Of those men and women whom we chanced to meet because we moved around so much, no one greeted my companions and me otherwise than with a cordial smile: they look at you, and the face in which those two eyes shine as they embrace you in their field of vision, instantly lights up. I admit that a joviality so immediate and unanimous (among the old scarcely less than among the young) may not necessarily be a spontaneous expression, but perhaps rather a matter of politeness; nevertheless, even if there was nothing but convention in those displays of joy provoked (or meant to be provoked) by the arrival of foreign guests, it is still true that one must regard as extremely civilized a country in which an attitude that is good-humored—and not in the least stiff—is in such circumstances required by etiquette. And it seems to me undeniable that a certain basis of true cordiality is, after all, necessary to anyone who plays this game: the actor who, too conscious of his craft, keeps his distance from his role only rarely manages to deceive, if indeed by chance he succeeds at all.

Of the vast fiesta—of almost continental or planetary dimensions—whose image had enchanted me from the very first minutes during that soiree in which it was presented on a screen, reduced to the relative poverty of a succession of black-and-white images, I saw an equivalent from which nothing was lacking, neither color, nor substance, nor any life-affirming qualities, when at Peking, on October 1 last year, I watched for nearly four hours by the clock the procession of the Chinese national festival.

Day after day we had seen the city hang up its lights, framing many a doorway with red and gold (thus dressing them in colors of which one was not sure if they were those of China or those of the Revolution); groups of male and female students, schoolboys and schoolgirls, practiced their dances in all sorts of places, including on the flat roof of our hotel; on the square where the procession would pass, and where people would be dancing that evening, great lengths of canvas (of the same oxblood tone as the walls of the old Imperial Palace and those of the adjoining constructions against which they had been stretched) formed the improvised partitions of street urinals capable of accommodating, together, hundreds of people. In overpopulated Peking, the everyday animation (that pullulation which is not hasty, not rough) was further increased, but on September 30 at midnight everything grew quiet, a part of the city having indeed been neutralized because some of the troops that were to march in the procession were housed there, along with their matériel.

In the morning, at the stroke of ten, the ceremony began with salvos of artillery thundering at will (as though to remind one that China was the original source of gunpowder); thus, the sky, already very mixed up, half cloudy and half sunny, was for a long time made heavier and somehow even lower by the great layers of smoke that hovered close to the ground. A big fat Chinaman placidly inhabiting his imposing frame, Mao Tse-tung, surrounded by other personalities of the regime, stood in the center of his platform, a sort of vast veranda hung with enormous spherical Chinese lanterns, near the top of the old restored edifice that bears the famous name of Tiananmen or Gate of Heavenly Peace.

The first movement—allegro—consisted of a very strict but rather unobtrusive military parade, without any provocative exhibition of warlike machinery and limited (it seemed) to what was indispensable for conveying the fact that one has well-trained soldiers and possesses modern weaponry. Next came—allegretto—the briefer parade of pioneers, little boys and girls in red silk scarves who saluted the Head of State by releasing before him balloons of all shades of color as well as doves (which one soon saw perched on the roof of the building where the officials were standing).

Whether the consequence of an elaborate staging or the happy result of chance, similar to those I would later come upon unexpectedly and which led me to believe that any crowd of Chinese was curiously apt to transform into a bed of flowers or some other work of art—not far from a train station, for example, a group of workers in blues, squatting amid heaps of red peppers, and behind them a drying structure like a house with no façade, its ridges hidden by clusters of peppers hanging in curtains, the whole forming a gay bouquet, with touches of black from crows or jackdaws in flight at the top of the picture—now, with the arrival of a cortège of people, in a confused and arrhythmical flood like a mass demonstration, after the marvelous parade of armed soldiers and the scarcely less orderly parade of children, the avenue was filled, so to speak, to the brim.

Workers, peasants, students pass, following a first wave of men and women representing all the national minorities of the Republic, arm in arm, presenting themselves in such disorder that the diversity of the traditional costumes they are wearing resolves into a single, shimmering medley. As had the young pioneers, the members of each delegation salute by waving or simultaneously raising sheaves of artificial flowers, and this produces sudden spatterings of foam—sometimes pink, sometimes red, sometimes yellow. Male and female workers alike wear the classic cotton outfit of a sort of blouse, but the skirts of the women students, of varying tints and designs, agglomerate into a motley pattern whose trompe l'oeil is continually formed, broken, formed again, and broken again with the stamping of their legs. A quantity of unnecessary flags, of which many are very short and very high, emerge from the cortège, much less standards than scraps of cloth (tender green, candy pink, pale blue, straw yellow) carried on poles for pleasure, as one would play with kites. Through the air move the multicolored constellations created by the balloons constantly being released, some of which, having reached a certain altitude, themselves release a small airplane that glides or a parachute from which is suspended a vertical streamer on which can be read a slogan such as: "Free Taiwan!" On the ground, I watch for a few moments one man among others who is walking on the right flank of the cortège with a child perched on his shoulder, as though—in this upside-down world that communist Asia doubly represents in relation to capitalist Europe—it were natural, for a civilian, to take part in a review with the same casualness as though this were a dull recurrence of Bastille Day. Some hot-air balloons take flight, and I observe with an increase of delight that there are balloons gleaming black as fresh ink among the colored balloons which have little by little composed a scene in perpetual motion and without any link to the ground. There are portraits of great men (Marx, Engels, Lenin, and several others, Soviet and Chinese), maxims composed by series of placards on each of which is inscribed an ideogram, doves of cutout wood carried at the ends of sticks by bonzes with shaved skulls and saffron robes, statistics on panels, simulacra of manufactured objects (machine tools, locomotives, houses), men at work represented in groups that one might think had been cast from life had they not been a little larger than life-size, fruits and vegetables immoderately amplified, a giant goose, a cow in silhouette, and other emblems of worker and peasant production, together forming, in this part of the procession, something reminiscent—though in a style at once larger and more graceful—of what was not very long ago in our country a popular procession like that of the First of May and, also, of that advertising caravan the occasion for which is the sort of circumambulatory ritual constituted by the Tour de France.

 This compact crowd that transported or carried along on its current various heteroclite burdens was succeeded without a hiatus by a group of strange creatures: factitious lions (each one represented by two men enclosed in the same imitation skin) came forward rolling grotesquely on the pavement and confronting individually an equal number of make-believe wild-beast tamers, who kept them at a respectful distance with some type of party-favor bludgeon. This surprising circus entry inaugurated the carnivalesque part of the procession, the part for which folklore groups and theater companies (professional or amateur) served as performers and whose chief attraction was, in my opinion (after some tableaux vivants presented on floats and many examples of the traditional game of fake dragons made of paper, cardboard, and light wooden armatures which young people caused to undulate over their heads by controlling them with a series of sticks), the appearance, in this case almost fairylike, of a row of equilibrists, mounted on high unicycles, and then the appearance, even more diverting, of the famous army of monkeys, marching in very good order and at the same time creating delicate rosettes with their long whirling canes, and displaying their faces painted in all sorts of wild colors, just as in the classic opera, where one sees those inferior and caricatural brothers victoriously attack the well-equipped troops of celestial gods, offering an image of the battles fought by the humble people against the feudal lords.

As though it had been thought morally or aesthetically necessary to show that legality regained its rights after the saturnalia, the sports organizations were the ones who closed the procession, in a species of da capo or at the very least a reminder of the handsome arrangement of the beginning: behind a flag bearer appeared a group of tall, strong girls in white leotards and pants, who advanced in step, flinging out their closed-fisted arms alternately left and right, in a very accentuated symmetry, as the soldiers had done with their free arms; other groups of adults and adolescents followed, maneuvering with a great deal of elegance and precision, some twirling their scarves, others knocking their barbells together in cadence. While fireworks exploded (noise and smoke in the brightness of broad daylight) and a new flowering of parachutes and streamers deployed, projected by the rockets, the festival ended with a sprint of all the civilian participants who, gradually assembling at the bottom of the square, walked to the foot of the grandstands waving bouquets and cheering. In the same way, at the end of certain shows, the entire troupe of actors will sometimes salute the audience standing in a line parallel to the footlights that moves forward from the back of the stage toward the spectators. At Tiananmen, however, there were neither saluters nor saluted (for all were applauding one another), and many hundred thousand actors surged to the far edge of the theater where they had just performed their maneuvers, in the extraordinarily sharp and at the same time silky light characteristic of Peking autumns.

During this procession, from which almost nothing was lacking except the hearses, for a complete representation of Chinese life, the people had been gazing at themselves for four hours straight, as though in a mirror. In a place where there is no great shared effort of construction, one will never be confronted with a festival like this: a parade in which one sees, gaily deployed, the full range of classes and activities is possible only if all these activities have a resonance for every segment of the society that offers itself this entertainment, more substantial than a lavishly produced play, and only if these activities find a common denominator in the great effort of which they are merely varied aspects. The fact that, for so many countries in the world today, the national festival is expressed essentially by a military parade shows to what degree such countries, and such numbers of countries, suffer from an incompatibility of temperament with themselves: far from being able to admire themselves in their everyday clothing in the full light of a good conscience, the people there are invited to contemplate themselves only from the terribly particular point of view of their military function and clothed in a disguise of which no burlesque counterpart is offered by an army of monkeys.

More grace than anywhere else, more ease or candor in joining together genres that are completely different—perhaps it is this that expresses the specifically Chinese nature of the national festival at which I was present. Never to so high a degree as at the time of my discovery of China have I seen a country in which aspects of nature, morphologies of manufactured things, and exteriors of people seem united by a complicity going so far, sometimes, as to materialize in a visible harmony: from landscapes furnished with trees more rounded than ours and with foliage in the shape of rice-powder puffs or feather dusters, to monuments that are not (as is almost the rule in our part of the world) a single edifice served up on a plate or endowed with an exaggerated importance, but rather a group in which empty spaces and approaches count perhaps even more than the constructions themselves, which are also rounded and all mossy with polychrome ornaments, from fish with vaporous fins bathing sometimes in basins of stone whose prodigiously soft patina offsets their density and rigidity, to ideograms so complicated as characters but of a design both so elegant and so firmly balanced in its imaginary frame, from the inert matter that always seems to know subtly how to arrange itself, to the human beings who, even when they are walking quickly, advance most often at a pace regular enough so that they seem to obey a rhythm dictated by the stars much more than respond to the uncertainties and incidents of what they have to do; all this would lead us to believe that from one extreme to the other of the long chain of living beings and objects that form the world of China, no break in continuity appears among the elements (disparate though they are) distributed among the three kingdoms, since one of the essential concerns of this civilization which allows us to speak of China as a "world" seems to have been (and to have remained) precisely that of maintaining or establishing this fabulous harmony.

Beds of flowers surmounted by metal disks, one red, one mauve, as I saw, not on a firing range but at the Nanking train station at the terminus of two railway tracks for which these mingled products of heavy industry and horticulture constituted the buffer-stop; a small crowd of young tomboys in sweat suits either garnet-red or wine (the color almost of glowing embers) frisking about near the Syndicate House in Peking in the light of electric floodlamps, throwing a basketball back and forth; the islet of flowers, also in Peking, that embellished the center of a vast intersection where there rose up like a semaphore the traffic policeman on his platform thus inserted into a ring of stems and corollas; the textile mill with machine tools painted in delicate tones to which signs and drawings of the company newspaper traced with various chalks on large blackboards corresponded here and there as pleasantly as the laughing eyes of the women workers above their antidust masks of white taffeta; urchins of both sexes and even tall adolescents perched on the graveyard sculptures (guardian horse, stele-bearing tortoise, or any other animal that can be climbed) just as in Rome on summer evenings at the monumental fountain of the Piazza Navona clusters of children playing hide-and-seek mingle with the beards of the river gods; the slight hiccup, half laugh and half sob, that often quivers in the throat when an emotional smile uncovers the teeth of a person taking leave of you by squeezing your two hands in thanks—this is what tends to show precisely the rather unusual good fortune it seemed to me that China enjoyed with regard to these sensitive arrangements (the play of paired contrasts or of correspondences either obvious or assumed or even suspended in the problematical expectation of a second term that would perhaps not exist except as a function of our desire to see the echo found in us alone by the supposed first term ascend to the rank of truth), exceptional contingencies whose more or less spontaneous felicity makes one think that a country well and truly possesses grace, if it produces them in quantity. But if, in trying to analyze China's charm, I resort at last to pleading grace because I can't justify otherwise the facts I have summoned as evidence, it is certain that I have explained nothing.

All the sorrow of the world in a single cup of wine that will not be drunk, like—near Hangzhou—the mountain suspended in the fat teardrop of a convex mirror, on the pediment of a temple that is not that of the Source of Jade. If I analyze the meaning of these lines (written almost as soon as I returned and based on the conjunction of two memories, the first of which did not have to be located, because its only setting was the false space of a theater stage), might I derive something from them that would help me define what formed the enchantment I experienced?

Except for the Source of Jade, which is here only an embellishment (since this is the name of a temple close to but different from the one in whose pediment the landscape was reflected and whose name, in the course of the walk on which I visited both of them, I neglected to set down), except for the very temple I was talking about (pure element of localization, as is the city of Hangzhou), a cup of wine, a mountain, a mirror are the concrete bases of that sentence which is articulated using the parallelism of the two negations. In preference to what *is*, to feature what *is not*; if I have chosen this peculiarity of phrasing it is not, of course, out of a simple taste for preciosity, but because I think I cannot express what China is for me without distancing it by means of the margin I have thus contrived and, perhaps even more, because the truth inherent in that immense country appeared to me of a quality too delicate for one to be able to capture it in the crude presumptuousness of an affirmation instead of seeking, rather, to approach it by taking one's inspiration from the protocol (based on reserve and moderation) that requires the Chinese systematically to indicate the insufficiency and the lacunae, that is to say the negative aspect, of what they are doing or giving. The cup of wine, the mountain, the mirror: was it from a perspective, here too, of negativity, opposed to all kinds of inflation, that I brought those three terms into play?

The mirror and the cup are counterparts, for one contains the immensity of the mountain and the other a pain just as inordinate, that which, at one of the high points of a Chinese opera which is among the most often performed today, the lover Liano Chan-po experiences when his beloved Chou Ying-tai insinuates that he is not the suitor accepted by her father, a minor squire with a feudal white beard, and when, with all her grace as a rich, refined young girl, she offers him the wine of hospitality, a ludicrous offering for someone who was expecting her hand in marriage. A mountain in a mirror, *all the sorrow of the world in a single cup of wine*: like a trick in physics-for-fun, immensity reflected in an object of modest dimensions and, as though the extreme of tragic purity should be reflected only by the mirror of theater, a torment that will deliberately not be exteriorized, except in an allusive manner and through all that either of the two lovers can put of themselves into an exchange of gestures and courteous remarks, those lovers who will be so broken by this torment that they will not survive it (the female lover's black hair-piece falling behind her like a single-paneled curtain with a single loop, the male lover whose rather ducklike way of walking emphasizes his masculine nature, customary in the style of Shaoxing opera, in which all the roles are played by women, some of them in men's clothing). Reduced to being a jewel on the front of a delicately ornamented edifice (and inserted in one of the judicious combinations of fullness and emptiness that constitute Chinese temples or palaces, with buildings arranged in an ensemble of courtyards or gardens in such a way that the terraces, bridges, and stairways seem to have precedence over them, unlike what we see in Europe, where the esplanade, the park, or the avenue is ordinarily only a jewel case for the monument), the mountain thus denied, in its absence of proportion, and reduced to our scale affirms more intensely its baroque structure as mountain. As for the cup left full, the cup that was there only in order not to be drunk, and whose wine remains intact, like the hoped-for woman now torn from her lover by an old man with chin concealed by an opaque rectangle of snowy whiskers, below a face almost that of a little girl, the emptiness that surrounds it and that is so suddenly perceptible once the cup is abandoned, produces the most glaring significance through the interposition of a *less* that can be manifested.

After our visit to these temples, of which some were ornamented, toward the top, with a landscape strangely deformed by the strong curvature of the polished surface in which it was reflected, we stopped to drink green tea in a café wide open to the elements and reminiscent of those airy pleasure pavilions in which—in many Chinese paintings or prints—one can discern small gowned figures chatting in the heart of a more or less wild spot; for a good period of time we remained there, ourselves chatting, with our interpreters, while gazing at a mountain stream in which some adolescent girls in cotton jackets and pants were elegantly dipping their feet (a rest after a long walk highlighted by a picnic—what must have been the occupation of that particular one of their schoolgirl days). It was at Hangzhou, that very morning, that we had been shown the curious tempest in a glass of water conceived during the Han Dynasty for the amusement of an emperor: a small house in the museum contains a thick copper basin whose bottom is ornamented with four carved fish and whose edges are provided with two handles gleaming brightly from having been handled so often; asked by the director of the museum or his representative to perform this demonstration for us, a young girl rubs the two handles with her palms, pressing on them (it seems) quite hard and imparting to them a regular back-and-forth motion; like the distant, low booming of a bell, a humming begins; then the water that fills the receptacle starts to shiver, and the vibration propagated in the liquid mass, whose surface is now folded into multiple wrinkles, soon produces delicate projections of droplets that rise and fall.

The excursion at the end of which a few of us had been able to admire the charming and sumptuous plaything consisting of those pocket-sized stormy waters accompanied by a subtle background noise had begun on a lake, in boats rowed by slight but sturdy boatwomen. For the final quick visit to the museum that several of us made (other occupations having been planned for the remainder of our group), I no longer remember which of our interpreters escorted us. Did the two Wangs come with us, a boy and girl who were not brother and sister or even related, despite what a foreigner might conclude from their common patronym, being unaware that "Wang" is one of the most common family names in China? One was Wang Sien, about twenty years old, who had been educated in French Indochina, where his parents, originally from Canton, had settled; a collection taken up by his Viet Minh friends, then under the control of the colonial administration, had provided him with the means to make his way illegally to his true country; slender and handsome under his navy blue cap, which he wore tilted back in the fashion of sailors and modern revolutionaries, he was endowed with a marvelous smile which spread over his blushing face if one showed him the least kindness (for he seemed almost childlike in his shyness). The other was Wang Yuen-chen, whose given name could be translated more or less as "cloud the color of pearl" (a fact in which she took no pride, such poetic appellations being quite common among her people); she came from a southern province where she had fought with the partisans, and was a gentle girl of twenty-seven with a delicate face and charming pointed chin, thoughtful, studious, taking notebook in hand any time she could capture from our conversation some French expression she did not know, and again any time she could extract, from the most knowledgeable among us, some piece of information about her own country; most often serious, she was the one who, beyond her official role as guide, made sure, as hostess, that our stay was agreeable; she was capable of being vivacious, occasionally facetious, and she sometimes laughed with a pretty laugh that justified the pearly cloud of her name; her feet small and quite flat in her masculine shoes, showing ankle socks of a lemon or some other acidic color, she walked (like so many Chinese men or women) with her arms dangling, waddling slightly, at a pace that was slow but so continuous that one wondered just what obstacle could oblige this sort of person to turn back, though she was so petite and graceful, closer to a schoolgirl than a virago, her face docile within the severe frame of her stiff, short-cut hair. Had I wanted to experience *The Magic Flute* in a revised version, in which Egypt would be replaced by the Far East and freemasonry by Marxism-Leninism, no doubt the two Wangs, boy and girl, could—missing the third person, but quite naturally—be substituted for the three disciples or child genies whose mission appears to be to aid those protected by Zarastro, the priest of light. During the excursion which took up the greater part of our afternoon at Hangzhou did I not, in any case, pass through a setting as fantastic as one could wish to have, for the scene in which one is introduced to the most venerable mysteries? For the mountain stream by whose banks we took our tea flows at the foot of the hill of the Phoenix, with a thousand Buddhas sculpted directly out of the rock at various points in a complicated arrangement that includes abrupt walls and deep, narrow passages and even caves, and which human hands have furnished with innumerable threshold guardians. But throughout that day, as during my entire trip, I was certainly less inclined to dream of magical worlds than to scribble down reference words which would help me, once evening came, to record my observations in a notebook. Thus it is only now that I summon up one of the works I love most, out of all those composed by this musician whose unfettered genius has not been surpassed. I am using it (in a word) as a last resort and as though, relying on a magic issuing from Tamino's own flute and from his companion Papageno's Chinese hat or glockenspiel, I hoped at least to cause a little melody to sing over the libretto of these notes of mine, so dry that I rediscover almost nothing in them, now, of what China gave me, and so rapid, at the same time as they are so scattered, that they do not even begin, despite their abundance, to form a documentation that can be rationally used to advantage.

When I reread what I thus wrote in the form of an attentively kept journal—going to bed well after midnight and disturbing with my tardily illuminated desk lamp the first sleep of my roommate, rising if necessary at dawn because of a neglected detail that came back to me in my sleep and that I had to note down without further delay because the new occupations in which I would be engaged early in the day would inevitably thrust it away into oblivion—I can scarcely discover a few recuperable crumbs, in a jumble of pieces of information having to do as much with the history of the theater as with that of the workers' movement, with the instruction of illiterates as with agrarian reform or with propaganda in favor of hygiene, with what I had seen in one or another institute or museum as with the policy practiced toward minorities in order to transform China into a "multinational State." Behind a zeal all the more rarely abated because it was perhaps merely a comedy that I played for myself, I wonder today whether a profound indolence was not concealed: to seize on the wing all that passes within your reach demands a smaller effort than systematically to gather documents on two or three given points; it also allows one to choose (in all good conscience, since to observe anything at all represents, in a sense, a certain amount of work) the most attractive of the various programs that are proposed to you. Under the pretext that I had available to me too little time to conduct real investigations (as I did, in Africa and elsewhere, in the course of my several professional trips either in a group or alone), urging so-called scientific scruples for not attempting to study what, even within a narrow time span, could if necessary be studied, but also not daring to abandon any sort of seriousness and behave like a simple *flâneur*, I opted—conscious or not of my stratagem—for the easiest solution, in other words the middle solution: to make it my goal to visit the greatest possible number of places, like, in fact, a tourist determined not to lose a single moment of a tour he is afraid he will never go on again; to hurry by train or airplane from Peking to Manchuria, from Manchuria to Shanghai, then from Peking as far as Sichuan and almost as far as the border of Burma, which was as fatiguing as it was pleasant; to go from a factory to a monument, from a people's park to a movie theater, from a conference to a guided tour, from a first-class meal to a show, regaining a semblance of seriousness at the hour when I wrote up my notes, punctually and (as though to prove to myself cheaply that I was a conscientious traveler) losing some time making a fair copy of what I had recorded too elliptically in the course of my peregrinations. As is most often the case with compromises, I was quite wrong to opt for this attenuated solution, and this is, perhaps, one of the reasons why my trip so quickly seemed to me rendered valueless: by not methodically restraining myself, I collected nothing worthwhile except, at best, the crumbs I have spoken of; by trying to capture as much as possible of what I saw or heard, I did not allow myself to live, and, because I did not yield to the rhythm of China without trying to be clever, I was not able to bring back anything from a vast and exalting country but those infinitesimal crumbs. It is certainly a foolhardy enterprise to try to interpret these trifles now: isn't it unrealistic to take what I embraced so poorly, at the time, that I held only dust in my hands and try retrospectively to make it substantial by examining a few minuscule grains taken from this same dust?

Their faces allusively bound, and painted just enough so that they are no longer ordinary, these girls of wax [cire] *(or of Saint-Cyr) glide from west to east, dividing the meridian of the stage. Exit to the side without change in level, as though on a conveyor belt* [tapis roulant], *since they lack the flying carpet* [tapis volant] *on which the goddesses take flight.*

In contrast to the very natural gait of the girls of the new China (who seem happy to step firmly on the ground which the atrophied feet of their female elders touched only with pain, walking cautiously forward, something one still sees here and there among old women who stumble like birds who are ill), in contrast to this placid and slightly swaying gait (the weight of the body bearing down freely on one leg and then the other), to this motion which ill-tempered people will call clumsy whereas I would identify it as precisely the way people walk who are in the process of emancipating themselves, there is the sophisticated gait of the actresses, of those, at least, who in classical theater play the parts of female characters of the feudal era. A perfectly horizontal gait, the sight of which gives one a pleasure similar to that which is sometimes offered by the sight of the trail of light left by certain meteors which, apparently larger than shooting stars, cross the sky of the warm regions with a slowness that is of course illusory but, at first glance, stupefying. *A body in motion animated by a movement of translation* . . . If it weren't that their rectilinear gliding is just as nuanced as, in declamation, the fascinating modulations (between speech and song) of their high-pitched voices, such a formula—a vestige, I think, of the wording of problems I used to find in my math books when I was in school—would more or less account for the way these sovereign creatures displace themselves, creatures you are surprised to discover, when you see them offstage and without their beautiful pallid faces and carmine-painted cheekbones, are girls similar in bearing and dress to those you might meet in the street, and endowed, not with a faculty for propelling themselves that is in some way astral, and disembodied, but with the same good and likable swaying gait. So that we are now charmed—and doubly so—by the lack of reserve of those who just a moment ago captivated us with their extremely refined gestures and diction. How can one pass from a disguise that is perfect because its wearer seems to have no reality except disguised, to an equally perfect absence of disguise? *Mystère et boule de gomme* [heaven only knows]: this is what Wang Yuen-chen might whisper to me, if she were present, since she had been taught this expression by one of my companions and used it somewhat randomly without ceasing to be amused by it.

Although (strictly) half in disguise, the lovers already halfway turning into beetles . . . It is in male clothing that Chou Ying-tai spends a year with a professor in the capital, for during the period in which her legendary love is situated, the studies that she has resolved to pursue were not open to girls. It is therefore to a dissimulated boy that her fellow pupil Liang Chan-po becomes attached, moved by a feeling that he will not recognize for what it is until the moment when he will at last have grasped the secret of the cunning metamorphosis. Now, all masquerade having been put aside, it is through a metamorphosis in which nature joins mythology that the idyll will end: when the lover, whom the father has rejected in favor of a wealthier suitor, has died of sorrow, and when, amid thunderclaps, the beloved has ended her dance of death by throwing herself into the dead man's tomb (that hemisphere of stone next to which she has ordered her wedding procession to stop, and whose cocoon has just been cracked open by a bolt of lightning), two butterflies will flutter in the sunshine of a lull in the storm; two butterflies that are the two lovers, incarnated by two actresses now enveloped in filmy veils and moving in front of a stage set of flowers and rainbow, two actresses of whom only one will have been more than half a young man (the other having played only a temporary simulacrum) and who both have abandoned their cast-off clothing of tragicomedy for a dance whose silent spinning represents the earthly apotheosis of the transfigured couple (the old beliefs relating to metempsychosis merging here with the idea of biological transmutations), a dance which, at the same time, expresses the triumph of the two actresses whom we see smiling at the ovation and crossing with hasty little steps the entire expanse of the stage, describing vast insect circles with drunken wingbeats. A "happy end" in two senses, since the timeless happiness of the lovers reunited in the form of butterflies is identified with the present joy of the protagonists, and since the cheers of the public applaud the actresses' talent as much as the happy outcome of a story that made it weep.

The state of ignorance in which most women were kept, the omnipotence of the parents determining conjugal unions as they pleased—such are the failings of feudal society exposed in the old tale of *The Love of Liang Chan-po and Chou Ying-tai*, the source, early on, of the play I saw performed in the most common of its modern versions. A representation of a way of life outmoded today, since the emancipation of women and the liberalizing reform of marriage are part of the great progress that the Chinese people owe to their present leaders, that comedy of manners, of which each fragment attains the lapidary poetry of a motto or proverb, conceals a critical meaning in harmony with the new faith. Even its conclusion, in which the marvelous comes fully into play, can (if necessary) be reconciled with Marxist-Leninist ideas: if immortality is only a dream and if a materialist cannot possibly believe in the eventuality of a rebirth, is it forbidden to him to seek, at least, a shadow of consolation in the thought that a human body is not condemned to disappear completely and that the elements of which it was composed will be embraced anew in a series of combinations whose infinite diversity constitutes what we commonly call *nature*, nature that is divided into three kingdoms in one of which is ranked, among other living creatures, the delicate little winged beasts that are butterflies? Closer to the real truth than Tamino and Pamina passing victoriously through fire and water by the power of the magic flute, Liang Chan-po and Chou Ying-tai share a fate that scarcely departs from the law of nature, in this case not so much violated as bent, as in the case of those pagan dead who are destined to recover a small bit of existence in the form of plant food that will grow in the very field where they have been buried.

As though I had taken for my model one of those Chinese paintings stretched on rolls too long for the eye ever to be able to do anything else but travel across the succession of mountains, valleys, and watery surfaces that are depicted in them, I reel off a succession of notations introduced—in the manner sometimes of explanatory commentaries, sometimes of elaborated glosses or free *marginalia*—with a few of the bits of text with which I tried, once I was back in France, to give a little solidity to certain of my too fluid impressions. Since I have been pegging away like this, working on a few details without managing to raise myself to any sort of general view, and also without coming upon one of those personal strings which you have only to let vibrate once they have been touched (when everything, if it hasn't organized itself, at least insists upon itself as a succession of truths of which the first that one succeeds in grasping makes one guess there are others of the same family that, by paying out the right amount of application and wisdom, one will also be able to grasp), what surprises me a little more at each new effort is, precisely, that I don't manage to go beyond these details, whereas my trip had appeared to me in the very beginning as an event that, in a happy sense, would mark the rest of my life—this was (it is true) once I had "torn myself away," for though I still believe in the need to travel, I experience any departure more and more as a wrench, even if its destination is a nearby country and my absence will not last long.

But wasn't it exactly because there was a danger of a gross disillusionment—as for someone playing his last card—that I had so much trouble tearing myself away when I left for China? And isn't it, also, because I feel such aversion to this disillusionment that I now cling to details like someone clutching at debris to survive a shipwreck? The fact is, however, that the details in question represent what, in China, was for me a certainty that I experienced and that touched me to the quick. What else should I talk about, therefore, if not those things that moved me and to which, despite their exiguity, I can firmly attach myself? If I am devastated today, the disaster probably remains entirely in the limpid glass of water of this twofold statement: my life hasn't changed because of the mere fact that I saw a part of the great progress that a great country is in the process of making, and I believe that it would not be more changed if extensive observations had freed me of all uneasiness as to the purity of the means—only through persuasion, I was told constantly—by which this great country is pursuing its modernization; for my life to have a chance to rectify itself, it would be necessary that in the chosen lands things would be so arranged that the work, for instance, to which I am dedicating myself when I seek to define my Chinese experience on the basis of details that are tiny, but precise, and moving to me, be judged by my friends from that place (if they knew about it) otherwise than as a kind of bad workmanship compared with the militant testimony they evidently hoped for from me and that alone would tally with the idea of a literature whose sole standard of value is the help it brings to the people. Posing the problem this way, I pose—as usual, indirectly—this fundamental question: am I forever incapable of having faith in anything at all that would be sufficient for my personal anguish to melt away, or is it the socialist construction that I must incriminate, insofar as it is effected—even in China—along paths too geometrically traced for such a vital anguish, with all the technologically useless products that may derive from it, not to be eliminated from consideration from the beginning by the heroic artisans of that construction? That socialism provide a remedy for everything (including the anguish of knowing oneself to be mortal)—such a demand amounts to asking for the moon, and if it falls short, one cannot take that as a pretext for abandoning it. But wouldn't it be natural to expect that labors whose aim is to fill, somehow or other, the hole of that original anguish should in any case be accepted by a Marxist society, since such a society ought by definition to be making it its goal to achieve the true human society? Nothing, of course, was asked of me, and I am completely free in testifying (as well as, moreover, in refraining from testifying). Nevertheless, everything I saw there, of the titanic enterprise in which the Chinese are engaged, incites me to believe that there they concede, at best, only a small and precarious place to anything that does not directly serve that enterprise. A great deal of importance (I am happy to stress this) is granted to the theater, to archeology, to the traditional arts, in short, to the various aspects of national culture, and an often brilliant cinematographic production proves, too, that even outside the immense effort to educate the masses, an intense cultural activity is taking place in this country which so many Westerners imagine to be inert. But the central factor, in all this, remains the building of socialism in China, and I have trouble seeing how an activity of the kind that absorbs me could be categorized there otherwise than among those bourgeois residues—or even feudal ones—that call for rehabilitation. Here, I agree, I am reasoning as an egocentric, and it will be quite easy for one to tell me that the man of letters is showing, in this case, a little more than the cloven hoof. On the scale of the collectivities and on the level of their immediate needs, it is only too certain that I am wrong, for what is urgent is—of course—to give a better life to hundreds of millions of people. Bad conscience aside, the rigorousness of the creators of plans makes me uneasy and obliges me personally to ask myself this question: is one pursuing the right path (for oneself as well as for those who will come after) if one works at something of which one knows that each person must devote himself to it fully (half measures being excluded where revolution is concerned) but of which one also knows that to adhere to it without reserve may lead one to deny oneself in what is most intimately one's own and thus to nip in the bud what would be one's real contribution to the collective work? Liang Chan-po and Chou Ying-tai, in the legend that portrays them dying and then changing into butterflies, benefit from this wonder: to undergo metamorphosis without thereby ceasing to be themselves. Must I draw a line through all hope of reconciling myself, or, on the other hand, must I affirm that it is in no way fantastic to imagine, on the level of militant action, an equivalent of the two lovers' miraculous metamorphosis?

> *De vos jardins fleuris fermez les portes,*
> *Les myrtes sont flétris, les roses mortes!*

> Of your flow'ring gardens, the gates now close,
> The myrtle is withered, and dead the rose!

On the eve of our departure for Europe, our interpreters had given us a banquet at which the toasts had been numerous and we went so far as to sing songs over dessert. In reply to a number by one of my companions (who, by exhibiting himself thus, had no other thought than to start the ball rolling), the small Chouang Sien—that pretty female translator of the English language whose parents lived in Shanghai, whereas her colleague Wang Yuen-chen came from Kunming, in Yunnan—sang a Chinese song for us, in a voice richer than her childlike face would have allowed one to expect, then in my turn I stood up for that tune from the past century that seemed to me, mediocre and fragmentary as may have been the execution that I was able to give it, to express better than my too prosaic declarations the melancholy in which I was plunged by the prospect of the imminent separation. "I ask you to drink to the health of my courage," I had said during dinner, in a toast whose theme was the pain I felt and the courage I would need the next day to leave this country, where I did not doubt I would have liked to put down roots. Thinking now about the whole path traveled since that moment of effusion in one of those restaurants in Peking whose courtyard is also its poultry yard, since upon occasion one sees limping about in it, fully alive, the ducks that are destined to be eaten lacquered, I wonder whether my comradeship, apparently so frank and so destined to last, with our interpreters, will not suffer the same fate as—when one is young—so many beautiful (but soon to fade) vacation friendships!

Meal finished and tables abandoned, we had chatted for some time without constraint and I, expressing myself like someone who is determined to follow the golden thread of his emotion, had set my heart on explaining to comrade Wang what I had learned from this trip, which was to end the next day: that the building of socialism, instead of being accomplished in boredom and with rigidity, could be done with good humor and gaiety (as testified by the very attitude of the woman I was talking to, as of all those who had gone out of their way to satisfy our many desiderata without ever departing from their smiling eagerness)—this was the great lesson I had learned from our few weeks in the new China. But the good Wang, initiate in ideas which were as regular as the cut of her hair, answered me that, where the building of socialism was concerned, it could not be otherwise. The admiration I was professing for something that, to her, was quite natural had to appear to her to be the surprise of a perfect philistine, and I realized this at the very moment I was talking to her; thus, I insisted strongly on this point, on the one hand in order to demonstrate to her that there was nothing in this so obvious that it would be superfluous to mention it, and then, on the other, in the hope of leading her to measure in a useful way what would be amazing about China's success were it to conduct its revolution from beginning to end without deviating from such a style. The young fanatical follower of the magus the color of ripe wheat or the color of the first moments of a September twilight over the North Lake Park on the outskirts of Peking would have been closer to winning me to her cause if she had shown herself more conscious of the good fortune that appears to be presently that of Chinese communism and less sure of the benefits, in some sense automatic, of the doctrine in which I cannot doubt that by devoting herself to it body and soul she found a great moral comfort.

The little sugar candy girl, with braids of licorice, takes our hand to lead us to the club of the butterflies, a Marxist-Leninist Monelle.

What anarchy and nihilism (of which Marcel Schwob became one of the prophets with his *Le Livre de Monelle*) were for French intellectuals of the symbolist period, communism will have been somewhat the equivalent for those of my generation: in whatever way we judge the present conjuncture, and even if we were to consider this great movement to be misguided today, it is impossible for us, anyway, not to regard the revolution of October 1917 as the major event of our epoch, the one that for the most perceptive of us will have marked the beginning of a new age or, at least, will have represented the last hope of seeing humanity apply itself to a task certainly fraught with perils and difficulties but defensible in its aims. I was sixteen when this overthrow took place, and I really have to say that at the time I attached no special importance to it, compared with the other events reported by the dailies and periodicals, solely concerned with the fortunate or unfortunate developments of the war being fought by the Allies. After the assassination of the monk Rasputin, there had been the takeover by Alexander Kerensky (whom I would encounter a few years later in the streets of Passy when, having fallen from office as chief of state, he had been reduced to the condition of an exile, and would walk along the peaceful sidewalks of the sixteenth arrondissement, a gray, sour-faced would-be Napoleon). Bourgeois opinion had at first been optimistic about the fall of the tsar, expecting that the result for Russia would be a recovery in the way it was conducting its war; but it had soon become disillusioned, worried by the intrigues of those who were called "maximalists" and "minimalists," and soon it had given vent to its indignation, when the Kerenskyite government had been toppled by the maximalists (those who, of those two extreme left groups, were in the minority, contrary to what seemed to me indicated by their French name, an approximate translation of the term *bolshevik* as opposed to that of *menshevik*). Lenin, who had crossed Germany in a sealed railway car, Trotsky the Jew, jumbled together with the pacifists of Zimmerwald and Kienthal, soon took their places alongside the spies and defeatists, the flashy foreign adventurers Almereyda and Bobo-Pacha, Mata-Hari the beautiful Indonesian, and others of smaller size, including the actress Suzy Depsy or the "traitor Guilbaut," whose name was never printed except preceded by that epithet comparing him to a modern Ganelon. When the characters of Lenin and Trotsky acquired some substance for me, a long time had already passed since Saint Petersburg had become Leningrad, after the transitory and now almost forgotten period in which its name was "Petrograd." At that time I had learned, from my contacts with a few artists and writers with whom I had allied myself, for reasons at first completely aesthetic, that one cannot limit oneself to being a nonconformist where art alone is concerned, and that one should assert independence also in the face of certain realities of a social or political kind; militarism, with the particularly revolting forms it assumes when it becomes disciplinary (as in the Bat' d'Af') or colonial (as in the Moroccan war), was the most emblematic of these realities, and, for me, everything probably crystallized around that one: before being the great leader of the proletariat, Lenin was, in my eyes as in those of the surrealists, the man who had dared sign the peace treaty of Brest-Litovsk. However much I may have vacillated since then (as I sometimes become indignant at the authoritarianism of Stalinist methods, sometimes believe them justified by the need to protect and strengthen Russia on its way toward socialism), I have never ceased to consider Lenin the apostle or the saint of this, the twentieth century, which is crossed by such diverse currents but of which, deep inside the capitalist world, an Andalusian and a Londoner—Picasso and Chaplin—are the two glorious and fully alive purveyors of imagery.

At Tientsin—baptized with another name since the new regime, like many other Chinese cities—we were taken to visit a community center for children, and there we were received, with great demonstrations of friendship, by a crowd of little boys and girls, the latter delicately made up (lips reddened and cheeks touched with pink) even though most of them were barely adolescents. The boldest of the little gang, grasping our hands and not releasing them, busied themselves guiding us and doing the honors of their club for us. As a sign of welcome, we were given some of those little plush birds dyed in bright colors (as are found in Peking and elsewhere in shops), nice presents to which were added gifts of a more comical nature: pretty apples with good ripe tones that melted into liquid if you held them in your hand for very long. Those of us who actually wanted to take part were dragged into folk dances, and fresh bursts of laughter, too frank to be in any way offensive, greeted the clownish efforts that several of my companions and I made to play our part in figures difficult to execute without some instruction, despite their relative simplicity. During the whole of my visit, my companion was a very small girl who, when I first arrived, had given me a plush bird and had seized my left hand, which, sometimes, she squeezed tightly, lifting her eyes to me and smiling at me with her whole face. Between her and me, there was not, of course, any possibility of conversation, but the pressures of fingers made up for it. We walked about in the courtyard and then, for a little while, I left my young escort to take part in the dances to which other children invited me. As soon as these frolics were over, her hand found mine again without my needing to look for it, and in this way we continued our walk, now touring the inside of the building, going from room to room and sometimes passing through a recreation room, sometimes a room for studying, this, as far as I can remember, and if indeed I have precisely identified these different locations, whose intended purpose, for lack of a common language, could not be indicated to me by my little guide. To the walls of one of these rooms were affixed some chromolithographs representing revolutionary scenes, and visible in one of them—a reproduction of a Soviet picture—was some episode or other from Lenin's public life. We marked a pause before this one, and the little girl, squeezing my hand a little harder, pronounced distinctly the word "Lenin," as though she had been happy to find in her vocabulary a term by which our accord could at last be expressed in speech, since I evidently knew this famous name and recognized it all the more effectually because it designated someone who must be, in her eyes, almost my compatriot. In the same way that Latin was for Christianity a sort of esperanto and the symbol of the fish served as a sign of recognition for the champions of the new faith, a name such as that of Lenin and symbols like the hammer and sickle or the dove inspired by Picasso's engraving can today form a living link between people separated by race, language, and even age. The inestimable virtue of communism, in my opinion, is that it effectively connects, through their having something in *common*, individuals who, without that, would remain altogether foreign to one another, scattered as they are to the four corners of the globe. But, completely based as it may be on social realities and not the vapors of religion, such a community is nonetheless fluid, for this world too possesses its theologians, who have been quick to excommunicate those they regard as heretics.

A crime every five days and the highest prices in Italy. I am in Palermo when I read this on a propaganda sign, in the trim English Gardens where the local section of the Communist Party is giving a fête to benefit the newspaper *L'Unità*, a sort of fair with merry-go-rounds, lotteries, and various attractions, including the election of "Miss Palermo Vie Nuove 1956" (but just as I will not see the happy winner, I will not know if these *vie nuove* are the new paths opened by socialism or the new streets of a neighborhood recently constructed or planned, in this city that abounds in slums). I am at the end of a vacation here with my wife, and for this last week we have settled in a place quieter than the one where we lived during our first trip to Sicily and where we stopped off again at the time of our arrival not long before: the "Grand Hôtel et des Palmes"—*Grande Albergo e delle Palme*—a palatial establishment that fell into disrepair some time ago, and where one can still see the apartment occupied by Wagner while he was finishing the composition of *Parsifal,* and where we had visited, nine years ago, the room within the four bare walls of which, in 1933, Roussel died in circumstances that suggest that it was in fact death he was seeking by consuming (as he did) too large a quantity of barbiturate. The hotel where we are now is a vast collection of buildings of an outmoded ostentation, in a park that overlooks the sea and is encircled by suburbs so poor that the presence of such a stately caravanserai in the midst of neighborhoods literally in ruins has something absurd at the same time as profoundly shocking about it; in a spacious room with "modernstyle" decor whose walls depict scenes of ancient Sicily, with pretty girls in enticing tunics populating an improperly flowery spot also frequented by swans and peacocks (whereas the dining room exhibits decors vaguely reminiscent of Pompeii mingled with chinoiseries dating from a fake eighteenth century and refinements more difficult to classify), a meeting of jurists is being held today. A small problem of the sort (neither legal nor moral but relating rather to civility) that often present themselves to bourgeois people like me who are imbued with "leftist" ideas and too disturbed by the excess of injustice not to be communist sympathizers: if, as I walked among the booths of the Party fête, I had been asked to buy a badge, I would certainly have acquiesced; but wouldn't I, who would also not want to wear a decoration or any other sign of affiliation in my buttonhole, have felt it highly unsuitable to keep that badge pinned to the lapel of my jacket when, returning from our walk, the moment came to enter the hotel lobby and ask for the key to our room from the little man with gray hair and sad mouth who wears with so much dignity his black porter's livery? *A crime every five days and the highest prices in Italy* . . . Whether determined or not to display it permanently on my clothing—and even if, by not resolving to do it, I would have evinced most prominently an unfortunate fickleness—I can only align myself with those who have written this slogan, for the sight of the wretchedness so extensive in certain parts of Palermo serves to confirm it.

"Lenin," had said the little girl who was leading me through the various parts of her children's club as though fate had designated her to be my cicerone in the magical country which was the source of the bird she had given me—a red country instead of the white country of which Monelle speaks to her historiographer. "Lenin," had said the chromo, accurate but unlovely, in which the great revolutionary was identifiable at first glance by anyone and everyone. The not very engaging product of an art conforming to the principles of socialist realism, that (and nothing more) is what this banal image would have been for me, had the little girl not endowed it with a function quite other than illustrative by pronouncing the word "Lenin," which was, in the most limited sense, only a useless subtitle but, in a larger sense, elevated the undistinguished educational chromo to the dignity of a symbol through which a positive understanding at last became possible.

I, who, in even my most ordinary courses of action, suffer from an almost maniacal doubt about my capacity to explain myself as I should (to the degree, for example, that I can scarcely enter a shop to buy something without first going over and over the turn of phrase, innocuous though it may be, and without any aspiration to elegance but merely simple rigorousness, by means of which I will indicate what I want, so that it often happens to me, doing an errand on foot in Paris, that I lose a good part of the pleasure of my walk in thus ruminating, instead of enjoying the spectacle of the street, over a phrase very different, anyway, from the one that will come to me once I've crossed the threshold); I, who converse only with embarrassment—except by chance or having a rare trust in the person I am talking to—because of my very fear of not knowing what to say or how to say what I may have to say; I, who, in addition, prefer, in semipublic places where I go (restaurant, barber, shirt-maker, tailor, or any sort of supplier) that the person serving me not only treat me like a customer too well known for one not to agree to trust him blindly should the occasion arise, but, if possible, that he give proof of our personal relationship by calling me by my name (as though having a name, for people before whom a quantity of clients file past, and being, for them, defined by syllables that do not have the impersonality of a registry office label, but cleave strictly to your skin, signified that they acknowledged in you something like a soul and was thus reassuring)—it goes without saying that I, more than most, was induced to listen, with as much emotion as though a key word had been spoken, to the enunciation of this name whose meaning was rich and universal enough to be common coin between an urchin of the yellow race and the awkward Westerner I was. I'm quite sure that in response to this word, whose sudden blossoming simplified everything, and which derived its vitality even less from an idea than from the living memory of the man it continues to designate, I said nothing. What would I have answered, anyway, except "Lenin" in turn, and could I therefore have done any better than to squeeze the little girl's hand a bit more, in a gesture identical to hers?

The liveliness of the children, the cordiality of the men, the charm of the girls and women, free of vain coquetry, count among the firmest reasons I have for loving China and, if these are virtues that did not require a revolution in order to manifest themselves, one must at least recognize that this revolution has not annihilated them—far from it. The girls and women, whose condition has to such a degree been transformed, can furthermore be regarded, in large measure, as products of this new China; had it only produced this, it would be a great and beautiful thing that ought to be set down to the credit of Chinese communism. And the news that has appeared in the French papers this month, October of 1956 (shaken by so many convulsions since the latent war persists in bloodying North Africa and, while there is increasing agitation in the Near East, Hungary is mounting a rebellion because it was governed with too harsh a hand for so many long years), the news, still vague, that has come from China regarding the democratization of the statutes of the Communist Party can, on the other hand, only tend to restore the confidence of those who, like me, have begun to wonder whether this revolution, too, was not going to lose sight of its humanism in its too immediate concern for developing national production at whatever cost. The match has not been won—far from it!—for the supporters of a free communism, whose adversaries are the partisans of an iron-fisted socialism as well as those of the classical reaction. But news of this kind suggests that in fact something has changed in a happy direction since what is conventionally known, in our circles, as "destalinization."

A single thread that has never been broken, from Sinanthropus Pekinensis *to comrade Mao Tse-tung.* It was close to Peking that, in the first half of the century, the bones and various other remains were discovered that defined Sinanthropus, which seems to represent the oldest known attestation of humankind and is now for the Chinese a sort of national glory. Little history textbooks intended for children include as prefatory illustration its reconstructed profile—something like a snout—and end with the portraits of the principal artisans of the revolution. Even though there is ample matter for discussion here, and one must also take into account the change of perspective that discoveries in other parts of the world might possibly entail, China can be proud of the fact that this Adam appeared here: the first being intelligent enough to produce fire and to fabricate a stock of tools. From a glance at these history books—the sort I saw in Chongqing when I was on my way toward Yunnan—it would seem that the Chinese educators were determined to show that their country had not waited for the modern era to place itself in the avant-garde of civilization, since the very existence of the remains of Sinanthropus or "China Man" proves that it was already there, really, at the dawn of time.

I am prepared to assert that there is a continuity to China, that the communist revolution did not descend on it like a disease; I am prepared to declare that the ancient wisdom and precious art of living that, for many of us, have long conferred on it a great prestige, find in what is happening in the new China their true culmination, as though a single thread connected, through the quiet periods and the sudden upheavals of its history, the various incarnations through which this part of the world has passed. And now, for me, a thread that has been leading me for several decades and that was entangled most intimately with that other thread, has abruptly been severed: the Soviet army has crushed the Budapest uprising, and apparently that army from a socialist country was, in the eyes of the Hungarian people, what an army of occupation is for a people that sees itself as independent. At first reticent, China has ended by aligning itself with the Soviet Union, and today it is applauding the action of the Russian soldiers, praising them for not having hesitated to spill their blood once again in combating fascism. After despairing of so many things, has the time decidedly come to despair of communism, too?

Self-confidence, without fanatical violence. At the bottom of one of my working notes (one of those with the heading "Bit of China" on which are consigned the tenuous observations I am using here), I had inscribed these few words, an aide-mémoire for the optimistic conclusion to be drawn from the note that forms the essence of the content of the slip of paper: "At the Mountain of the West, near Kunming, a fully active Buddhist temple (presence of bonzes, offerings of fruits on the altars, sticks of incense burning, etc.). Among the various buildings—which include the lodgings of the bonzes, a restaurant for the pilgrims, etc.—there is a progressive reading room with a portrait of Mao Tse-tung." Let the pilgrims, if they like, indulge in their masquerades, and let the bonzes draw a supplementary profit from the management of their tabled'hôte! No one forces anyone else, and one only hopes that the reading room will *also* be visited. That truth which sooner or later will be revealed has only to be put within reach of the people (more and more numerous) who are now capable, thanks to the method of accelerated teaching invented by a soldier, of deciphering the indispensable quantity of ideograms, if not all of them in their huge numbers.

But—just as I was at that point in my critical examination of China, and as though, in my perplexity, I had vaguely summoned up a diversion—a dream comes this very night, slipping in and presenting itself like an ideogram that I must urgently decode. A dream that has (as is often the case) fragmented since my awakening into disparate pieces not always immediately identifiable, but originally, I know, constituting a single whole. A dream, of course, with references to events from my real life (sometimes obvious, sometimes tricky to separate out); with references also (more vivid but whose meaning is no less problematic) to a past dream that seems to be linked to an even older dream by the fragile footbridge thrown from one to the other by an aspect of the Mountain of the West as I saw it at Yunnan—the farthest point of my Chinese trip—six months after the manifestation of the second of those dreams which an interval of almost thirteen years separates from the first, but which shares with it, as with the other links of that chain, a curious family resemblance.

A more or less vertical wall of rock, which is sometimes the natural balcony at which I arrive after a long journey on foot and from which I see, unfolding below, a fascinating spectacle; sometimes the high façade whose grandiose ornaments I contemplate, at the end of my climb, with a feeling of ecstasy mingled with an anguish that is not merely vertigo. This is the element common to my three irregularly spaced dreams, as well as to the walk I took in the environs of Kunming, during one of the obstinately rainy days we spent in that region where (according to our friend Wang Yuen-chen, who was affected almost to the point of tears by the mediocrity of the view that we thus had of her native country) we were supposed to encounter an eternal springtime.

*Il vole sur l'étendue de la neige
et le voilà perle blanche . . .*

It flies over the expanse of snow
and look, it is white as pearl . . .

In the dream that preceded by six months my trip to Yunnan and that visit to the temples, one of which included a building devoted to Marxist-Leninist propaganda, I noticed—far below the mountainous site where I found myself, and almost straight down—a horse of indeterminate color, the only living creature my eyes could clearly apprehend in the uniformity of the plain or plateau within my view. The horse's mane, also colorless, seemed to represent the whole life of the animal, to which I attached some sort of private and distant signification, as though an obscure but exact connection had bound it to what escapes me the most about my own person. In this dream which, waking me in the middle of the night, I noted was "beautiful and melancholy," as I described it to the person who had also woken up, as though just at the right moment to listen to me tell it, no other event occurred but this: at a certain moment, the horse moved. A completely rectilinear movement of constant speed that, without perceptibly diminishing the distance between us, which was measured most of all by our difference in levels, brought it closer to the point where my gaze would have plunged had it followed the direction of a plumb line. The displacement happened silently and without any part of the horse moving, except perhaps its undulating mane. I then uttered the words that identified the color of the horse and of the whole panorama—that snowy white with the softness of pearl which my eyes had not observed—at the same time that, representing the culmination and in some sense the moral lesson of the dream, they seemed to reveal to me its essence in a manner such that the reflection I would apply to it in the light of day, once I was back on the other shore, would only express in discursive terms what, at the time of the dream, had been given to me poetically. An image of destiny to some extent mastered if one succeeds in considering (as though from very high up) its imperturbable course—this is what was in that moment suggested to me by the horse, displaced by its motionless gallop over a flat surface. A guarantee of an everlasting existence gained through the projection of oneself onto an object (a work of art) whose history continues independently of your own and which is both something else and you yourself—this is what it became when I returned, the next day, to this dream and to the phrase that concluded it, and forced myself to derive the whole lesson from it.

At the beginning of my dream of the other night ("other night" and already no longer "last night," as I now approach this second account), there is also an abrupt cliff, which I reach after an excursion into the mountains. But the animal I will see running across the sort of rocky wasteland one sees down below does not have much in common with the fairy-horse that, a few months before I left for China, had appeared to me as I was sleeping in the country house at Saint-Hilaire where my family and I would go spend each weekend, before a pernicious series of events introduced a rather long break in the periodic accomplishment of this ritual: the death of my mother (occurring at Saint-Pierre-lès-Nemours, at a time when she was so old that one would almost have believed she had been victorious in a stage of life fatal for most people but over which some would be capable of triumphing forever); an accident of which my wife was the victim at the very time when the physical condition of my mother was beginning to worry us seriously (a false step she took on a tread of the stairs leading up to our bedroom in the house at Saint-Hilaire, and a fall from which we lifted her with a sprain, a dislocated knee, and even a fracture of the small bone called the "tibial spine"), a private grief and a personal inconvenience which were accompanied, on the level of public violence—as though everything had to come apart at the same time—by the sinister Hungarian affair (which hasn't yet ended) and the pitiful affair of the Suez Canal, of which one result that is evident right now—without prejudging the probable gravity of its more distant consequences—is, with respect to life in France, a shortage of petroleum products which affects many industries and which—an obviously minor repercussion, but annoying nevertheless—complicates things a great deal for those who were in the habit of spending weekends in the country.

The animal that I saw running after a bird in my recent Paris dream was neither the same size nor the same color as the horse from the other dream and had in common with it only the fact that it was a quadruped. A prosaic animal, specifically rustic, for its prototype in waking life lives in the house at Saint-Hilaire (where, to my greatest vexation, some dull French country people have replaced the Guadeloupeans who were its caretakers before their refusal to comply with the most minimal rules led them to leave us, not at all peacefully, as we would have liked, but in an atmosphere almost of passionate drama, which included an appeal for supernatural vindication, when the mulatto housekeeper called down a solemn curse against my wife, who was compared to a slaveowner worthy of feudal times, and against our house), this animal of a completely rural robustness, and of a good breed, though without a registered pedigree, is none other than my bitch Dine, whom I hadn't seen for a month and whose society I was beginning to miss when that night came, on which, toward the beginning of a dream, she escaped from me (as is customary with her on our real excursions), plunging down to the bottom of the cliff—as only a cat could have done without breaking its bones—and hurling herself in hot pursuit of a bird. When that gallant animal, as good-hearted as members of her breed, the boxers, generally are, but impetuous, and whom I have never succeeded in inducing to obey me, escapes like this—like a maddened huntress—during one of the walks we often take across the fields, when she ends by losing herself in the distance after having swum through the tall grasses of the Beauce—like a small terrestrial dolphin clothed in fake fur, now diving, now emerging with the help of her two large brownish ears, whose beating lofted her in long flights—even though it is well known that a dog always finds her way back again, I ask myself each time if I will ever see her again. And in my dream I experienced this same perplexity, not knowing how far the fugitive would allow herself to be borne away, and not seeing, moreover, how she could rejoin me on the top of that cliff at whose edge I found myself. However, this fear did not last long (as is the case with the pranks of the same sort which the ebullient Dine plays in everyday life) for I saw her, after a few minutes, appear at another point on the cliff and come back toward me at a gallop.

The scene then changed completely, its new setting a place very different from that cliff overlooking a barren plain, that cliff which had already appeared in the oldest of the three dreams, but in such a form that I never could have made the comparison if, near Kunming, I had not also gone to a rocky escarpment and gazed out at certain things: besides the Taoist temple with its series of structures perched there like eagles' nests (chapels set at intervals one above another, each abundantly decorated and embellished with statues, with other sculpture here and there in niches exposed to the open air of the extraordinarily steep site); besides that astonishing chaplet of constructions vertiginously suspended at various heights, I had looked—with a more peaceful gaze—at the lake that extended below with its sandy or muddy bottom breaching the surface and which, toward the opposite bank, appeared, on that day of almost uninterrupted rain, covered with a sheen as though from the saliva of snails, glints of silver close to the golds laid down on the terra firma by rays of sunlight passing through breaks in the clouds, a lake not very deep, yet navigable, since I saw a string of junks pass, reduced by the distance to the proportions of a toy. If it had not been for the sculptures in human form and the other sculptures (a tortoise with a coiled snake, a young buffalo, a phoenix) with which that real escarpment was ornamented, either in the interiors of the chapels, or on the outside, on one or another of the platforms on which the wayside altars were set one above another along the zigzagging itinerary the visitor had to follow (toiling over a succession of very steep slopes, sometimes paths and sometimes steps, and even following a narrow passage in the form of a ledge under natural arcades); if it had not been for the presence of these sacred sculptures, no precise analogy would have connected the wall of rock that loomed up in a dream more than thirteen years old to a section of mountain breathtaking in its composition as well as in the view revealed as one ascended it; and if the section of mountain thus doubly endowed had not made the connection, I would probably not have noticed how close the old wall is to the two cliffs, no less unreal, of which I have just spoken. For that first wall is clearly distinguished from the other three—that of the Mountain of the West so amply loaded with figures, and those of the two dreams, each animated by the gallop of a quadruped—in that I saw it before me like a wall instead of being perched on it. Of course what was involved, there, was also an excursion into the mountains, in that case motivated by a visit to a church; but the only spectacle there was the church itself, its back against the mountain in a spot with an extreme declivity. On the wide and lofty façade, conjoined so tightly with the mass of rock that it more or less merged with it, were sculpted enormous colored figures having something in common with the kings and other wax figures that are one of the curiosities of Westminster Abbey, and with the giant angels with long trumpets surmounting the high altar of the cathedral at San Juan de Compostela, as well as with the mannequins of musicians with which the organs of merry-go-rounds were adorned when I was younger. Figures so beautiful and so grand (in both senses of the word [*grand*: "grand" and "large"]) that seeing them at a distance I was overcome with vertigo, and filled with anguish, imagining what that vertigo would be when I saw from closer up—and, then, of a truly extreme *grandeur*—those sculptures carved directly from the exterior walls of the church and, perhaps, standing out from the very mass of rock itself.

China, where the red spot of hope is growing larger, my great friend the poet Aimé Césaire said a few years ago in a speech addressed to the people of Fort-de-France, when he was a strictly observant communist and the horror aroused in him by the full revelation—in Russia itself—of Stalin's despotic methods, as well as the inertia of the French leaders after that official proclamation, in addition to his desire to direct the workers of his country toward strictly Antillean goals and to remove their action from the oppressive weight of Soviet centralism, had not yet led him to separate from the French Communist Party. Now, Aimé Césaire (one of whose children has been entrusted to us, my wife and me, while his father is conveying the good word over there) is central to the second episode of the dream I had during one of these past nights.

The setting, now not at all picturesque, is simply the country. The country, in the very imprecise meaning that this term assumes for the person listening to me if I say, today, that next Sunday I will be "in the country," as others speak of the visit they will make "to the seaside" or "to the mountains." Like this monotonous setting (a house that is the one at Saint-Hilaire but does not resemble it, a very thickly wooded garden that is perhaps based—with certain vague memories of the villa "Les Gaules" where my mother lived, near Nemours, and that I feel I have always known—on a photo received that same day that showed me my mother's tomb entirely covered with flowers concealing its stony angles and giving it the rustic aspect of a tumulus), the last episode of the dream is only a confused accumulation in which old memories mingle with my current preoccupations. In this house where I am hosting Aimé Césaire—a detail probably derived from the fact that for the moment I am lodging one of his sons—a crowd of people of color who have come to see my guest are pressing into a sort of long corridor-veranda that leads from the bedroom he is occupying to the little room where I am temporarily encamped, a sort of cubicle without a door and missing one side. Césaire and I are supposed to go out together and, perhaps, take a country bus with a few of our family as a sort of excursion (since "country" for city dwellers evokes "vacation"). Entering my cubicle to get ready, I note that a part of the crowd from Martinique has invaded the room, which is open to the elements anyway, and has thought fit to shift all my belongings (among them the pair of laced boots that I wore riding a mule during the trip, at once so remote and so present, that I took to Ethiopia more than twenty years ago). To these people, who have set up a refreshment bar on my table, where soft drinks and syrups are being sold (more or less as in the *ajoupa,* or temporary shelters, of the patronal festivals that number, along with the funeral vigils, among the great moments of the life of the communities of Martinique), I explain that they must leave me so that I can get dressed, and that they shouldn't have upset everything like this. Pleasantly, they help me put things back in order, and together with a young woman of color I suspend from the arm of a sort of tall scales, by means of poor-quality iron wires curved into hooks at one of their extremities, the drawer or other container in which my belongings are put away. Passing through the crowd as I left Césaire's room, I have spoken for a moment to one or two Antilleans, prudently, for I wondered whether they were partisans of the one I support or bourgeois curious to find out what has become of the dissident deputy.

Nobly begun in the aridity of a mountain landscape, and pursued in the hubbub of an overpopulated house, the dream, soon an election festivity, after the vertiginous leap of an animal intoxicated by air and freedom, culminates in a crude repair job for which we shamelessly employ a delicate object at the risk of ruining what gave it its dignity: its balance, because of which the scale is a symbol of rectitude and justice. Thus summarized, the intermittent succession of phantasms acquires the logic of a fable, to which I would be tempted to assign the following meaning if I ignored the uneasiness of the atmosphere in which these events took place: our completely pure, and in some sense animal, aspiration to a life that is not closely confined is relegated to the background by political action; but this antinomy between natural demands and the rigor of an idea can be resolved practically—in a manner that, true, verges on acrobatics—with a little determination and ingenuity.

If this representation were to be oriented differently (retaining not so much the apparent success as what is laborious and problematic about the crude repair job at the end), it would still be quite poor, and by definition misleading, like anything that, being oversimplified, has been stripped of details that were hastily judged superfluous, or like what plain prejudice has induced us to extract, at whatever cost, from its radical incoherence. There is no reason, certainly, to consider that representation more suspect a priori than that which I would apparently have had to adopt if, starting from the episode of the beam of the scale (that eminently mobile shaft from the two ends of which I suspend a drawer as best I can), I had set off down the troubled path for which that bizarre object may be taken as the signpost and had interpreted the whole in sexual terms: the bitch and her breakneck plunge as image of irrepressible amorous desire, my celebrated friend as substitute for the father or older brother whose virility I have always envied, the tinkering work I accomplished, not without difficulty, with the help of a kind female assistant as expression of the tour de force that will one day be represented by the proper use of the scale with its two fibrous globes that is the engine of procreation. But there is no reason, either, to consider this representation more valid than that which I would obtain if I emphasized data of a linguistic order: isn't the bitch who runs after the bird a bitch *"en chasse"* [hunting; in heat] in the proper sense of the word? Isn't the countryside in which the subsequent scene is set automatically called an electoral *"campaigne"* [countryside; campaign]? Isn't it true that the table which I ask others to clear of its bottles, and the quadrilateral of which the beam of the scale and the drawer constitute, precariously, the two horizontal edges, have issued from the word *"trapèze"* [trapezoid; trapeze], which physically evokes an apparatus to which gymnasts cling in a certain insecurity and which I know is etymologically related to the ancient Greek τραπεξα, ancestor of the word for "banks" in modern Greek—something I learned during my first trip to Greece, when I also learned to use an equivalent of "logarithm" to ask for the check at a restaurant—and a word that, if it is actually based on the table or the counter, since the original word means "four feet," at the same time thrusts out antennae toward the *balancing* of accounts, the *balancing* of the budget, etc.? Even if I were able to show that these various analyses complement rather than exclude one another and, in the end, that they support, by confirming, one another on many points, I would find them too mechanical to come anywhere near touching what is most important, and I would accord only a small value to insights of which almost at will I can extend the series, discovering, for instance (without great effort), a fourth Ariadne's thread in astral mythology: the course of the bitch like the course of the hours set in motion by the solar bird at the dawn of the dream; the radiance of the friend, at once poet and popular speaker, who in life is not exactly an Osiris (despite what is African about him), but well and truly the incarnation of that *black Orpheus* around which an essay by Jean-Paul Sartre has caused some intelligent minds to gravitate; the dead-leaf complexion of Isis or the Queen of the Night, who, as the dream is coming to its end, tries to put back in order what has been scattered, then joins her efforts with mine to hang something in the sky of that scale whose pans (if I could see them) would obviously be two identical copper moons. This last explication is a caricature, of course, but also a magnifying mirror reflecting the insufficiency and slightness of the interpretations I sketched out before. It is a demonstratio ad absurdum, after which there would apparently be no point in trying any further . . .

Yet, like those astonishingly perforated artificial rockeries which one finds in many Chinese gardens and whose form is defined by the holes that are drilled in them even more than by the contours of their surfaces, my dream is riddled with gaps which, I must assume, have their own importance. If I examine them in their turn instead of considering only the full parts, will these gaps possibly become the *eloquent silences* starting from which I will be able to comprehend the whole truth of the dream?

The most striking of these lacunae, the one that would lead me to believe I dreamed two dreams in the course of a single night, if not for the fact that when I woke up I did not doubt for an instant that there had been only one dream, is the emptiness that separates the episode in the mountains from the one whose setting is a country house. What connection is there between the leap made by my bitch in a more or less deserted place and the whole political and social sequence whose protagonist is Césaire, toward whom a crowd of visitors is flocking? I would see none if, looking at it more closely, I did not notice that in the full parts of the dream, the theme of travel appears at various times and in various forms: it is in the course of a ramble in the mountains that the bitch Dine escapes me to go for her own ramble, and it is an excursion—this time by country bus—that Césaire and I are supposed to make; the crowd that spreads through my house in order to meet my guest is a crowd of people of color such as I came in contact with during my visits to the Antilles; lastly, the only things that were specifically identified, among the vestimentary or other objects that I rather ridiculously strained my ingenuity to tidy away, were the laced boots from my first contact with Africa, too martial an accessory for me to be able to think of them now without irony. Viewed thus, it appears that the disconnectedness of the dream, if it is due in part to deficiencies of memory, also reflects the disconnectedness—the sudden breaks, changes of view, dizzying slippages of things and feelings to their opposites—in other words, the sudden shifts of wind and changes in mood inherent in any true voyage: using a broad range of means of transport, now private and now collective; knowing, even when you are settled somewhere, that you are there only temporarily; collecting, for your imminent departure, effects and implements you have only just taken from your suitcases or other containers; passing from a wild spot to a place that is overpopulated; contemplating nature in all its isolation and then melting into the midst of great rivers of humanity; being irked by those specimens of mankind who originally charmed you or, on the contrary, being won over by those whose manners had at first irritated you; in motion even if you are sitting still, experiencing with them and with what surrounds you something analogous to the emptinesses and fullnesses of passion, as when, your heart calm, you wake up saying to yourself that you're not in love anymore and feel, then, prey to such sadness and regret that you fall in love again; asking yourself, as you arrive somewhere, what in the world you came here to do, and deriving from this acknowledgment a masochistic joy, as though the trip does not reveal its true essence until the moment when its reasonableness is called into question, that is, when homesickness shows its cloven hoof; but, lastly, feeling dispossessed when you are back inside the walls of your own house.

It would be easy, of course, to give a semblance of unity to many of the dreams that present themselves as made up of bits and pieces, if we supposed that their mad succession of adventures, lacking any visible links or continuity of setting, were framed by a journey we were taking in our imaginations. Should I then yield to this sort of facility by regarding the dream which began with the maddened race of an animal to the foot of a sort of cliff, and whose conclusion (purely virtual, since the dream stopped short of it) was an excursion in a rural bus, as, in fact, the dream of a trip I was taking? This is a question I would have to ask myself, if there did not exist, in the case of this dream, which is also in bits and pieces that I can join together through the idea of a voyage, a prior difference: from the moment this idea comes into play, not only a logical armature, but a whole emotional background, is revealed.

I spoke of uneasiness when, with a single word, I wanted to indicate the dominant note of the whole dream. But, attending to the most urgent things first, I did not try either to define the exact nature of that uneasiness or to locate precisely where and when it manifests itself.

Toward the beginning, I do indeed feel a certain anxiety concerning the dog: will she survive her plunge, and then, when I see she has survived, how will she manage to climb back up to me? However, the prompt return of the dog does not give this anxiety time to assert itself or to be more than a small flaw in the euphoria that I feel at finding myself in a *high place*, from which I can see a vast panorama. Since my fears remain groundless, I can even say that this curtain-raiser has less to do with anguish than with victory: to the somewhat lifeless majesty of the mountainous site, the sight of the familiar animal running across the stony desert adds, with its flurry of everyday intimacy, something like a gust of wind arising to animate the *pure air of the summits* rather than to trouble it. If the dream deteriorates, it is in the country house that this occurs and it is, assuredly, with the scene of the bedroom invaded by strangers that the uneasiness culminates.

Aimé Césaire lives in my house, in a room situated at the end of the veranda that is filled by the crowd of his visitors and at the other extremity of which opens the cubicle where I have temporarily installed myself. While knowing he is there, I scarcely glimpse him at all, and during that sequence of which he, though almost always hidden from view, is the central figure, I know, with the same diffuse knowledge, that the house possesses a large garden, so neglected that it has returned almost to wilderness. When the dream, long over as an action one thinks one is experiencing, becomes merely an imaginary adventure that must above all be accurately reconstructed, I will ask myself if the sight of this garden or even the mere sense of its existence was positively given to me in the dream, or if that enclosure half submerged in vegetation did not enter simply as a memory, a vague image that the *I* around which the present dream was organized had dragged after him like a fragment of a past that was not mine but his own, as would have been the case if that *I* had recollected the content, real for him, of earlier dreams of which my own memory had lost all trace. It seemed to me, however, while I labored at capturing in writing this dream of which I had been able to gather scarcely a few scraps, that that garden, very different from the one at the authentic Saint-Hilaire house, probably derived most of its mystery from the actual recollections on which it was based: the abandoned appearance of the garden of the villa "Les Gaules" at Saint-Pierre-lès-Nemours, and, perhaps, the photo my sister had just sent me which showed me my mother's tomb disappearing under a mass of sheaves and bouquets. Thus, in contrast to the distant tropics evoked by the radiant figure of my friend Césaire, there was probably, in my dream, an allusion to what represents the most stable and the most literally homebody element in my life: that childhood house now illuminated, as though by a black sun, by the effigy of my deceased mother.

To find the source of the suffering by which the dream's country episode is gradually infected, in which direction should I turn: toward that mossy pole, intuited rather than shown, that is the intimacy of a garden too close to everything of which I am woven to be clearly separated from it? Or toward the torrid pole represented by Aimé Césaire, himself almost implied too, since he remains in the wings and his existence is scarcely attested except by the people crowding onto the veranda and by my preparations for our shared outing? If the lacunae in my dream are as important as I think they are, it is not by happenstance that Césaire appears only, at the very most, in the chink of a door, and that the garden, when I tried to give an account of what happened under the roof of the country house, whose surroundings could logically include that garden, proved to be so confused that I don't even know whether it was only a memory or a thing actually seen with my own eyes, closed by sleep but open on the dream.

Though he is central to this whole episode, Aimé Césaire nevertheless seems to me cleared of any implication: if in these days anyone gives me courage it is certainly he, for I believe I can regard him as the only one of my living friends in whom art and politics—in other words the superabundance of imagination and the crude hardware of socially useful maneuvers—succeed in merging instead of excluding each other or merely coexisting after a fashion. He is neither a poet who has emasculated his art by subordinating it to the directives of a party, nor someone whose original revolt has been deflected or stopped in midcourse by excessively aesthetic concerns. Far from conducting himself like an intellectual who has become a militant as well in order to escape his own mirages, he is only a Black who, with all his genius as a writer, with all his knowledge as a teacher, and with all his farsightedness as a leader, is working for the liberation of all people by making it his primary duty to improve the fate of his countrymen. If because of the play of genealogies he belongs to the race that was flogged by the mechanized arm of the commanders, there is no doubt that morally he is of the race that—as Rimbaud says—*sang under torture.*

Césaire thus cleansed of all suspicion, what should I now say about the garden within whose tangle my mother's tomb is hidden and which tries so hard to conceal itself that its presence in the dream is only half certain? As I attempt to extract from it a secret that it perhaps does not contain, I can't help evoking the image of another garden that at a much earlier time I really visited: near the village of Ermenonville, whose château was apparently (if one believes Nerval) a meeting place for the *illuminés* before the Revolution, the marvelous English-style park, not very well tended nowadays but still orderly, that contains, along with a Temple of Philosophy dedicated to Michel de Montaigne and the remains of an archery range, the empty tomb of Rousseau, at the center of the Isle of the Poplars. As I pass, because of the dreamed garden, through a series of alternate certainties and doubts—I saw it, or rather no, I remembered it; it was a memory, but no, in writing about my dream I innocently invented it; even though it was invented, it was formed of real vestiges of my past; thus created from the truth, it is as though I had actually seen or remembered it—I think of the succession of enclosures that left me so thoughtful after my outing to Ermenonville: in the leafy fullness of the park, the emptiness of an expanse of water; in the emptiness of that lake, the fullness of the earth of an island; in the more or less round fullness of that terra firma, a smaller circle delineated by the poplars; in the middle of the emptiness created by the ring thus formed, the fullness of the stone of the tomb and, under the fullness of the stone, the hollow from which—as Nerval said—*Rousseau's ashes are missing.* Like the triple ring of fire protecting the sleep of a virgin warrior, barriers seem to have been symbolically raised around that tomb, which no longer is one since its occupant now lies in the Pantheon, where he was transferred, as though an increase in prudence required one to confuse things by removing him from his original resting place.

Arising in the course of the dream, or while I was in the midst of telling it to myself, in which case it arrived after a certain delay, but so spontaneously that the detail thus added could not have been the product of an artificial reflection, this garden with its configuration doubly indecisive (since its natural undergrowth is complicated by the muddle of my perplexity regarding it) appears to me tangled from the outset in the stems and stalks of a mystery that is part of its texture, under whatever flag its image has been navigating and even if I would no longer have, as regards that, even the slightest hesitation.

It is, theoretically, the garden of the house at Saint-Hilaire, but it is, in fact, the garden of my sister's home at Saint-Pierre-lès-Nemours. Wherever it is situated, it is the garden attached to the family house, and, being the patch of ground in which are rooted the most irreproachable references of our position in space and time, necessarily includes a tomb in the background. It is a garden that, to give a somber color to the dream, simply needs to be there and does not intervene otherwise than as a mute reminder of realities that one could not elude except by donning another skin. In contrast to everything Césaire's form contains that is warm and invigorating for the future there is, heavy with all its past burden, this rectangle of earth which the half-obliteration of its interior layout occupies without animating it.

An almost literal expression of a rootedness that seems to prefigure the last immobility toward which the seasons in their inevitable sequence are leading us, this garden would thus be the cradle, whose shadows are too dark, from which I have distanced myself each time that, separating, for a time, from those who touch me most closely, I have gone off on a trip.

That gardens should have a special place in the childhood memories of the middle-class boy from Paris or any other sizable urban center is not in the least abnormal. It was to the municipal garden that he was taken for at least some of his outings, and it was quite often there (among other open-air places contrasting strongly with the streets and their heavy edifices) that, after having run like an escaped horse, he would come back bathed in sweat to his mother or his sister, who would scold him for having gotten so warm that he was now completely soaked. The setting for great exploits and especially for mad fits of excitement, the public garden (like the one that in my house we called the "Town Garden") is, for the child playing in it, a place where, even if a guard imposes the observance of a certain discipline, space is not begrudged him. However lively his pleasure may be at feeling physically free, however, it is the private garden—less vast but subject to less strict prohibitions—that will sometimes be the plantation in one corner of which he tries his hand at horticulture by sowing sweet peas or china-asters, sometimes his Money Island or his Republic of Bears, if it is not the biblical enclosure where in the company of the animals he learns to taste the fruit of the Tree of Knowledge. Wasn't it in a garden that has lost for me all measurable surface, the one belonging to the villa "Les Gaules," now a pool of memories rather than solid earth, that one day my friend, the dog Black, standing on his hind legs and embracing my leg with his front legs, abandoned himself on my person to a piece of behavior that, without understanding the point of it, I guessed was obscene? And wasn't it in another family garden that, a few years later, finding myself alone with the bitch of the house—a sort of mongrel white-and-red spaniel—I allowed my hand, which was caressing her, to venture some improper touches that were endured without flinching by the peaceable Flora? With or without animals subjected to our whims or submitting us to theirs, it is in the tranquility of the garden, open to the skies, that one has all the latitude to believe one is a "savage," as during those days of our vacation at Viroflay when my brothers and I would play at being Redskins, and the oldest, assuming the role of the great chief, would utter the war cry he had invented— *Baoukta!*—a term that impressed me by its barbarous violence and intrigued me also because it was like a password or magic spell taken from a language of Martians or belonging to a secret vocabulary, pregnant with meaning, the key to which was possessed only by my older brother, principal officiant.

For the young city dweller, habitually confined as he is, the garden of the house one occupies in the summer, or of that which some member of the family circle permanently inhabits, is not only a place with less strict policing, but— however familiar it may be—a territory with numerous hollows always to be explored and favoring the manifestation of many singular things. Topographically, it is thus in part an unknown enclave inserted into the known world, and only later will it lose all exotic coloration in order to represent, on the contrary, the oldest and most stable intimacy, when one will recall, through the group photographs that were taken there, those gardens from which one derived the material for handicrafts as rustic as carving sticks or fashioning necklaces of chestnuts. It is remarkable in this regard that the garden in my dream, whereas its context made it the one at Saint-Hilaire, resembled more the one at Saint-Pierre with its older foundation and its history, going back to the time when, among the things that occupied me, there was a choice spot for "the garden," even if it was modest, like the one my parents rented one year near our house, so that my brothers and I could enjoy the fresh air, a meager bit of land situated in the rue Jasmin that, despite the propitious street name, never flowered very profusely. That the more recent example of garden should be replaced in my dream by an example that plunges back into that distant period gives an idea of what is so heavily equivocal about the apparition: the fatal seal of my membership in a group circumscribed and limited in time, that place, cultivated but half reverting to wilderness, is also the home port I would like to return to, not in order to put myself in dry-dock like Rimbaud's *fierce invalids home from hot countries*, but endowed with the extreme youth that allows one—because of the enticing projects that one foments there—to enlarge the frontiers of a place that is in fact cramped, and to bring infinity into its small space.

By noting, without explaining, this profound ambiguity, I have most likely exhausted what I could say about the enclosure attached to the house where I was lodging Césaire, and I am quite prepared to believe that my incapacity to go farther is due to the fact that with this theme I am touching upon something so fundamental in me that it is actually inexpressible. Will I approach a little closer to the truth, or will I simply be covering over what cannot be said with a deceptive veil of chatter, if I describe what tenderness as well as what agony has been aroused in me by other gardens I have dreamed of: the poorly lit groves where (after a macabre sequence beginning in an attic) I encountered, her heart bared as in a butcher's stall, the friend who had revealed to me that the female body is a garden of Armida, but without teaching me that in less than four years we would have exhausted the joys of the body or the soul in which we melted; the walkway, perhaps flanked by thickets and covered in gravel, where I was overcome, a few years ago, by an inexpressible pity whose nature, and, even more, that of the creature that was its object in my imagination, led me to compare it to that emotion which, when I was very young and found myself probably in our quite real garden at Viroflay, I experienced seeing a few steps from me a small bird that had fallen from its nest. In this ordinary stretch of walkway, which no specifics in the dream allow me to locate even approximately (there being only a suggestion that we are close to Paris), someone in my group has beaten a bird. "Beaten" meaning that (without intending to be cruel, but hard enough to wound it fatally) he has struck it several times with a leafy twig, in such a way that it will fall to the ground and we will be able to catch it. Leaning down to pick it up, I pass my right hand under the belly of the bird, which is a nightingale even though it does not actually show any of the characteristic traits of that species. This movement scarcely completed, I feel that the greater part of my right hand has become damp, for the bird is bleeding. Someone who is near me and who, no doubt, is in fact my wife says to me then: "They've beaten it, beaten it. Its eyes have been cut!" That the little creature should have been so unfairly mutilated, and that this should have occurred in those delicate organs of sight in which the spark of consciousness and life seems to reside, fills me with an emotion close to those inspired by love and poetry. There is no relation (I see this, now that I am going back over this dream) between such an emotion, profound at the same time as nuanced, and the horror, more intense but also more exterior, that would be aroused by the tortured humans displayed in a Garden of Torments. Is this difference—which is not a matter of degree, but has to do with the very quality of the sentiment—due solely to the fact that an emotion experienced within the terms of a dream belongs to the domain of art, since it is connected (either as the initial trigger or as repercussion) to an imaginary world that we create? Or should I rather recognize in this the proof that a certain ardent pity by which we cling to the creature whose object it is, is not the same as simple commiseration, so that we do not weigh our words carefully enough when we designate by a single term the love that we may feel for a person or a limited number of persons because of affinities that defy all arithmetic, and the love that we may pride ourselves on feeling for great indiscriminate masses: a nation, for instance, if not the whole of humanity?

All the sorrow of the world in a single cup of wine, a tempest in a copper basin and, under a bird's plumage, the fragility of all those whose existence I hold dear. Having thus delivered my long commentary, I would gladly congratulate myself on having topped off with a moral lesson the little drama I dreamed. However, I cannot do it, knowing very well that—precisely when I was preparing to conclude—I was neglecting, for my convenience, an essential element of the question. It is impossible, in fact, to wash my hands of the bird's death, for I, too, had wanted to capture it. If I was as moved as I was, wasn't it because of the blood-red remorse that colored my pity? In a single piercing thrust, I identified myself not only with the bird but with the person who in his eagerness had been too rough, whence this nameless sadness, close to that of a child who is not unaware that it is his own fault, because of his extravagant boisterousness, and not in complete innocence, that he has broken his toy. The words around which my emotion crystallized certainly constituted an implicit reproach, or even, if indeed it was my wife who uttered them, a bitter allusion to moral havoc which—the oneiric mask being cast aside—I believe she would actually have good reason for holding against me.

Starting from a garden that was not the one at Saint-Hilaire but rather the one at Saint-Pierre (which I have dreamed about once again, encountering my mother there standing straight up on one of the flowerbeds and restored almost to life but even smaller than she was and deformed here and there by swellings like a mandrake or a survivor of some plague), I have arrived, by traversing other gardens, at the ordinary stretch of walkway where, through the intermediary of a bird, I have now been confronted with this reality: correlating to my love of life, as well as to my horror at seeing how precarious it is, my enduring attachment to people whose fate I recognize is closely bound up with mine, and my inverse tendency to be unkind or detached when the idea of what awaits us, one and all, becomes intolerable to me. In one encroachment after another, and adding one slight modification to another, I have tried to fill, with the substance of my experiences, which for me take the place of arguments, the emptiness which is always carved out again after each attempt at a response to a question. In so doing, clearly I have discovered nothing I did not already know; but it is no less clear that, in order to elucidate certain facts I feel are important, I needed the evidence of that deserted garden whose calm (as much as its apparent uselessness) contrasted so with the bustle of the Antilleans. Now these details take their place among those of the problems concerning which my trips have forced me to question myself, whether those trips were attempts to find solutions for what was already obscurely worrying me, or whether they were the means by which I was led to ask myself other questions that in the end appeared to me inseparable from the first.

Apart from my two missions to the Antilles (from which issued the crowd that pushed into my dream), if I do not include a brief interval such as the visit I was invited to make not far from Blidah in the valley of the Chiffa (whose great attraction was the band of monkeys that at a certain point on the route, and in response to the simple call of a peanut seller, descended from its mountain to be regaled by the tourists), and if I also disregard two earlier stopovers in Spanish Morocco (with the encounter, on the outskirts of a village that was not, however, very remote, of a group of children among whom there was a very small girl who, having never seen Europeans before, touched fearfully with her brown fingers the paler hand of my wife), it has always been as a single man that I have traveled outside Europe, as though I were constrained to return for a time to an old vocation as a person uprooted from his home environment.

When I left for Egypt, still very young and married not even a year and a half, it was a flight—so to speak—*to a pure state*, in response to a violent need for a change of air, without my being really curious about the country I was going to see. My wife and I occupied, at Boulogne-Billancourt, a room fitted up especially for us in the house my wife's family lived in, surrounded by modern paintings and sculptures side by side with a quantity (excessive in my opinion) of bibelots and old things, including a medieval German Pietà, some glasses painted with religious or profane subjects and, next to other exotic objects, most of which belonged to African paganism, a wooden figure from Easter Island. Like many of my surrealist friends, I had belonged to the Communist Party, so one evening each week I attended the meeting of the street cell to which I was assigned. Although it might appear justified by the idea of transforming a rebellion that had been until then completely ideal into a revolutionary practice, this semblance of militant activity was, in fact, only one more form of servitude in a life that I regarded—precious as may have been many elements of its setting—as a sort of engulfment in familial banality. Whereas I had wanted to be a poet, I was now a publisher's representative, which (of course) left me enough leisure to write but could signify only an abdication, for me who, very surrealistically, had denigrated work in the name of poetry. Having posed as a person who yearned for the absolute, whom nothing could tie down, I was uncomfortable at seeing myself settled in married life, and I experienced the shame of having thus demonstrated that I had abandoned my furious intransigence. Given my partisan spirit, I also reproached those around me for their opinions on art and how life should be lived, opinions that I judged to be more conformist than mine, in that they did not go as far as those of the movement whose guiding principle was Rimbaud's idea of "changing life." Less assiduous with respect to my Parisian friends, now that I was living in the suburbs, I felt I was guilty of a twofold betrayal for which—it goes without saying—I tended to blame my wife and her family. To this was added the impression of lamentable deficiency from which I have suffered since before that time: a small-scale Hamlet, a coward as lover, a would-be rebel—such were the images of myself that no mirror needed to reflect back at me for their daily contemplation to give rise to an uneasiness that would soon verge on suffocation.

So many years have intervened by now between me and the crisis that led to that first departure that it is impossible for me to say what its immediate motive was. My job bored me, and it also humiliated me insofar as it was a job that bored me and that I nevertheless accepted (bringing to it, moreover, less and less zeal). A member of the union, as is proper, I could certainly tell myself that by thus playing my part as a cognizant and organized wage earner I was avoiding what is degrading about the exercise of a profession, but that did not help anything: the official who had seen me when I had gone to register at the union of traveling salesmen and business representatives had in fact asked (a natural thing since I flattered myself that I was a writer) whether I would contribute to the bulletin he edited, and I had agreed, for lack of a valid argument to answer him with; however, I could not without feeling sick imagine writing something that would be suitable for this professional paper, so that my membership in the vast workers' organization which is the C.G.T. gave me only, in the end, another reason for having a bad conscience. In the ranks of the Communist Party at that time, we discussed the arguments of the Trotskyite opposition, and I was sent as a delegate, along with one of my comrades from the cell, to an area assembly. This took place on a Sunday, on the premises of a school in the boulevard Jean-Jaurès. For hours I listened to the speakers from the two opposing groups dispute the question of the Russian kulaks, the balance of prices between town and country, what opportunity there was for Chinese communists to stay or not stay within the Kuomintang. A few images seemed convincing: one, offered by the members of the minority, was to bring together urban and rural prices like the two branches of a pair of scissors as it closes, and another, by the members of the majority, *China as the rising main cable carrying the electricity of the Revolution*. In theory, I sympathized with the oppositionists, but the plain commonsense arguments of those who would soon be called the Stalinists, and the appeal they made to the grand theme of the October Revolution to justify the decisions of the Russian comrades, those people who obviously knew more about it than we, since they had behind them that formidable experience, seemed to me unanswerable. In order to put myself openly on the side of the opposition, moreover, it would have been necessary for me to be better informed, for if one takes the part of a member of the minority, one really must be able to hold one's own. Whether what is involved here is an insufficiency of dialectic, too scrupulous a propensity to weigh pros and cons precisely, a fundamental doubt which leaves the door open to any challenge, or a simple lack of character, it is certain, anyway, that I have never been able to help allowing myself to be persuaded, in a discussion, and not for nothing has my companion often thought it useful to remind me how important it is to have the "courage of one's convictions." I therefore limited myself to listening as attentively as I could and remained quiet from beginning to end of the session, not emerging from my apathy even when a delegate from one of the cells from Renault challenged the street cells by saying that we weren't doing much. What most depressed me was the report I later had to give of this assembly to my comrades in the cell: endeavoring to sum up the debate, I became lamentably muddled when describing the error (denounced by some) that would be committed in underestimating the kulak danger, the need (affirmed by the same ones or by the others) for measures to be taken so that the two branches of the scissors could close, and that Chinese electric cable in which one should have confidence (as was declared by the last speaker, a representative of Soviet orthodoxy). No one understood a word of my account, and, in the end, I was sharply reproached for not having protested vigorously when our cell was criticized. On this point, I wouldn't have had to turn my tongue in my mouth seven times before replying, and the blame was only too justified; so that there was only one thing to conclude about my conduct during the whole of that Sunday, that I was annoyingly lacking in presence of mind and in the other virtues, intellectual as well as moral, without which one will perhaps be a devoted partisan but never a true militant.

To help the proletarians cast off the yoke of the bourgeoisie presented itself—logically—as a solution to a number of my problems: wouldn't it mean leaving my grotesque situation as eternal misfit in order to join those whose efforts are directed toward a healthier adaptation of things, to move from a completely verbal denunciation to a positive struggle, and, in the sphere of my private life, to react against the gentrification that marriage signified for the romantic I had remained? But I still would have had to be somewhat more than a mere shadow of a militant for this fine edifice of reason to have any chance of holding up. However, on that count too, I proved to be a failure. So the day came when escaping in one way or another from this imbroglio imposed itself as a vital necessity.

Had I returned, once again, to our house in Boulogne-Billancourt a little too visibly agitated by the drinks I had consumed with one (or several) of the poets and painters who, despite my relative remoteness, continued to be my friends? Had I yielded to one of those fits of disturbance in which the horizon seems so closed off that you feel like an animal caught in a trap and you make remarks so uniformly pessimistic that the person who shares your life must deduce from them that she is no help to you? Determining exactly which drop of water made the vase overflow would have, in truth, only an anecdotal interest, and it is therefore without regret that I am able to give up that useless research. There is nothing else to say but this: to go join, in Cairo, where he was teaching French, someone I have always regarded as having emerged pretty much without retouching from the mold in which Rimbauds are made, my friend Georges Limbour, seemed to me likely to put me to rights again, and it was my wife herself who advised me to take this trip.

I thus *left everything behind*, or, at least, made the gesture that seemed equivalent to this when the idea of "departure" had assumed some appearance of reality for me after having been for a long time only a romantic subject for daydreaming. What I accomplished remained, in fact, closer to playing hooky than to any tabula-rasa fresh start, for it was understood that I would come back as soon as I had drunk my bowlful of air and crossed out the scrawl of equations that had managed to spoil a brand new page of my life. But the thought of such a spoiling—without remedy other than absence—did not cease to be overwhelming and it was with an unsteady heart that I envisaged loosening—even for a time scarcely longer than the summer vacation—an emotional bond that had scarcely just been tied. Beyond that, a concern that was at the very least without nobility: having ceased to live with my mother only to take my place in another family, I had never had to count only on myself; and here, this time without any framework, I was going to have to shift for myself in the waters where I had been thrown by what a remnant of childish helplessness presented to me as a vertiginous plunge. In short, when I embarked (not as an emigrant but as a second-class passenger) on the steamship *Lamartine* bound for Alexandria, the very excess of my mental distress gave rise to exaltation, the thing occurring in my eyes as though a most tragic fate—a burning sign of the gods' attention—had led me to undertake a fabulous long journey. It was, in fact, to the degree that the petty bourgeois homebody I had always been had trouble leaving that he thought he was a great traveler and decorated with fantastic colors a displacement in itself quite without any element of adventure.

La fière . . . La fière . . . This was one of the almost immemorial fragments of the time that I persist in hauling along inside me and that comes, in this case, from one of the installments of *Morgan the Pirate*, a tale of adventures at sea and on land that used to be published by Editions Eischler, in medium-sized booklets of which other series were devoted to the detective *Nat Pinkerton* and the Indian *Sitting Bull*. Somewhere in Central America, in that area where buccaneers made certain names famous, like those of Vera Cruz and the Isle of the Tortoise (which was governed by the famous M. d'Ogeron whose fortified residence of Basse-Terre took the form of a wretched hamlet where one could still see, in 1948, long, heavy cannons half buried near sections of crumbling walls), the companions of Captain Morgan painfully sought their way through the inhuman region into which they had strayed, moving their feet like masses of lead as though they were sleepwalkers half dead of hunger, thirst, and fatigue, ills to which was added the torment of the fever [*fièvre*] of which, perhaps, they complained in their half-delirium in a sort of litany limited to the gloomy repetition of the word designating the fire that was overwhelming them. I myself said *"la fière"* [the proud], either because of a misprint attributable to the inattention of the typographers, or because of my own erring ways as an unskillful reader or listener in whom many words were deformed at the pleasure sometimes of his ignorance and sometimes of his imagination (for I don't know if it was really I who would decipher the mediocrely printed installment of the series whose general title was *Under the Black Flag* or my brother who would read it to me). Was it at about the same time that our sister, invited to visit a girlfriend who was staying at Noirétable in the mountains of Forez, went to see the Gorges du Fier? It would be dishonest of me to offer it as proof, but I believe I can say that between this "Fier" [proud] in the masculine and that "fière" in the feminine, one as arid and steeply sloping as the other, a link was established such that this single syllable summed up for me all that one could find that was bitter and magical when one approached remote and difficult places.

Begun in a state of distress that, as soon as the thread was cut, became lyrical intoxication after having brought me so low that, not long before my departure, I had been very close to throwing myself on the rails at the moment when the metro came in to one of the stations on the elevated line that passes through La Motte-Picquet, this trip, whose pretext had been to rejoin a friend whom I admired literarily and of whom the marginal life he had chosen seemed to me exemplary, ended up in a solitude greater than I had anticipated: once the school year was over, Georges Limbour left Egypt to spend his vacation in Europe and as for me, I went to Greece, a country of which I was wary because of my anticlassical ideas but whose beauties Limbour had praised to me, saying also that the summer would be less torrid there than that of Cairo and that there, in drachmas, I would live more economically than here in Egyptian pounds. It was at the end of this solitary tour through Attica, Argolis, and the Peloponnesus that I encountered, without recognizing it at first but as though my true rendezvous were with it, the species of fever of all fevers which is malaria.

During my stay in Egypt I had more than anything else taken advantage of the presence of the friend I had rejoined: conversations, reading, walks in the streets of Old Cairo, excursions in the environs (on the motorbike with which my companion had traveled through Syria a short time before), the inception of a poetic novel that I had baptized *Aurora* and in which I was trying to give form to my torment had sufficed to occupy me. Having gone, in sum, for a cure and with rather slender financial means in a country where the cost of living was high, I led a sedentary life, encouraged, in addition, to visit almost nothing by a hostility in principle toward tourism, an activity in which the reverence it involved for the high products of culture seemed to me incompatible with surrealism. Of the little I had seen, what had moved me the most was, without a doubt, the outlying site of Cairo from which the eye discerns, along with the flight of rapacious birds, the ashy monuments that are the tombs of the ancient khalifs and down at the very bottom, stretching out as though at the foot of a cliff, an incredible swarm of modest houses that look as though they have been gnawed to the bone by calcination and penury. *Seeing, far off, the town minced with light . . .* said Apollinaire, speaking of dazzled eagles and sketching, in a line, a marvelous picture that it seemed to me was realized here.

As soon as the Anglo-Egyptian boat that was taking me from Alexandria as a bridge passenger was within sight of Piraeus, the perspective changed: the Greeks on board jostled one another to see the Acropolis, and this joyous tumult swept away in a single stroke my preconceived ideas; I was arriving not in a country decked out in its Sunday best of colonnades but in a fully living country, where the very image of the Parthenon—pale in the luminous sky— received me in a summer dress rather than in a Renan-style frockcoat. Being alone now, I had nothing else to distract me but to visit this country my predispositions against which had dropped away and, more at ease materially than I had been in Egypt, I could walk here and there in complete freedom. I made ample use of it, and, sometimes over land and sometimes over sea (in skiffs whose flotation seemed a matter of chance as much as of engineers' calculations), I went all over the place, no longer reading anything but the *Guide bleu* (the only book that I had brought away with me when I left Egypt), inspecting ruin after ruin, going from antiquities to Byzantine constructions or to vestiges of the Crusades and, in certain little-frequented spots, arousing the curiosity of the peasants, who asked me if I was looking for treasures. Most often, our means of communication was the rough English introduced by the emigrants who had returned from America, those they called "Ameriki," certain of whom showed off their provenance beyond the Atlantic either by smoking fat cigars and wearing boaters with saw-tooth edges, or by sticking the star-spangled banner on the roof of the house that had just been built for them. Whereas I had not had any real contact with the Egyptians (in fact having nothing but antipathy for the pretentious bourgeois of Cairo), I felt on an equal footing with the Greek population as soon as I was outside the capital, a commercial city with beautiful neighborhoods too proud of the white marble that gives their buildings a nasty look of being newly rich. Sometimes, seeing me all dusty and sweaty in the course of an excursion I was making on foot for pleasure as well as out of a concern to save money, a peasant would invite me to rest in front of his door and, too hard up to offer me any wine, would bring me a glass of water. I held conversations, after a fashion, with the people I met in trains and one of them — a man visibly very poor — once insisted on making me a gift of a pencil he had on him, as a souvenir of a few hours spent in the same compartment trying to make ourselves understood. There were hardly any places or any situations in which the note of hospitality was not sounded. A tobacconist from Athens, a mature man who liked to speak French and had been my table companion for a certain time in a small restaurant in Nauplia, put me up for a few days at his sister's home in a mountain village of which the latter's husband was the mayor and where he himself was welcomed for the end of his vacation. It was here that I heard, sung by shepherds in kilts, a long epic tale the subject of which was the following: the great Marcos Botzaris is dead and his companions, in great trouble, come to his tomb to ask his advice; a coryphaeus lends his voice to the shade of the deceased rebel, whom the whole of the chorus questions. On a second-rate steamer that was ranging the coast of the Peloponnesus and which, coming from Sparta, I had taken at Gytheion (where a small fort dating from the Turks reminded me of the crenelated papier-mâché fortified castles that children play with), a warm bond was established between me and the captain, who, toward the end of the trip, since there was almost no one left on board, on his own authority moved me into a first-class berth whereas I had embarked as a passenger without a cabin. When we exchanged views on current French politics (a cause for embarrassment for me, because I was less well informed about it than was allowable), the tobacconist was quick to wonder what the cunning Ulysses would have done in the situation we were talking about, had he found himself in the place of the head of the French government. One day of stormy weather, when we were chatting on the bridge as we watched the waves' assault, the captain of the steamer complained of old Neptune, who, that evening, was really "not good for us." In the everyday world as in that of the statues, myth was always present and I saw, one night when the full moon spread out above some town I can no longer identify, an itinerant telescope renter whose placard informed idlers that he would show them Artemis for a few drachmas. As for me, the myth I was living was that of the traveler, having no more than a very reduced baggage and walking about in clothes that would soon be worn down to the thread, eating frugally and believing, when I drank resinous wine (that nectar that smells of leather and woodwork), that I was consuming all the truth of Greece, a country whose harshness the academics have failed to note, just as they have disregarded what is baroque and composite about it.

As regards the malady that the vague plural "fevers" tends to situate in a mysterious and indeterminate remoteness, I have always thought (rightly or wrongly) that it was not in Egypt but in Greece that I contracted it. Toward the end of the stay of a little more than two months that I made on the peninsula, a foolish matter led me, in fact, to spend two nights in a place infested with mosquitoes against which the detestable conditions in which I was lodged prevented me from protecting myself. A piece of negligence on the part of my bank, from whom I had requested money for my return, now imminent, caused me to remain stuck in Olympia because I could not pay my hotel bill. Kindly, the proprietor was patient for a few days, but as I was his only guest, in the end he made up his mind to tell me that, really, he could not keep the establishment open for only one guest and one who was not paying. A telegram that I had sent to pester those who were providing me with funds had gone unanswered and my host concluded from this (which was logical) that I should no longer hope to receive the money I was expecting. Sincerely grieved (his contrite attitude showed me this indubitably) to be obliged to ask me to leave, he announced to me that he had rented for me in the nearest town, Pyrgos, a small room where I would be lodged for another three days without having to pay anything; I would leave my suitcase at Olympia, taking away with me only what was strictly necessary. This was done, and I went and installed myself in a wretched place, where the windows did not close properly and where the bed had no mosquito net. I was very warm within the four walls of that room, which one could not ventilate without being invaded by a cloud of insects, and the bites of the innumerable little beasts that found their way in despite everything because of the poor joints made sleep impossible for me. The fatigue due to my peregrinations, often made under a leaden sun, as well as to my alimentary carelessness, the difficulty into which my bank's silence had put me and the impression of abandonment that resulted from it could only make heavier for me an atmosphere already appreciably pestilential. Planning to hold out as long as possible with the infinitesimal sum that I had in my pocket, I decided to simplify my meals in the extreme: a portion of a coarse bread I bought and a few bunches of grapes that I went and filched from the vines thereabouts were enough to sustain me during one or two days. I cheerlessly envisaged the moment when I would have no other resource than to go on foot, in order to ask for my repatriation, to a town situated some sixty kilometers away, the least distant among those where I could find a consulate (as I had learned from the *Guide bleu*, from which I had not separated). In the most natural way in the world, and without my having to impose on myself the additional fatigue and tiresomeness of such a proceeding, this unpleasant affair came to an end: before undertaking my pedestrian escapade, I decided to make, on the off chance, a complete tour of the banks in Pyrgos to see whether any transfer had been effected there in my name; in one of them, I was told that an order had indeed arrived but that they had not notified me, thinking that my bank in Paris would have taken care of that. I returned triumphantly to Olympia and lunched at the hotel before getting on the train again. Happy for himself as well as for me, the proprietor brought out from his cellar a good bottle of Demestika with which he watered my lunch gratis. I drank the entire bottle by myself, which would have been much too much, had I been in better form. And I thus left Olympia in a state of excitation and euphoria both at once, after having exchanged demonstrations of the greatest cordiality with my host.

It was to Patras that I was going, in order to embark there for Brindisi, whence the train would take me back to Paris. I had decided to make, before returning to France, a pilgrimage to Missolonghi, where Lord Byron died, in conditions that succeeded in making him into a legendary character: laid low by fever, as he had just put himself at the service of the Greeks to help them free themselves from the yoke of the Turks. I attached to my gesture only the vaguest political meaning for, if I still thought that a true poet is necessarily an enemy of oppression, I had, at the time of my *abandonment of everything*, taken an eraser to my militant inclinations. Simply, I regarded Lord Byron as one of the most eminent literary figures of the past century, and it was as a romantic that I went to pay homage, wanting to breathe the air in which there had still to be mixed a little of the last sigh of the lame aristocrat who—after so many passions, debauches, and scandals—had gone off to end up far away as a hero of liberty.

Missolonghi was in truth a sinister straggling village, endowed (to the best of my recollection) with a statue of the lord in the middle of a small square on which there was also a Café Byron (or rather "Mpiron," according to the Hellenic orthography). The sea wasn't even the sea, at least in its coastal part, which looked like a swamp covered with a crust of dirt. A bad smell prevailed and it seemed that in fact no stranger, poet or not, would have been capable of enduring such miasmas for long without being weakened by them as though by a poison. It was, I'm quite convinced, when I had returned from Missolonghi to Patras that I felt prey to a discomfort so persistent and so profound that I couldn't attribute it simply to the effect of fatigue and the heat.

The alert was given me when I drank a glass of ice water while resting on the terrace of a café: from the first swallow, it seemed to me I was consuming a beverage of a frightful bitterness and I thought it was a matter of the water being unwholesome. A little later, drinking something else, I found it just as bitter and realized that this detestable taste was not inherent in what I was drinking: the most delectable liquid in the world would have revolted me in the same way since it was from me, and not from outside, that this bitterness emanated.

After the incident that had kept me in Olympia and then in Pyrgos, revealing to me all at once the reality of my remoteness, I confess that this discovery frightened me: I saw myself ill and forcing myself to be admitted to a hospital in Patras, an ugly and depressing town, so dilapidated that in the hotel where I was staying—the best or one of the best—it rained through the ceiling of my room. Without waiting further, I therefore made my reservation on the first steamship that could take me to Italy.

Now, I had to struggle against an abominable fatigue and it was very late at night that my boat was supposed to weigh anchor. The wisest thing would have been to wait up until the hour appointed for the departure, but I didn't have the courage to do it. I went to bed, giving the hotel desk instructions to wake me at the proper moment. At about five o'clock in the morning a bellboy came and knocked at my door and, quite abashed, announced to me that the ship had left the port. I was so shattered by this that I do not even know if I had the strength to become angry. The price of my passage lost, I would have to telegraph once again for someone to send me the money necessary for the payment of another passage, this with the same hazards as at the time of my preceding request and, in addition, the risk of being quickly overcome by the illness. But at Patras as at Pyrgos things, in the end, worked themselves out: in the course of the morning the deus ex machina presented itself in the form of a dragoman all trimmed with braid, who had learned through his office what had happened and offered to get me out of my difficulty. In return for a large gratuity, he procured me, without its entailing a new disbursement, a cabin in a boat that was leaving for Brindisi that same evening.

This time I was at the port well in advance and I embarked in order to go to bed almost immediately, worn out by a day during which I had not succeeded in finding the long interval of peace I had hoped for. One of the servants at the hotel had in effect persecuted me by knocking at my door pretty nearly hour after hour to demand his tip (which I had certainly decided to give him but only when I left, not at all by capitulating to a solicitation that was insolent because of the distrust it indicated), a conflict in which each of us on our own account remained stubborn and in which we were both losers: if it cost me my rest, it cost him the drachmas that he was reckoning on for, exasperated, I finally threw him out and slammed the door in his face with the firm desire to knock him senseless.

At Bari—where the boat took me without an additional payment, having arrived at Brindisi very late, so that they could not oblige anyone to disembark in the middle of the night—I had to submit to another kind of victimization: toward the end of a walk in the town and in the port, I was suddenly accosted by some customs officers, who took me into their guardhouse, searched me, and despite my protests relieved me of my pocket knife, jeering. But the irritation that this incident caused me was compensated for by the little I saw of Bari (of which I haven't forgotten the candy-colored houses in one of its poor neighborhoods) and then by the long rail journey I made all the way to Milan, which revealed to me an Italy less desolate than Greece without, for all that, modulating to a postcard sort of charm and offering here and there its displays of clustered grapes suspended from trees or from the intersections of lofty poles.

The disease took hold of me *rinforzando* once I was in Milan. Sitting in a café, I heard around me a buzzing of conversations that appeared to me to be held in French and not in Italian as they obviously were: absolutely pointless family stories about which the other customers seemed to be talking to one another and that I had to follow in all their most insignificant details, without anything being spared me, this having the same absurd and obsessive character as those dreams I have occasionally had whose content is reduced to a long text (dictionary or treatise) that I decipher without skipping a line, believing it is given to me by the dream whereas in truth I am inventing it as I go along, a horribly fatiguing and tedious work that seems to me to last the entire night and is perhaps only a caricatural image of the way I have of going back over each sentence before passing on when I read a book, even a prefiguration of the activity that for the past fifteen years or so has been the number one occupation of my life: the written formulation of this immense monologue that in a certain sense is given to me, since all of its material is drawn from what I have experienced, but which in another sense obliges me to make a constant effort of invention, since I must introduce an order into this indefinitely renewed material, shuffle its elements, adjust them, refine them until I succeed in grasping something of their signification.

At the station restaurant, where I went to have lunch, I ordered—so as to dope myself as much as out of greediness—a bottle of sparkling red wine that was probably a lambrusco (that wine of a dull red with a somewhat rough taste with which my wife and I regaled ourselves in 1954 in Mantua at the Ristorante Albergo ai Garibaldini, a gastronomical place but simple and homely, whose founders were said to be three Garibaldians, "two fathers and a son," we were told without further specifics by the waiter who was serving us). Perfectly lucid at the end of the meal, I paid the check and tried to stand up: to my great surprise I found that my legs refused to serve me, and, even though I was not properly speaking drunk, since I was quite rational, I managed to leave the table only at the cost of a considerable effort. I had scarcely reached the street, where the sun beat down hard, when I was overcome by dizziness and had to lean back against a wall for a certain time in order not to collapse, seeing before me—as though I had entered a bizarre state of ecstasy—only a formless, intensely luminous mist. This momentary dissolution of the visible world, accompanied by a sensation of faintness—the whole perceived quite coolly—was the final blow that plunged me into anxiety and I began to recover my equanimity only when I was on the station platform, suitcase within reach and ready to step up into the train after having undergone (without being able, this time, to derive the least metaphysical pleasure from it) the assaults of an intestinal disturbance of which I had had precipitantly to go relieve myself.

In the railway car, knowing I was finally embarked on the last stage, what I felt was a great wave of euphoria. I who ordinarily avoid as much as I can any conversation of the sort that so often comes into being among people who are traveling together, chattered abundantly with my traveling companions. There was in my compartment a troupe of musicians dressed in blazers such as are frequently worn by those who perform in music halls or in casinos, and there was in addition a needlewoman who also, now that the season was over, was returning from the Lido in Venice. The fact that they thus had somewhat itinerant jobs endowed them for me with the charm one ideally attaches to those of whom one can say to oneself that they are "charlatans" and "children of the trade." I exchanged with them, as with other strangers encountered in the corridor, impassioned remarks about what is intoxicating about the fact of traveling. A sort of profession of faith which was easy for me to make now that I was returning to my home in all tranquility, leaving behind me the trip and its hazards. I believe that on certain of those I talked to I made the impression, if not of a madman of whom it was best to be wary, at least of one of those terrible bores whose overtures I am usually careful to reject, whether they are made to me on the bridge of a ship or in the compartment of a railway train.

At Paris, descending onto the station platform, where no one was waiting for me (which was natural, since I had not announced the hour of my arrival, but even so was unpleasant to me), I felt really uprooted: the ground sliding beneath my crepe soles (those soles of which it amused me to say that they were made of "calves' lungs," like the rails on which rests the statue made of corset whalebone described in *Impressions of Africa*), my clothes continuing to fray around a thinness in keeping with the idea I had always formed of the sort of asceticism involved in a stay in a "hot country," the fatigue that I was experiencing and the absence of anyone close to me come to welcome me made me think that my first attempt at a departure had perhaps made me more of an outsider than I had wanted.

The very day after my return, I was reduced to taking to my bed. I had a fever of over 40 degrees centigrade, and the doctor summoned to examine me declared in favor of an attack of malaria. He treated me energetically, and a few days sufficed for my temperature to fall. I who ordinarily read only very slowly and at the cost of great efforts of attention occupied my period of reclusion reading, at the rate of about one volume per day, a part of the Parisian romancero in which are narrated the adventures of *Fantômas*, the bandit with many and varied experiences. I have not forgotten the proud impression of extreme acuity of mind that I experienced during this whole period. There were, of course, moments of slackening in which I projected on one or another of the walls of my room a succession of images issuing from my plunges into a half delirium, but a conscious effort always allowed me to recover my lucidity as soon as someone entered the room and spoke to me. When the fever relinquished me, I sweated so much that my sheets were quite wet and one might have thought that the disease that had left me, sucked up by some other blotting pad after that of my bed linen fit to be wrung out, was resolving into an immense spot of dampness spreading over the wallpaper against which the couch where I lay was placed.

In a position, now, to look at this with a cooler eye, and knowing myself better (for I have taken, with the passage of time, a clearer and clearer view of my narrow repertory of gestures repeated with few variants), I can say to myself that beyond any deliberate trickery, but as though I had astutely gotten out of a venture without loss, I emerged gaining rather than losing from an escapade in which the adventure had been experienced without seriously testing me: in effect, because of this crisis involving malaria, a disease that was certainly benign but that had swooped down on me like a punishment from heaven, I ended in a blaze of glory my several months of leisurely wandering and I was anointed in my own eyes as *one-greatly-pursued-by-a-fate-that-will-never-grant-him-rest*.

To appropriate the world symbolically by roaming through it, to live in new settings in order to enlarge my mental perspectives and break the thread of the calendar, to slake a certain thirst as cerebral as it is emotional by establishing other human contacts—these are, on a level deeper than the immediate need for change, some of the most important reasons I have for traveling. But I am discovering, in the light of this first departure, which at first had Egypt alone as its goal, another reason, more secret but no less decisive, that I had for effecting, even though nothing obliged me to do this, distant displacements that substantially removed me from those close to me.

To substitute, for my presence, which I managed so badly, an absence that was certainly not total, since I continued to exist for those I had left, but such that I existed henceforth *at a distance*—this natural consequence of my first departure was also one of its most exciting aspects: moving about in a world different from that in which my family lived, I escaped them, without, however, entirely burning my bridges—quite the contrary, since between us there was now the connection created by the flattering notion which my letters and postcards, with what they said about my unsystematic way of living and my itineraries, would lead them to form of the traveler I had become, and by the notion (on my part), almost mythological and no longer simply social, which, through being without her, I would form of the companion from whom I was separated. As though—having for a long time now been impressed by a famous example— I had wanted to relive, in my own way, that biblical legend of which a transcription in the form of silhouettes had been published, toward the end of the previous century, in an album that I had, in the old days, complete freedom to leaf through, among the works in my father's library acknowledged to be within my reach, I was playing, in sum, the Prodigal Son in his period of destitution, the runaway who will see his return fêted by the slaughter of the fatted calf and will be looked upon with an eye all the more tender because he has gone wandering off in a foolhardy way. But unlike the Prodigal Son, who has not foreseen the fatted calf and risks everything when he goes away, in my case I had always planned on returning and pursued an end fundamentally alien to the satisfaction of a curiosity of which you do not know where it may lead: wanting to be not there, yet not at all expressly enticed by what I might find elsewhere, I had left home not so much in order to see as to be seen traveling, taking, without cutting any ties, a little distance from the one who would follow my journey with the eyes of Penelope, and bent, certainly, on being a solitary creature but being so only for a time.

Thus, even in the course of this flight (if I may designate by such a name a voyage that truly had as its principal object to withdraw me from my family circle but was accomplished in broad daylight and not surreptitiously, as flights are), I took care not to do away with the thread that, over broad expanses of sea and land, connected me to my household gods, those gods who in my recent dream showed through under cover of a garden and who, after the fashion of most gods, present a double face, since they are at once that for which, out there, I feel homesick and that, in which, here, I do not want to root myself.

"How one seeks to break through one's isolation, to be no longer alone, to be understood by another. How, once one has revealed everything (or has *believed* one is revealing everything), been understood, it is even worse: an impression of promiscuity, and that the *other* has all rights over one." When—in the very middle of the year 1934—I wrote down this reflection, in which this same *I* (who speak now as such, no longer taking cover behind the least defined of the third-person pronouns) made the scales lean in the direction, not of communion, but of silence and withdrawal into oneself, it had been a good sixteen months since I had returned from the longest of the trips I took: the one during which I was initiated in the ethnography of Black Africa and which, begun in 1931 and completed in 1933, will have occupied in truth a large part of my life, if one includes not only the period of preparation and the period, just as tumultuous, that followed my return, but all the sequelae of an episode that represented a serious turning point in the course of my life, if only to the extent that it endowed me with a profession.

This second departure—the one that in a certain sense I ought to call the last, since none of those that followed assumed the romantic tint that could legitimize the use of the lovely word "departure"—this second departure, even more distinctly than the first, was motivated by the need to violate my parole. Things going from bad to worse, for me, without my being able seriously to incriminate external circumstances or the attitude of those around me, I had had to recognize that at the source of my breakdowns and more and more frequent outbursts, there was something rather pathological—an observation that was humiliating but that did not exclude a touch of optimism, for, if there was an illness, there was at the same time a chance of curing myself of it. I therefore had recourse to the care of a psychoanalyst, and it was from him, naturally, that I asked for advice when I had to answer with a yes or no the offer that was made to me to join, as secretary, a mission whose goal was to work in Ethiopia, where it would go by way of Dakar instead of taking a more direct route. Thinking that such a change of air, and long months of studies, combined with an active life, would be beneficial for me, it was yes that my adviser urged on me.

The length of this voyage (foreseen as necessarily occupying us for a year and a half or two years); the character of the countries traveled (those black countries with "indigenes" similar to those described to me at one time by my Uncle Prosper, the sergeant in the colonial army who had served in Madagascar under Gallieni, whose name was almost as thick with tropical heat as the word "indigenes" itself or the words "Cochin China," thrust back to the far end of the world by its ricochet of syllables; with "indigenes" whom, despite what I had learned about the too-quickly-dubbed-primitive peoples of Africa, Oceania, or

America from reading a certain vulgarizing exposé of the theses of Lévy-Bruhl, I was quite prepared to imagine endowed with the conventional features of the savages one sees in Châtelet-type spectacles in chocolate tights to imitate negro skin; that unsubjugated country that was called Abyssinia or Ethiopia and whose sovereigns up to Menelik II, to whom Rimbaud sold arms, traditionally traced their genealogy back to Solomon and to the Queen of Sheba); the harmful climates and harsh living conditions that I would have to confront (I, whose taste for a burning-hot sun, for strongly spiced dishes, for non-liqueurlike alcohols, for meat that was red and rather firm, this taste that has always deterred me from those too soft beds in which one sinks down and for a long time induced me to regard a military bed with supple steel springs as representing the height of comfort, I, whose taste apparently hostile to all softness does not prevent me from being a sybarite revolted by violent exercises as well as by cold water or from loving to linger lazily in overheated baths) — these were the essential traits that placed this new departure in a more rigorous perspective than the kind of trompe-l'oeil to which the first had more or less conformed. Mingled with the idea of accomplishing my redemption by performing my role on a team that demanded certain manly qualities from its participants, was the idea of a sort of perdition: to plunge, as I was going to do, into the heart of the black continent, to grapple with its reality, sometimes too dry, sometimes too luxuriant, to live on an equal footing with men apparently closer than I to a state of nature, was to break the circle of habits in which I was locked, to reject my mental corset as a European for whom two plus two makes four is the ABC of wisdom, to throw myself body and soul into an adventure from which I could tell myself in a sense I would never return, since it seemed out of the question that I would be intellectually and spiritually the same when I emerged from this swim in the waters of primitivism. If the voyage I was undertaking was likely to give me direct knowledge of that negro world which, ever since the advent of jazz, had won me over beyond all reason and if, far from being a solitary flight marked by the stamp of misanthropy, it had the signification of a humanist quest that the team of researchers of which I was going to be part would fervently pursue while straying as little as possible from a preestablished plan, it remains true that, despite its indisputable justification and the eminently academic auspices under which it would be effected, I attributed to it the same flame color as to a daredevil enterprise, if not one of desperadoes, a color scarcely attenuated by what constituted for me, as for my companions, the very basis of this voyage: the somewhat heterodox science that ethnography was at that time. Beyond all desire for study, it is certain that I was preparing myself to play the parts — without concern for the flagrant incompatibilities among these characters — of various of Conrad's heroes: the sailor, fallen, then regenerated, in *Lord Jim*; the perfect gentleman in tropical suit in *Victory*; the hothead whom, in *Heart of Darkness*, the narrator discovers negrified "in the outposts of civilization."

These reflections on the spirit in which I prepared myself to cross Africa—a state of mind I am trying to summon up again, since that would be desirable if I am to talk about it, but in vain, so anachronistic does its naïveté seem to me—are being written during a trip. However, this circumstance is of no help to me, for this trip is, in truth, too different from the one whose amplitude would almost have permitted me to think myself possessed of the whole world, and, isolated to the point where I soon felt it, despite living within a group and having multiple contacts, something like God or like Lucifer in exile: the sojourn that my wife and I are presently making in Florence (after the hydrotherapy that took me, at the beginning of this month, to the waters of Montecatini) has, in fact, no other purpose but rest and amusement. Such a sojourn—merely a way of relaxing among monuments and other products of culture just as one relaxes in the mountains or at the seaside—is thus as distinct from the "committed" trip I took when I visited the new China (since to participate in that tour made in a delegation was implicitly to declare oneself a sympathizer) as from the voyage made, if not in solitude, at least in celibacy, from the west to the east of Africa, driven by a need that was neither to occupy leisure time as a dilettante nor to seek a sort of salvation in the contemplation of a country presumed to be less removed than the others from perfection.

However keenly I experience it, this dissimilarity would not in itself be capable of thrusting Africa and what I expected from it so far away that, in the present conditions, such an evocation would appear as an anachronism. But it so happens that my stay in Tuscany, of which the tourist phase is only an extension of a medical phase, followed, without a break, an episode adventurous enough so that I may say to myself, with respect to it, with more certainty than for any other of my geographically locatable peregrinations, that I returned from afar when, like a dead man who is wrested by magical operations from his plunge, I emerged from the darkness into which I had ventured.

Am I in a fit state, right now, to relate this episode, or would I do better to let it lie, waiting until the wound that caused it, as it might have caused a bad fever, has finished closing over? Whether or not I have the distance that would allow me to make out its design rigorously (at least the larger elements of it) and without in the process scorching myself too badly, it turns out, in any case, that I cannot speak of anything here without its having a false ring to it, after what will have been for me—almost literally—a descent into hell. What is more, the wound in question is probably not close to scarring over. Why, therefore, would I wait, and what would I gain from a suspense whose end I cannot foresee in any near future, and which, as long as it prevailed, would be for me a sort of paralysis? If it is still too soon for me to be capable of telling *everything*, it is nevertheless possible for me to explain myself regarding the most important thing: how, one day, my sempiternal reverie on the theme of departure as a means of drawing a line through the equation—when one's life seems too tangled for one to find a way out of it, even temporarily—took concrete form in the most desperate of acts.

Speaking of the difficulty I had detaching myself in order to go off to China, and of the happiness, so quickly disintegrated, that I derived from the five weeks spent in that country, I have already indicated how profound was the illness from which I suffered: having opened, with harsh creaks and groans, the parentheses of that trip (which seemed to me the last of my great displacements, the one after which I would no longer have either the occasion or even the wish to make any important moves, and the accomplishment of which would have led me once again to distance myself from my companion, whereas the years remaining to us to live together are now terribly numbered), it was with creaks and groans no less harsh that I closed the parentheses at the time of my return. Depressed when the time came to fulfill the desire I had had to fly to Peking, I was equally so when I returned to Paris, everything occurring, again, as though, whichever way I turned, I encountered nothing but uneasiness and could not avoid it except almost by chance, for rare and ephemeral satisfactions.

To be or not to be: this is not the question that is giving me so much trouble. To be or not to be there, to be here or to be elsewhere: this, rather, would be the burning question, where I'm concerned. When I would like to be elsewhere, I'm afraid of going away from here, and elsewhere, when I am there, scarcely brings me any rest, whether because it continues to be elsewhere and I feel disoriented there, or whether I am followed there by a regret for what I have left behind, or whether that elsewhere cannot be a here except in a manner too fleeting for me to regard it as other than derisory. Whatever is involved, whether the most benign things or the most serious, those having to do only with my surroundings or those involving the plot (daily occupations, large changes in mind or heart, and not merely journeys), this useless action of the pendulum, wherever I may be, whatever I may be doing, allows me only with difficulty to escape from its devastating exactitude.

As anciently anchored in me as may be my mistrust of literature—without, of course, excepting my own—it is literature which, indisputably, colors my life. My first trip to Africa represents in this regard a paradox that verges on buffoonery: having discovered ethnography and wanting to devote to it henceforth the largest part of my activity, I had gone off on this expedition wishing to turn my back on everything that seemed to me no more than a contemptible aestheticism; but it so happened that the travel diary I had strictly obliged myself to keep (making concessions to a far too inveterate habit of a man of the pen), this diary, published almost without any revisions shortly after my return, was, in fact, the start of my being published otherwise than in a quasi-confidential way, the one, in short, that situated me as a professional writer. The effort I had made to distance myself from the business of literature thus had an inverse result and merely endowed with a second calling—ethnography—the man of letters that I have remained. As for my recent trip to China, it can likewise furnish ample material for my irony: whereas in China I had said to myself that, as a Chinese in the people's China, I could quite well adapt myself to a society whose members have as their ideal to take industrial and agricultural production as far as possible, in the same way that their recompense is eventually to be anointed "work heroes" (the strongest in weaving, manufacture of steel rods, or pork raising)—just as in other societies one can be consecrated a great writer or an artist of genius; and whereas on my return from China, properly literary preoccupations had become almost alien to me and I could not see what justification one could logically propose to men except the growth of their ascendancy over nature, I found when I arrived at my house a packet of press clippings proving to me that the book I had sent out a few days before going off—*Scraps*—had been received much more favorably than my preceding books had been. This relative success, occurring when I had just become convinced that my life could very validly have been constructed outside of literature, was a mockery that could only lead me to some bitter meditations on things that arrive too late: as a young writer I hoped (without admitting it to myself) that one fine day I would have a certain following; having grown older in harness, and believing less and less in the need for my message, I was in fact obliged to acknowledge that I did not derive more than a slender pleasure from this success and that my life, though it had become that of a respected writer, was in no way changed. I found myself, in short, in the situation of one who, where his love life is concerned, begins to enjoy good fortune though he is now too old to have the capacity—or even the desire—to profit from it.

Aside from two or three studies pertinent enough to help me take stock, which I read with interest, I had the feeling, as I studied the clippings gathered for me by my wife, as well as some articles that came after, that what I saw before me were obituary notices: having been bound and determined, as I was, to create a statue of myself, and having spoken only of myself, it was about me that they were speaking when they spoke about the book, and that statue which I had taken such care to sculpt—I saw it now, with horror, rise up like a tombstone in the external reality that it had assumed. Far from encouraging me, the welcome given to *Scraps* was thus for me a cause of depression and a constraint in the continuation of my work. The two feelings, of horror and mockery, of which I have just spoken were soon joined by a sort of stage fright, entirely new to me in this area, and it, too, was paradoxical: as if I now required this praise, although I declare that it caused me even more ill than good, and as if, having tasted this poison and consumed it with many a grimace, I was nevertheless afraid I would suffer for lack of it, I began asking myself if the same kindly reception would be reserved for the following volume, these "fibrils" on which, ever since China, I have been working with a difficulty perhaps connected (I have been thinking about this for some time) with the fact that China played no more than an infinitesimal role in the exoticism of my childhood, so that it lacks certain resonances, a difficulty based undoubtedly on my concern for truth, but carried to an extreme by this new worry. The dread of no longer doing as well, of being judged someone who perhaps had his hour but is today a finished man, the idea that I have now told the essential thing or, in any case, the thing that had enough attraction in itself to tolerate being narrated without too much art (so that I will need to deploy an art that is greater and greater as the attraction of what I have to say dwindles, and that I will have to resign myself sooner or later to silence, if I am incapable of inventing beautiful fictions when I reach the point of no longer finding anything in my life worth being recounted)—such thoughts plunged me into a state of uncertainty and almost physical disgust, aggravated by the opinion, more detestable than ever, that I formed of myself, as vulnerable as most men of letters to the judgment that may be passed on them by their readers. One myth at least was destroyed forever: that of the writer as rebel, so marginalized that he is no longer strictly speaking a writer. If writing still answered an almost visceral need in me, this was no longer because I hoped to find, at the end of my written discourse, a rule for a better way of living or because I had something on my heart of which I had to relieve myself or even because I needed at all costs to obey an inclination to tell about myself; it simply seemed to me that to say nothing would amount, in some sense, to dying, in the eyes of the men and women who had followed me thus far. No visible change had affected my person, and I had not decked myself out in any almeh's baggy trousers; yet I had become Scheherazade, worried when she thinks she sees that the sultan has taken less pleasure in her tale of that night than in that of the preceding night, Scheherazade who cannot run short of stories under pain of being put to death by the sultan.

Through most of the published studies of *Scraps* or of my work as a whole ran one leitmotiv, my obsession with death, and as I read them it seemed to me that it was the same with my writings as in the Cards aria of *Carmen:* in vain had I mixed, cut, shuffled, hoping there would at last emerge a happy card; what showed up in the arrangement of figures and imageless values of my game was *Death again, always Death.* I saw a recognition that what I am is indissolubly linked to that from which, precisely, I want to disengage myself; and, whatever the praise was, anyway, I had to conclude from the great mass of these articles that my attempt to escape from the unbreathable atmosphere created by the constant presence of the idea of nothingness had failed. Certain critics spoke of my masochism, whereas I dream only of the fullness of life, and, though they clearly wanted to see my disturbance as an interesting case, they treated me as an ill man in love with his illness. I would seem blind, certainly, if I denied my inclination to lean, to the point of vertigo, over our inner abysses, and it would, furthermore, be ungracious not to pay their due to those whose commentary, in one way or another, helps me positively in my effort by allowing me a clearer view of the point to which I have come. But I may—without acrimony, though firmly—protest against the opinion advanced by some, that, under the effect of a morbid impulse, I strain my ingenuity to diminish my enthusiasms and systematically seek to destroy all reasons for hope. Refusing to be deceived is not the same as proposing to reduce everything to mere deception. True, I want to accept nothing that I have not submitted to a severe examination; but if what results from this is the destruction of many illusions, that does not mean that, with a perverse joy, I set out to disqualify all things. It seems to me, in any case, only too natural to have to fight inch by inch against the idea of death, and that, without being a neurotic, one may well resist this invasion only with difficulty; if they were not in the majority, I would, in fact, consider abnormal those who apparently think so little about the thing by which I am said to be obsessed and, in my opinion, thus give proof either of a never-failing courage or of a deficiency of perspicacity that could not be justified by its happy consequences.

Those praising me (I must emphasize) were not at all unanimous in regarding my statue with the mixture of respect and commiseration one owes to the noble forms that may be assumed by one who has been defeated. One of them, in his friendly kindness, went so far as to conclude an essay (which contained comparisons that were ingenious and for me revelatory between my various writings) by attributing to me this triumph: the discovery of the system that allows one to eliminate all distance between a personal life and mythology. But whatever egotistical joy I may have derived at the moment from the pages of my "supporter," these pages soon ceased to be a balm and became, rather, a knife in the wound, for I knew too well this about myself, that, even admitting I had managed to transform my life into a myth, it has become such only *in writing*, in the past-tense tale I have made of it and not in itself, in the present in which I live it. I was therefore stricken, in the end, by this victory announcement (whose extremist nature could hardly escape me) scarcely less malignly than by the tributes of those who were saluting my defeat.

Never happy, said the title in gold (or black against a gold background) of one of my childhood books whose theme was the following: the naïveté of a young boy and his sister, who imagine that the early centuries were better than ours but encounter only disillusionment as they experience, in a dream, life in these epochs, none of which proves to be without a fault. "Never happy," I could say with reference to myself, accusing myself of a lack of wisdom even worse than that of those two children, whose mistake is to underestimate what they have as their lot in life and to attribute marvelous characteristics to what they do not have, but who at least are led by their successive disappointments finally to appreciate what the present gives them. Uncomfortable if someone honored me while pitying me for my bad fortune, but also uncomfortable if someone sang my praises extravagantly; sensitive to judgments that I myself have provoked, and acquiescing to only a tiny part of them; disheartened by the series of clippings that I had to read when I arrived home, but annoyed when that dried up; depressed almost as soon as I saw that I was the recipient of a prize honoring me for my work in literature (the same prize that I would have been vexed not to receive once I had known I was in a position to obtain it); depressed, on the other hand, when I am incapable of continuing my task as writer and say to myself that if this goes on I will soon cease to exist for anyone, it is certain that in my chosen area, as in those from which arise, not only long trips, but other ways of searching for a Promised Land (like the little boy and girl who wanted to leave their own time for another), I behave like a sulky child, as though, despite my desire to come to an end of it, I intended to be the living illustration of that "never happy."

I present myself as a morose sort of person, I depict myself first and foremost as eternally dissatisfied, and yet I protest if someone other than me should happen to accuse me of pessimism. Is this a desire to be contradicted, or a vulnerability associated with a concealed coyness, is it a complete inconsistency, or an illustration of that paradox from which it would be difficult to escape once one has become caught up in it: to be loved for what one is requires that one reveal oneself, and one proceeds to do so, risking all, but, the confession having been made and received, one is irritated once one sees oneself taken literally and unmasked? If there is something so unfair about my reaction to the simple belief accorded to what I said that it can make one laugh or merit an annoyed shrug of the shoulders, this is not even the height of my oddness. As it happens, in fact, just when I declared that I was not in despair, and rebelled against those who attributed too black a meaning to my writings, I indulged in what one may regard as a suicide attempt, and this, when I had just achieved what for a long time I was calling a piece of good fortune, the love affair of which, I had begun to think (many years ago, by now), the other adventures of one sort or another in which I might involve myself represented only, if I wanted to see things in their intrinsic nature, timid substitutes: the vain distractions from my boredom which were, in the end, my flights to other countries, my humanist research, my vague political inclinations, from which (if it were not for what is happening today in North Africa) I would probably have turned away, after the events in Hungary, which made me see the odious sort of religious quietism into which I had sunk when, after the Vienna Congress of 1952, I had become more or less what people of the right call a "cryptocommunist."

About the crisis that motivated an action the result of which (according to conventional thinking) was nearly fatal to me, I will confine myself to giving a minimum of information. I remain too involved in it to be able to talk about it at greater length.

I should say first, therefore, that for several months I had been stockpiling, instead of using, the small tablets of phenobarbital which a doctor had prescribed for me in order to improve my emotional stability. A complicity had arisen between a woman I was corresponding with and myself on the subject of the "eight grams of soneryl," the fatal dose of sleeping pills it is good to have on hand, since to have permanently available a sickly-sweet means of doing away with oneself can only help one to live. Not having this product, I had accumulated, without telling anyone, not even my correspondent, a quantity of barbiturate that had amounted to some six grams by the night I ingested it.

I should then say that the love so much desired, even though its advent, along with the exaltation that accompanied it, delivered me from a part of my torment, gave me a clear perception of the following harsh truth: except during short periods of true peace, I seem to oscillate between a boredom such that I believe it will drive me mad and the state of intolerable tension into which I am thrown by the conflicts of feeling that surge up as soon as I embark on a love affair in order to escape this boredom. What could be poetically described as the incarnation of a beautiful dream is labeled bourgeois adultery in the language of social relations, and I suffered from that dichotomy as I suffered from the game of duplicity to which I was led, in practice, endeavoring to maintain secrecy vis-à-vis the companion to whom, despite the difficult turbulence of which I have spoken, I am joined too deeply, and have been for too long, to want to leave her, and having no other choice than to betray her by saying nothing to her, or to betray the other by revealing my secret.

A lie does not merely attack a truth; by this lie, the whole truth will soon be called into question: to love within a lie led me to ask myself whether that love itself was not a lie, to what extent my partner was telling me the truth, to what extent also were we not feasting on a Henry Bataille sort of play whose lines we were feeding each other and if, when I hoped for an encounter that would banish the idea that before one dies, one can do no more than go quietly along one's chosen path, I was really anything other than the victim either of the need to revive my slackening forces by giving them a new point of application, or of one of those violent lusts that seize men as they enter old age, most especially men like me, who, not having lived enough, and having always doubted themselves terribly, are determined to test themselves while there may still be time. What came to me then—from a woman who will remain, in this picture, a formless figure by virtue of a stupid way of proceeding that seriously falsifies perspective: the one that obliges me often to say nothing about a certain detail that matters, whereas I have all the accommodation in the world for other, secondary details—presented itself (I do not deny it) as a favor from destiny, but a favor that came to me too late, as came to me too late a certain literary consecration, and that, in addition, turned out to be impossible for me to seize without thereby seriously burning myself. I found, in short, that I was confronted with the following alternatives: either suffer this burning (knowing, furthermore, that my double life could scarcely last very long) or else remain in my rut. It was this exact point that I ran up against, believing I was in a situation with no way out and sinking more deeply than ever before into a nauseating state of mind of which I did not know what parts of it I ought to assign respectively to its physical and its mental causes.

Ancient cosmogonies describe the formation of the world as a degradation of the original unity, which split into fragments that split in their turn, so that the integrity of the whole decomposes finally into the dust of multiplicity. My own unity was first of all split between two women, and the harm, painful as it was, would perhaps not have become too extreme if the division thus begun had stopped there. But this division continued the same way as in the cosmogonies to which I have alluded. At the time of a visit from my correspondent (who had come to Paris from the Germanic country where she was feverishly trying her hand at writing while finishing her medical studies), a second and intolerable dichotomy occurred when I heard, from the mouth of this rather gruff visitor, who pleasantly accused herself of having betrayed me by seeking, for her attempts, other advice than mine, a phrase that I heard without restraining (with a greedy gesture) my emotion, but that overjoyed me only to torment me, for what I would have wanted was to hear it from another mouth: *There is something heart-rending about you . . .* This happened in the office that had gradually turned into a simple retreat, for me, in the basement of the Musée de l'Homme, which is today quite sleepy, after having been the most modern of the ethnology museums at the same time as a bastion of antiracism. Wretched as he felt, just as much so when he was at home as when he was in this lair, within the walls of which five days out of seven he enclosed himself for a few hours, the rake which I was not could not tolerate a farce in which Grace and Truth—the Cat and the Bear—took turns bringing him out of the torpor of which he was the victim. This was why he lost his grip, as they say.

The idea of suicide had been preoccupying me for a long time, it is superfluous for me to come back to this again, except to say that its ascendancy had grown starting from the moment when, no longer having my previous blind faith in the human value of what they call the "socialist construction," I saw myself not only deprived of a sort of religion, but stricken even in the activity to which I devote myself with the most consistency, since, lacking henceforth a gleam of light, even if distant and intermittent, to guide me, I would become bogged down once and for all in the slough of my book. How—now that I had been shown in black and white how very many pitfalls lie along the path of Marxism and what numbing analyses one must perform if one wants to take part honestly—how was I to take this book to the conclusion that I had glimpsed, the rejection of which would only mean (if I still wanted to conclude) its replacement by an abrupt lowering of the curtain—that is, the recording of my defeat: this conclusion being the key I had found in achieving the fusion of the poetic and the social in the direction indicated to me by the experience I recounted at the very beginning of *Scratches*, an experience that was in some sense my *cogito*, when, learning that one says *"heureusement"* ["happily"] and not *". . . reusement,"* as the little fellow I was then had just done, I had discovered the existence of language as an external reality extending beyond me, from which one must deduce that *one does not speak all by oneself* (others, even if absent, being implicated in the act of speaking, since it is their words that one employs) and that as soon as one speaks—or writes, which amounts to the same thing—one admits that outside of oneself there exists an other, so that, if one speaks or writes, it would be absurd to reject the knots that attach one to the indefinite circle of humanity that, beyond time and place, is represented by one's faceless interlocutor? To this difficulty, not altogether new, was added, as though to make the cup overflow, the fact that something happened to me of such a nature that, knowing it would be henceforth out of the question to say *everything*, I saw myself committed to a form of cheating that consisted in continuing to talk about myself while keeping silent about this thing, which was, however, more important than many others about which I had gone on at length with perhaps too much complacency.

In such conditions, I ran the real risk, by wanting to finish my book whatever the cost, of disappointing those who had followed me attentively until then and whose signs of sympathy had proved to me that one could, without deluding oneself, believe that there was some kind of communication. With my wife, life appeared doomed to degenerate little by little into a dance of death since, preferring hypocrisy to separation, but incapable of betraying her in so exquisite a way as to inspire her to forgiveness, I would discredit myself so much in her eyes and become so impossible to live with that in the end she would despise and hate me. For quite some time, moreover, our relations had been corroded by the bad conscience I harbored about her, reproaching myself for the flights that my trips had been; the almost parasitical role I had in our association (our resources coming most of all from her job, while my work at the museum represented only a little extra, whence, also, an embarrassment with respect to my colleagues, all the more so since this work was not even the one that primarily interested me); the displeasing way in which I had implicated her in my literature (that literature à propos of which I also told myself that "I was not playing the game," not having to depend on it financially and thus protected from many temptations); the lack of an imponderable gold thread that I could have mingled with the tight bonds that united us (moral, intellectual, physical also, until the beginning of the nasty period during which only by enclosing myself in the most bristly humor could I tolerate being subjected to failures that went sometimes as far as complete fiasco); the regard, lastly, that from the outset I had for her rigor (appreciating, in defiance of all my principles of equality and liberty, the fact that she was a Penelope or a Lucretia, whereas I was nothing comparable).

In addition to these reasons for feeling demoralized, there was another, of a more general sort. Even though I had not turned into a millionaire, or a king, or an international celebrity, I was now in a situation such that to complain of it would have been like finding one's bride too beautiful: in consequence of a change of locale imposed by fortuitous circumstances, the gallery of modern art that, from the time of the first anti-Semitic measures proclaimed by the German occupiers, has borne my wife's name had become the most spacious and the best outfitted of galleries of that sort; we had the use of a country house known in the area by the pompous name of "château"; I had, for my own part, acquired my bit of fame as writer and ethnographer. But regarding this promotion, by which I should have been delighted, within the limits of what it was worth, it seemed to me that my life had objectively attained a sort of horrible culminating point, such that from there on, with regard to social success, I could reasonably expect nothing more. The end of this life, as it appeared to me, somewhat resembled the last days of my stay in Florence: just as in the Tuscan city we explored so thoroughly there remained a few trifles for us to go see, there remained to me a few trifles to do during the time I still had to live—to finish *The Rules of the Game* simply in order to finish it, to compose a thick tome on Negro art to which I had committed myself with a contract, to write a study of Aimé Césaire that I had promised. I had no more plans for distant travels, or even any idea of a tourist holiday in some spot that I would have liked to know. There was the pleasure of seeing a few friends, a few shows, but no more real attraction to anything at all. I would be cut off from everything, as I had been shortly after the last war, when, in the railway car that was bringing me back from Le Havre, my liver and my nerves affected by having drunk too much wine, coffee, and hard liquor, I had felt the first violent attack of this disease and had been afraid I would suddenly begin to shout and gesticulate like someone in the grip of an uncontrollable delirium, as I looked at the countryside (wintry but sunny) in the declining light and thought of that Africa of the past that I had loved but that had lost for me all mythological dimension. It was a frightful anguish, aggravated by my confinement in a cramped railway car filled with other travelers, but its source was the idea of a peaceful group of African huts seen by the setting sun, as I was seeing the landscape on either side of the tracks; it was a grief without fangs or claws, which I may define as an impression of perfectly naked and dry objectivity confronting a countryside that in other times I would have been able to admire. Did I foresee the state that would truly be mine some seven years after, when I expressed in a note dated June 1950 a doubt about the value of the treasure I may find at the end of the imaginary road on which I walk every day more and more tired: "When—through a patient effort—I was able gradually to rid myself of everything in me that was superstition, aestheticism, snobbery, childishness, etc., I observed that my life thus pruned, improved, stripped of superfluous embellishments, was less open to criticism, no doubt, but no longer represented much of anything that was worth being lived."

Having thus come to a standstill and wishing sometimes that my uneasiness would take a turn sharp enough to gain me the diversion of a stay at the *manicomio* (as I said, using as a joke the term which, as my wife and I knew from having read it on maps of Italian cities we had visited, designated homes for the insane), I was, even before the love complications that occurred, absolutely ready to effect the true departure: by dying, I would leave those close to me an effigy that was intact, and, as for the book, the fact that it would remain in abeyance appeared to me less serious than to finish it by lowering myself to fakeries that would destroy its significance; the slips of paper I had amassed would be published by a friend just as they were, as we had arranged when he agreed to be my executor and if necessary undertake this publication. I think I can conclude from all this that the conflict that shook me would have led me to something I am not exactly sure of, but undoubtedly not to an attempt to do away with myself, if the idea of suicide, despite the change that had restored some savor to my life, had not pursued its course, under its own momentum. For me to come to the point of gulping down the stock of phenobarbital that I had created for myself (making use, in order to augment my provision, on the very eve of the day on which I performed what I would like to call the "act of the soneryl," of a rediscovered prescription that entitled me to another bottle), what was still needed was an almost accidental cause, which seemed to me, in my disturbed state of mind, like a catastrophe, and released the trigger.

I was very nervous that late afternoon, because of a rendezvous that had not taken place, a rendezvous that was in no way formally designated and was hardly more than a prospect of a meeting. Away from her, I was reduced to division, conflict, laceration, nausea. The only thing that could make me forget the uneasiness into which her irruption in my life had precipitated me (while rescuing me, it is true, from another sort of uneasiness) was her presence, that presence which I knew, at the same time—with a crushing certainty—would not have had this luminous intensity if, having become constant instead of merely intermittent, a thing settled once and for all and no longer problematic, it no longer appeared to be a piece of good fortune that one could welcome while wondering whether it would be followed by another, similar piece of good fortune. On that particular afternoon, this was worse than ever, for I had not seen her after having hoped to, and I also knew that the time was fairly close when she would be going away for several months, as she did every year. In a very bad state, I went off into the strange neighborhood of the Marché Saint Honoré, certain aspects of which were almost working-class even though one was, there, two steps from the Place Vendôme and the Ritz. A cocktail party whose object was to fête a very *highbrow* English essayist passing through Paris had been my reason for going into that area, topographically not far from my own neighborhood, but separated from it by the mental abyss that opens between Right Bank and Left Bank. In the apartment, modern with antiquated surroundings, where I was expected, I found, besides a rather large number of individuals who did not matter to me, a few people I liked very much, beginning with the hosts, he an Englishman who went through a surrealist period and is now working on a biography of Picasso, through whom I had met him very shortly after the Liberation (and I can still see him in his handsome British Army uniform), she an American brimming with vitality, built like a caryatid, her attraction residing in that grand demeanor which she mixes comically with a touch of the preposterous. To one and the other both, I was grateful for a few good, cordial times: a weekend on their farm in Sussex the last time my wife and I went to England; a morning walk I took with her alone to admire, in her Paris neighborhood, a shop selling fowl and game whose window exhibits even whole boars, then to visit, at the Magasins du Louvre, still as no more than gawkers who would just as readily have gone to see Christmas crèches, a department devoted to the divinatory arts—astrology, cards and tarots, palm lines—and I'm sure I'm forgetting some of it. At the time of the cocktail party from which I made my departure for a journey whose last stage would be worse than adventurous, both of them had just taken a trip to Belgium.

I have never liked these kinds of receptions, once they reach a certain size and I feel lost in them—standing there, awkward—among a majority of strangers, contenting myself when necessary with conversing with someone I have not seen in a long time, then someone else whom I know a little, neglecting (if there are any) my closest friends but on the other hand not willingly accepting contact with those to whom I am introduced. I like these cocktail parties even less now that I have been forced into sobriety: formerly, I drank to abolish the distance between me and the others, which sometimes succeeded, but, in certain cases, resulted only in humiliating drunken episodes; today, I lack this recourse, and I do not know what to do with myself, the idea of being preserved from the danger of getting ignominiously soused being, in this regard, of no help to me.

When the cocktail party I am speaking of took place, which was very recently, a whiskey now and then (but not more than one) was still allowed me by the very old friend and doctor to whom I had appealed for help at the time when the hope of something a little new had opened up in my life, inciting me to do everything possible not to spoil my chances: apart from the fact that I could shamelessly, and without hesitating to go into the most meticulous detail, complain to him about the impairments from which I was suffering, he had read my writing and knew me much better than his colleagues knew me and was thus certainly the one most capable of putting me back to rights. My intention that day was certainly not to drink too much, but, as I have already said, I was very much on edge. Whereas for some time, by then, I had submitted with fairly good grace to the interdictions imposed on me, I was not able to resist temptation at this party, where, despite my friendship with my hosts, I was prey to a discomfort all the more insidious because it was grafted onto the state of extreme tension I had reached and was complicated further by the disturbance into which I had been thrown by the failed rendezvous, that rendezvous which, however, was not one. I did not at all like the idea of drinking a single whiskey and then remaining empty-handed indefinitely after having gotten rid of the glass, which I would have finished so quickly, and, even before the party, I had said to myself that two or three glasses of champagne would be worth more than that single whiskey, without being more harmful. In fact, it was not two or three but numerous glasses that I swallowed greedily, one inviting the next and my nervousness contributing. Among other people I knew was a couple at whose house there had been, the evening before or the one before that, a party to which I had declined to go, alleging my state of health but in fact taking into consideration this cocktail party, to which I had long since promised to go, and seeking to reduce as much as possible my occasions for overindulgence. These people, who, logically, ought to have expected anything but to encounter me, did not seem to resent me for being there and even appeared very cordial; but I was nevertheless embarrassed at seeming not to be in bad health except where they were concerned, and it is very possible that I was driven to drink even a little more by this embarrassment, whose original cause had been a desire to be sensible.

I therefore drank in a little more than an hour a quantity of champagne that was certainly excessive but still not enormous. Having always had a very poor tolerance for drink, I have never really drunk *a lot*, even in my more wicked days, and before alcohol was for me more than contraindicated came a moment when, if I abused it, I had such aftereffects that for me its taste was in large part spoiled by that in the very moment when I was drinking: it seemed to me I was consuming a beverage whose exquisite flavor could not conceal a perceptible promise of my mind agitated, my mouth pasty, and my head at once leaden and cottony. Since this impression grew progressively more distinct as I drank, I was soon restrained without having to control myself, so that my worst excesses no longer went very far, starting from that time, when an almost organic connection was established for me between the notion of alcohol and that of deleterious potion. In the home of my friends of the Marché Saint Honoré I was therefore drunk, but with a rather mild drunkenness, and not at all to the point of rambling or ranting.

More talkative than I usually am, I was chatting with various people and, my original depression changing into the sort of exuberance that is quite often combined with a feeling of emptiness rather than lightheartedness and conceals the grim pleasure of quite consciously emptying the cup of absurdity, I ended by flirting outrageously with a young woman whom I had known in Brussels—

through her mother, who was then sharing the life of one of my friends—and whom for the past ten or twelve years I have seen now and then, not without recognizing her charms but without ever having dreamed for a second of paying court to her. Even though this took place in a social circle too lacking in moral severity to take offense at a few kisses exchanged openly, I soon became aware of my incongruity: not only should I not have brought so much passionate ardor to these effusions, but this lack of restraint, beyond the fact that it was no longer really appropriate to my age, seemed to show that in the absence of my wife I did not hesitate to give public signs of complete indifference toward her. Rescued from my enchantress by the hazards of the entrances, exits, and unexpected movements that tend to shift groups of people, I was ashamed of having yielded, for a few minutes, to a dionysian enthusiasm during which I had transgressed the laws of a *savoir-vivre* that I believe is quite distinct from a meaningless etiquette.

Things would probably have gone no further and would not have snowballed to the point where they did if I had not had to go, after the dinner hour, to a second gathering. Assuredly I would have been mortified to have behaved so badly after my relapse into a weakness that I thought I had overcome, and I would have felt even worse about having conducted myself, after the missed rendezvous, like an adolescent who does not know which skirts to throw himself at. It would have increased the sense of intolerable fragmentation I had experienced when I had not been able to restrain my emotion at hearing the phrase that came from my correspondent and not from the one from whom, at the moment it came to me, I had hoped it would come instead. But I am convinced that these new torments, added through my own fault to my other torments, would not have had any measurable consequence if my program for that evening had been merely to go to bed brooding about my bad day.

This second gathering, to which my wife and I went together, had a more intimate character than the one to which circumstances had caused me to go alone, at the end of the afternoon. A philosopher whom we have known for a long time was bringing together a few friends in his apartment on the boulevard Saint Michel, perhaps five minutes from where we live, a little beyond that naturalist's shop whose windows are crowded with skeletons and skulls of animals of all sizes and all species. I did not need, in this case, to drink in order not to be ill at ease, since I was already doped and since the guests, most of whom I had met many times or who belonged to my usual circle of friends, did not in the least appear to me as members of an anonymous crowd. However, I had adopted a certain attitude, and the incident that had occurred some two hours earlier had not lessened my nervousness—far from it. On the Right Bank I had drunk some champagne, on the Left Bank I started in on whiskey and soon lost control of myself to such a degree that, in order to continue my story, I must call upon (my memories are so vague) what my wife told me about my words and deeds of that evening, much later, when I had more or less finished gathering my wits after returning to myself between the rough sheets of a bed at the Hôpital Claude-Bernard, where, behind me (as I soon learned) yawned a gulf irreparably opened by three and a half days of coma. I will confine myself here to noting down the little I retained, either on my own or with the help of the catalyzing role played, in activating my dormant memory, by what my wife has told me.

On the Right Bank, I had displayed a momentary inclination toward an adolescent licentiousness. On the Left Bank, when I was farther down the road of drunkenness, I sank into the suspect waters of sentimentality. Among those people who seemed to have no other concern than to chat peacefully in this apartment, rather gloomy despite the lights, there was one couple with whom I maintain relations not just familiar but almost familial. When they were married, I was best man to the groom (the musician in the small circle of my friends from work), and a twofold feeling of affection and admiration is what I have for his wife, an American whose kindness and simplicity are rare adjuvants of her beauty, already great. Lost as I was, it was to her that I clung when I was tired of talking with others and disposed to give precedence to exchanges of the heart over exchanges of ideas, with which I am not so enamored and from which the mists that the scotch whiskey had amassed in my head contributed to deflecting me. *I have a great sorrow,* I said to her, without being more specific, speaking like a little boy who is trying to get someone to comfort him. Then, with a tender and childish avidity, I huddled up close to her—she could do nothing—and I remained by her side for a long time, sitting on a narrow bit of couch or on the edge of an armchair. (As I was convalescing, having found out that during the entire latter part of the evening I had persisted in staying so close that she was inconvenienced by it, I apologized for having importuned her in that way, but she laughed and immediately reassured me with a few friendly remarks.)

About the improvised supper that my wife and I had afterward at the house, settling in the kitchen with two or three of our close friends who had left at the same time we did, I recall almost nothing, and would even be incapable of saying whether the musician was present along with that American with the pale triangular face whom I had clutched as someone who is drowning may clutch a buoy or a child its mother's dress. I can glimpse only the form of my friend Limbour (whose silhouette has always seemed to me that of a pirate climbing up the rigging), and I know that during the meal I drank a little more wine.

Our guests left us close to midnight, and this was, for my wife and me, the moment to go to bed. Either I sobered up a little as I undressed and prepared for bed; or, tormented as I was under my outward appearance of childishness or frivolity, I perceived with alternate subsidences and recrudescences of acuity what had continued to unfold deep inside me while I was distraught in my outward behavior. Whatever the case, I recall fairly clearly the rush of appalling reflections that had just invaded me all at once when, standing in front of the bureau where my linen is kept, I opened with a sudden angry gesture (the way one picks up an object in order to break it or throw it out the window) the drawer in which were deposited—among woolens, gloves, and other clothing accessories—my bottles of barbiturates.

During those past few days, it was decidedly an odd game that I had been playing—something that I will compare now to a bizarre contest of blind man's buff. What was I, then, if not (but I don't claim to have really thought, at that moment, of the Mozart character I will allude to in order to be better understood, keeping in mind, also, that at the very most I can only *interpret* what I felt much more than thought) if not a Cherubino almost sixty years old who is maddened by the sight of each desirable woman, but who, unlike Cherubino, is down to his last reserves and not waging his first campaign? I had betrayed everyone, and, attaching myself to people whom I reduced practically to the level of shadows, each of which faded away to make room for another, which would vanish in its turn, I had acted as though no one existed, and I had annihilated everything by thus denying the presences without whom nothing is left in front of one but emptiness. For me, who had for so long fondled the idea of my own elimination, it was now or never. If I waited, I would do it too late, or I would never do it, and I would only succeed, at the rate I was going, in purely and simply disgusting those who had loved me until then.

Carrying with me my provision of poison, I went into the bathroom, as I do every night before going to bed. Shut in there, and careful not to lose anything, I emptied into the hollows of my hands the contents of the six bottles and then, with a rapid motion, I crammed all the small tablets into my mouth. Their bitter taste did not seem too unpleasant when I chewed them. I knew, anyway, what this taste was, because at the time when I was still making a medicinal use of the tablets I had sometimes happened to suck, instead of swallowing, the little mauve-colored pill incised with a median line permitting one if necessary to break it in two. But I had never before tasted them in such considerable quantity, and this time, I felt a whole mass of vaguely sweet and purple-blue bitterness in my mouth, with an emotion not completely lacking in joy. Having swallowed down the whole thing and pulled the flush chain several times (without managing to make all the bottles I had thrown into the toilet bowl disappear), I returned to my wife, went to bed, and curled up against her.

If I had contemplated making use of a fatal dose of sleeping medicine or other voluptuous poison in case things went decidedly too badly, this had remained in some sense theoretical; and even when I was hoarding in order to form my provision, the first step toward putting it into practice, it was rather in order to reassure myself—by means of that last card that I would hold in my hand—and not with the deliberate intention of suicide. When I felt that the moment had come to take the decisive step, if—in that instant—there was truly on my part a will to destroy, it scarcely lasted the time of a lightning flash. Rather than kill myself, what I wanted to do by eating the poison was to take a great plunge, something that later—when, having been rescued and having resolved not to begin again, I had put on the agenda a large effort at correction—made me think of what had represented for me, in that dream whose exegesis I must not abandon for in order to find my feet again I need more than ever to clarify things, the plunge of the dog Dine rushing headlong to the bottom of a cliff before launching herself in pursuit of a bird: to perform the gesture of a daredevil, who hurtles forward, head down, in defiance of what will happen and gambles his life on the toss of a coin. Rather than annihilation, what I was seeking in consuming the poison (as though I had needed to crown my series of foolish acts with a last foolishness enormous enough to silence all criticisms) was to sink down into the depths of gluttony: pushing to a tragic extreme my pitiful behavior as vaudeville boozer, I wanted to stuff myself to the point of dying of it with a substance more harmful still than alcohol and in which (if one can put it this way) one is dissolved, in a well-being that is at the same time a nonbeing, within precincts that belong to the domain of death but are not exactly death, in the place (perhaps) where stands the majestic escarpment whose appearance I have noted in many of my dreams.

My deed done, then, I returned to my bedroom and lay down next to my wife, in the state of mind of a child that has just gorged itself clandestinely on sweets and would like her forgiveness without having to ask for it.

I have sufficiently insisted on the cowardice that is, in me, an almost congenital defect, to say without pointless reservation that in that minute I was not afraid. Moreover, if I was not unaware that I had played for high stakes and that my sort of bad farce had a chance of having extreme consequences, I did not in the least believe that my fate was sealed. It was, as I have said, a heads-or-tails toss rather than a gesture in response to the deliberate decision to put an end to it all.

Lying close to my wife, it appeared to me impossible to keep this to myself.

Wasn't one of the hardest aspects of my situation of these past weeks precisely the fact that it was in her that I would have wanted to confide and that she was the last one to whom it would have been possible to me to expose my torment for, by speaking, I would have violated—and profaned—the secret that tied me to another woman? Having suffered daily from not being able to impart all my confidences to her (to her who knows me better than anyone else) I imparted to her at least this one: a few words from my mouth half asleep informed her that I was holding a provision of phenobarbital and that I had eaten it.

I had scarcely spoken before my wife declared that she was going to telephone our doctor friend. But I asserted to her that it was useless to disturb him at such an hour (wishing perhaps, in truth, that he would come but not wanting to seem to waver). I was going to go to sleep peacefully now and, I added, as to what would come next, *I'll be free of it if they pump my stomach a few times.* Saying this, I was thinking of what my correspondent, the medical student, during the conversation that we had had on one of the preceding days, had taught me about suicides using products such as soneryl or gardenal and about the care that allows, even long hours after the ingestion of the poison, one to save those who have taken this bad step. I had confessed, my gesture had left the realm of the irrevocable and everything seemed likely—now that I had given way—to collapse into a lugubrious comedy.

I sang the praises (it appears) of the two American women whom I had seen during the day, my hostess of the Right Bank and my comforter of the Left Bank, qualifying them as "very good women." If I evoked their twofold image in preference to any other, it was (I suppose) because they were, in the circumstances, the only ones of whom it was possible for me to speak without remorse, among the figures of the constellation in which shone the one that (much later) I would associate with the Evening Star pricked out in a tender sky and inflamed like the skies of autumn that I loved so much when I was in Peking.

All that is literature . . . I asserted finally, meaning not only that literature had hurt me to the core and that I was no more than that, but that nothing could henceforth happen to me that would weigh more heavily than what was accomplished by ink and paper in a world without one at least of the three prescribed dimensions.

It was after that (according to the story told by my witness) that I plunged resolutely into darkness.

II

Maccheroni . . . was the suggestion (articulated as best he could and in his softest tone) of the white-jacketed maître d'hôtel who had been vainly trying, for a long time already, to find even one word they might have in common in whatever language possibly among those they might know—he, maître d'hôtel at the Hôtel de la Ville, via Sistina, Roma, and the two ladies, apparently Japanese though dressed in Western fashion, whose dinner it was incumbent upon him to order, a procedure with negative results given that they seemed not to know Italian, English, or any of the other languages attempts at which had been made, not only by him—notepad in hand, eye attentive, and torso slightly inclined—but by one or two acolytes summoned to the rescue in order to try languages that he himself did not know. *Maccheroni* . . . suggested the maître d'hôtel, his plump face suddenly beaming, as though illuminated by this inspiration that had come to him: maccheroni, the name of a dish known all over the world, is part of the international vocabulary and, on this point at least, the icy glaze of incomprehension will at last be broken. But the two ladies continued to smile with lowered eyes, and the beam on the face of the maître d'hôtel yielded to a desolate stupor: "maccheroni" is no more a magic word than macaroni a magic dish, and, since in this case it has not been the open-sesame which would unlock the door of communication between Europe and Asia, there is no point in trying any further.

It was not to the word "maccheroni"—widespread, though not universal—that I clung, as to the mysterious vocable that a spiritual being charged with guiding me through the underworld taught me with a whisper in my ear in order to resurrect me, when I escaped from that thing which, at the time, far from being positively a thing, was not even a subject of discussion, but which, now, I can represent to myself as an immersion for three and a half days in absolute darkness. If I got caught on something somewhere in the instant when I came back up from my plunge—and in fact I would probably stick closer to the truth in saying: if something coming from somewhere caught hold of me and caused me to emerge for an instant—it was the culinary idea of macaroni (and not the word considered as such) that, for a second, played this role by involving itself in the darkness that my mind had become. A sudden feeling of disgust—a feeling that did not, strictly, follow anything, or, at least, anything definable—seized me at the moment when I thought that in order to feed me they were trying to make me ingurgitate a long tube of macaroni, by passing it through one of my nostrils: this reminded me of the ignoble sensation one experiences sometimes when one vomits and does so with such abandon that a part of the vomit goes into the nasal fossae. In order to be capable of imagining that strange hands were being thus employed in feeding me, there must have accumulated behind me a number of confused perceptions on the basis of which I could already form a very vague sense of my situation. But this disgust, and my immediate revolt against this repugnant mode of ingestion, represent probably my first gleam of true consciousness as I emerged from the sort of death in which I had been: as I was convalescing, I reported this detail to my doctor friend, believing I was reporting to him a pure phantasm; yet he said to me, laughing, that the macaroni in the nostril was not in the least my invention, since during my period of unconsciousness they had fed me by means of a nasal tube; what ought I to conclude from this, if not that that disgusting sensation of a foreign body being pushed through my nose coincided with the end of my eclipse and that it is therefore (logically) the oldest in the inextricable confusion of impressions I have retained from my period of return to life?

To return to oneself on a bed transformed by the two boards edging it into a sort of oblong, coverless box, to find oneself with feet and hands squeezed within loops formed by a sort of sausage of padded cloth, and to feel, thus tightly bound, like a maniac who has been put into a straitjacket, whereas one knows that the excess that has brought one here was not a violent delirium but the most tender passion: this is what—unlike the torture of the tube of macaroni in the nostril—gives rise to a certain romantic outburst. In that Brussels hospital where nameless people were caring for me, I was something like a Peter Ibbetson separated by his prisoner's irons from the Duchess of Towers, a lover in an opera captive to the rival faction and singing his lament, a poor Tom on whom the gates of Bedlam have closed, or any other recluse whose pain, anchored in the depths of a supremely sensitive heart, would make the very stones weep.

I recalled clearly the moment in which I had ingested the contents of the bottles of barbiturates, but I was much vaguer as to what had happened next. I simply knew that, my deed having been done, I had jumped onto a train just departing for Cannes, wanting to go see Picasso and his friend Jacqueline as much to say goodbye to them as to open my heart and confess to an act most contrary, of any I could have committed, to the example Picasso continually gives, since to scuttle my ship was to deprive myself radically of many years that I would still have had complete latitude to use for creative work. In the company of Picasso and this woman Jacqueline, with whom I sometimes talk about the regions of Sudan where she has lived (which creates between us a sort of freemasonry bond), I had gone to the home of a friend of hers, a very nice doctor, who was a pilot during the period when aviation was something of a cottage industry, and whom I have met two or three times. There, I had drunk a great deal and, my drunkenness combining with the effect of the poison, my flight from home took such a bad turn that they had to rush me to that Brussels hospital. To have gotten drunk at the home of this doctor, in the presence of Picasso, who I know has little liking for the ramblings of a drunk, seemed to me an idiotic conclusion to my lightning-fast trip, and I was especially ashamed of this lapse because it was hardly in keeping with the almost filial spirit in which, even though severely affected by the drug, I had left the quai des Grands Augustins in order to make a leap all the way to the large villa with its ornamental moldings in the Mediterranean South.

What I can retrace, using only my own memory, of the day on which I returned to myself and of that which followed is decidedly quite confused. Not only have I no precise memory of the moment in which they removed from me the fastenings that had been imposed on me, they told me, because I was trying to get up, but I do not know how I discovered that I had beneath my Adam's apple an opening which scarred over only after quite a long wait on my part: perhaps I noted that some of the air that I exhaled was escaping noisily through this wound and that I could talk only at the cost of great effort, in broken phrases, in a hoarse voice, and with frequent pauses to catch my breath; or when, after having dressed me in a nightshirt of coarse white cloth (scarcely longer than a pajama top and which I disliked very much), a nurse had me eat like a child, bringing close to my mouth a plate filled with a sort of gruel of which she stoked me with spoonfuls, the person thus cramming me with an authority at once maternal and surly asking me if I could swallow without it hurting; or, again, changing the dressing I had on my throat, she made some reflection on the state of my wound. At that moment, I realized fully that I was in bad shape, but I knew nothing about the complicated work that had been done to bring me back up to the surface, nor about the fact that my saviors had been obliged to resort to tracheotomy—a procedure nowadays quite commonplace—in order to facilitate my respiration. I had only the obscure certainty of being a sort of Lazarus risen from the grave and—neither pleased nor furious at having survived, merely bloated with a violent gust *of love and melancholy*—I derived a certain pride from having hurled myself recklessly into adventures that had made me exceptional. I had gone to an extreme. *I was wrapt in gloom, the widower, the unconsoled* who treats death and madness as his equals. However, lying on a sickbed within the four walls of an unfamiliar room, and though certainly cared for humanely, reduced practically to the condition of a prisoner, I was no less oppressed than intoxicated by this quite special misfortune on which I prided myself. Thus (probably toward the end of the first morning) my joy was very great when I recognized, as a white and brown silhouette whose presence I had not detected right away, Jacqueline standing at my bedside and observing me with an affectionate vigilance.

That same evening (when my wife and our doctor friend came to pay me a visit and told me that I was actually in the pavilion of the Hôpital Claude-Bernard where they perform "resuscitations"), the absurdity of my entire odyssey appeared to me flagrant. How, drugged to death as I was, could I have run off from my home in the middle of the night and made my way to the Gare de Lyon in order to take the train there (that train, I think now, whose very late hour of departure would have been quite strange)? How, once the alcohol drunk at Cannes had knocked me out finally, could the hospital to which it had been necessary to transport me without losing a second have been a hospital in Brussels? But at the time, what is true of most dreams was true of this odyssey: none of these unlikely notions posed any problem for me, and I adhered totally to this construction, which was entirely emotional and which I had in my mind as a perfectly evident established fact about which I did not even have to reflect, far from it appearing to be the more or less successful result of an effort at reconstruction responding to my need to soothe my uneasiness as to the place in which I found myself.

A few phrases that fell from the lips of my visitors had reduced to nothing the fable of my incursion into the South, that fable of which I could not say either that I had invented it or even that it had appeared like something revealed when a veil is torn, since, as I regained consciousness, I had found it within me as a past which, as such, existed in the simplest way in the world. Through this contact with family and friends, whose testimony was heavy with all their weight of flesh and bones, the thread had been tied again: Jacqueline beside my bed was no more than a phantasm (or more exactly the result of a false recognition, for I realized that the silhouette thus identified was that of a nurse wearing the classic white uniform); I was no longer prey to any misunderstanding about the setting of the drama or the way in which I had entered this place; the very next day, I would escape from my condition as an almost anonymous patient, since my wife would bring me a pair of my own pajamas, for which I would exchange the odious nightshirt, at once so short and so wide, which they had made me put on like a madman's blouse. Everything seemed, therefore, to have returned to the order defined by geodesy and the ephemerides, in conjunction with the registry office. All that remained was for me to take advantage of this enforced stay on the neutral terrain of the hospital, as a suspension introduced by an exceptional situation into the conflict that was agitating me, and here allow to ripen—who knows?—the seed of a solution, since I, as a resuscitated man, had paid quite dearly for the right to be in love openly. I was to learn, however, that I was still only at my very first step in the path to the return to reality: my hope of détente proved to be the utopian daydream of a convalescent to whom the future seems rosy after the tunnel he has passed through, for my gesture had no other result than to show not only the extent of my disease but my lack of concern for the harm that my defection might cause someone else; furthermore, the visits made to me—at my own request—by the woman whose irruption in my life had brought my confusion to a head, especially the intimacy manifested by her coming—more revealing still than the looks, the grasping of hands that refused to part—betrayed quite plainly the feeling that tied me to an intruder, with a bond such that I gave her access to whatever place I was and that in any circumstances at all she was the one I desired; as for the very structure of my person (the foundation of any edifice that, whether or not in the manner of a castle in the air, I had to build all over again), many days were necessary for it to finish putting itself together again, so shaken had it been by my long period of unconsciousness and the various drugs with which I was saturated.

Mentally, the crisis having concluded with a plunge of more than three days into the nothingness of the coma, I had suffered a shock ruder than I imagined. For perhaps twenty-four hours, I was, during my vague moments of somnolence, prey to an idea in itself not so strange but that shows how fragile my sense of my own identity was. As though, all unity having been broken, my fate was definitely to be a person divided, two creatures were substituted, in the most natural way in the world, for my usual personality: I ceased to be Michel Leiris and instead became—against an unclear and rather bookish or iconographic background of chaises longues and lawns—a couple of very snobbish English writers, identifying now with the man and now with the woman, according to whether I rested lying on my left side or my right, not experiencing in any way the painful impression that can be caused by a delirious reverie, that one is too weak to deny but that is nevertheless disturbed by the dissonant and confused perception of the extent to which such a divagation is impossible.

When this fantasy, now a prisoner of my mind after having controlled it for a while, this fantasy that had taken me over, was reduced to the condition of a memory whose extravagance amused me, two ideas, also singular, occupied a part of each of my nights, one assaulting me during the two hours or so that never took me much farther than midnight, the other joining this one while

I oscillated between a too lucid wait for the first pallor of day and a daydream which, even when it slipped into dream, did not cause me to forget either this bed where I was lying or this room enclaved in a pavilion that I knew was itself integrated into a vast group of buildings. The remarkable thing, and perhaps more significant than it seemed at first, was that the keystone of both of these curious constructions was a personage belonging (in the one as well as in the other) to the world of the theater, as though they had come to complete my first illusion and to illustrate, in a way richer in imagery than the latter, which was confined to setting in motion an elegant household of aesthetes, the theme of artistic activity as a way—direct or indirect—of enticing others to look at oneself, even if only a small number of persons. I must now wonder why, scarcely out of danger, I was so obsessed by the idea of the artist as *theatrical* figure at least to some degree, and if a consideration of that order did not have something to do with the gesture that led me to a sort of temporary death.

To the first of these constructions, dismantled each day but rebuilt each night more or less without variant, a memory quite distant (since it goes back to the year following the First World War) is probably not unrelated: the weekend I spent, with a girl and two boys who for several months were my inseparable companions, at the Pont-aux-Dames old people's home, intended (as we know) for the least fortunate of the professionals of the stage and to which our little gang of four had been brought by one of the two boys, whose mother—a former actress—had a management position there. Nothing about this brief stay deserves to be mentioned, except perhaps the indiscretion—in truth quite harmless—to which I found myself led: having to separate from my confederates in order to turn up Monday morning at the office of the delivery department of the Cité Paradis, where I worked (because I had to do something, after all) and sickened by the thought of this departure, which seemed to me to signify that having ceased thus to be one of the party I would occupy in our zealously united quartet a position henceforth marginal, I decided to rid myself of a job that was proving more irksome than ever, and I sent my bosses a telegram in which I pleaded a health problem or some other accident but which, drafted without great concern for verisimilitude, was equivalent to a resignation.

An old star of the variety theater, now the director of a foundation which, depending on the night when I dreamed this, was sometimes a charity establishment like the Pont-aux-Dames, where I had slept without having had any right to, sometimes a private conservatory—this was the character I incarnated, lying in that bed which seemed to me to be the actual bed of the ancient celebratory of Paris, that actress who, in plays that were once famous, had been so fêted but who was saved from complete oblivion only by the philanthropic or educational foundation to which her name as well as all her inner passion were henceforth attached. Like a ship's captain who, even while he is dreaming in the darkness of his cabin, knows he is responsible for the vessel with which he has been entrusted, and that he is responsible for other people, I was this solitary idol from whom the little world over which she reigns seems to her to require all her vigilance, even in the hours when between her and this little world there is no longer any precise relationship. An artist of the grand sort; a beauty who without appearing ridiculous can recall the time when she would happily have destroyed her career in response to an impulse of the heart or a nod of the head; God the father or mother (like the captain on his boat or the respected matron of a whole little household)—these were approximately the features of the figure in which, in the first half of each night, I would yet again clothe myself. One of the last times she appeared, when a certain distance had opened up between me and that figure (for if she continued to haunt me, it was now in the third person that her existence inhabited my mind, a distancing first begun on the night when she had fleetingly taken as her official identity that of Mme Daynes-Grassot, whom I saw perform when I was an adolescent and she an old person whom my parents had applauded when she was younger), she bore a name reduced to the surname alone, as happens with the names of many stars: something like "Sandier" or "Sanguier" but whose two syllables, instead of sounding crisply like these, created a whole past full of passionate emotions experienced, at the same time as they were provoked, by this woman whose triumphs, achieved on stages and within a repertory that were not those of our official theaters, remained, for certain people, legendary. With this surname, as loquacious as a thick calendar of events, the identity of my visitor was, that night, once and for all affirmed.

An actress whose name, worshiped not so long ago, could scarcely have any meaning now except for those rare survivors of her generation or for the young actors who were her students, this creature who during so many nights was attached to me so closely that she became confused with my own person did not have (I believe) any particular prototype. As I thought it over, of course, I found two names that were probably models for hers: that of the political leader Marc Sangnier, whose *Christian socialism* my brother and I, as adolescents, approved of and whose name we wrongly or rightly pronounced "Sanguier"; and that of the actress Aimée Tessandier, star from the same period, a photograph of whom came into my hands afterward, showing her with a mouth at once pinched and fleshy, somber bohemian eyes, and dark hair tumbling down over her shoulders. But this (I sense) is an entirely formal filiation, corresponding to the mechanical use of two names—one taken as it is, the other with its first syllable amputated—in order to baptize a figure who, in truth, sums up in a motley sort of way the special qualities of those women of the theater of whom I had heard people speak when I was a child or whose portraits I had seen in the series *Célébrités contemporaines* published by Félix Potin, a numerous succession of photo-premiums inserted into grocery bags and depicting sometimes a leader in the world of the sciences, literature, or the arts, sometimes a politician or a member of a ruling family, sometimes an explorer or athlete, sometimes a big shot in the clergy, the army, or the navy, or someone else who had won renown in any one of the other fields—crime excepted—where one can make a name for oneself. Unlike this uncertain figure, a symbol whose form was muddled but lively and warm with the shadows and lights of the life of the theater, it was a personage duly situated with respect to me and clearly labeled in the album of my family memories—a cousin on my mother's side of whom for years now I have no longer had any direct news—who was the colorless and unradiant protagonist of the second of my nocturnal obsessions.

"Louis de Kipouls," "de Kipours," "de Kilpou" . . . this was approximately (formless the first nights, then fairly clear, even though probably lacking, here, one or two other syllables that gave it the odd appearance of a name of a remote principality somewhere near the Indies) the pseudonym with which my cousin, whose actual first name was Louis, embellished himself in my dream, in order to try to mount, in little halls in the sixteenth arrondissement, the plays that he wrote as an amateur, or, failing something better, to contrive to place his essays of dramatic criticism in the daily papers. In this cousin, an affable man of slight build who, until the age of retirement, was director of a patent office and devoted all his leisure time to the practice of equitation, I never knew the slightest ambition to be dramatist or columnist. But when his image came thus in pursuit of me, I could attribute to him connections to the world of the theater without this being a pure fantasy: the father of this enthusiast for advanced dressage whom we always childishly called "Loulou," even when he had gray hair, had taken as his second wife the Belgian singer Claire Friché, whose sumptuous voice and perfect simplicity of heart, along with her impressive physique, that of a popular heroine in whom Flanders and Spain would happily have united, enchanted a part of my childhood; though I don't dare affirm it, for this is inscribed for me in a much hazier remoteness, which is less a past than a random collection of oral traditions unequally retained, I believe, in fact, that my cousin's mother was an actress, in her case retiring early and remaining in complete obscurity while my aunt Claire had her hour of fame in Brussels and in Paris, as a soprano specializing mostly in verist works.

The whole time that I submitted to the intrusion, reiterated each night, of what was not even a semblance of a character whose features I could have perceived or divined, but a dry scenario made still more irritating by its total insignificance and its vacuity, like something that comes to you by way of a piece of gossip or an inattentive reading of the newspapers, I did not know why the memory of this cousin—with whom I have always had good relations but whom I have lost sight of for a long time now—came back to me with the same insistence as if I had been one of those whom, in his tireless attempts to be performed or printed, this imaginary nuisance had had to solicit all day long. Centered upon an individual with a pseudonym at first indistinct (the given name "Louis" flanked by a name with a particle) but soon clear enough to seem, through the action of a mysterious correlation, to define its bearer as a person at once minuscule and ridiculously sophisticated whom I might have seen, for example, by looking through the large end of an opera glass, this construction—as it became more precise and solidified into a figure with unalterable relief—tended to situate itself at a distance and to persecute me, not in the manner of a fixed idea, but as might have done some sort of strange thing set permanently by my bedside. Having achieved its final form, the construction relating to my cousin, even though lacking any visual aspect (or even a sonorous one) that would more or less have connected it to the tangible world, appeared to me localized in the right part of my room. What I knew, in fact, of the machinations of the failure to whom I was connected by the impalpable thread of kinship, took place, with as much obviousness as if the thing were a physical construction, in the portion of space that extended to my right from the edge of my bed to the side wall of the room, a portion occupied only by a washbasin and a limited number of pieces of furniture or other objects including a bed with no occupant, whereas the left portion (beyond a nonworking television set positioned opposite the door) was dominated by a patient who could not speak and hardly moved—someone who, stricken some weeks earlier by a malady whose nature no one understood, was sunk in a coma and lay next to me living a larval sort of existence that was sustained through the most varied artifices, including, as part of the program, a session of physical exercises to which, from time to time, a graceful physical therapist in a small white beret submitted the inert body. It was, in other words, as though I had chosen the part of the room that was not haunted by this living dead man, in order to lodge there what had neither the need nor any conceivable possibility of being lodged anywhere: not even cobweblike, this construction, more abstract than a blueprint, in which entered only the *idea* of my cousin, in the absence of any image that would have allowed me to see him as I knew him (with his pleasing smile, his delicate mustache, his pince-nez, and his unfailingly well-groomed manner of dressing) or as he became, apparently (an old man, reclusive and almost blind, who telephones one of our mutual relations every day for no other reason than to escape thus for a few minutes his isolation as a widower without children).

In a parish bulletin or some other rag of his Vaugirard neighborhood, and occasionally in a thin booklet, the paternal uncle of my cousin Loulou—a cripple afflicted with a clubfoot and often referred to as "Louis the lame" in order not to confuse him with his homonym—published, signing them "Louis de Lutèce," columns through which, in the *Bottin mondain* (where he felt it flattering to appear), he could promote to the rank of "art critic," and decorate with a name which in Chat-Noir manner smacked of the big-city scholar, the humble Parisian pen pusher with artistic and somewhat bohemian tastes which he was. From "Lutèce" to "Kipouls . . ." the path is obviously the very same one that leads from the fantastical descendant of Gallo-Roman nobility to a Parisianized Hindu like the very select maharajah of Kapurtala, from the self-righteous follicles of the fifteenth arrondissement to the real or fictitious little theaters of the sixteenth, and—obliquely connecting two generations—from the amiable would-be dauber whose Cour des Miracles leg and druidical beard seemed to be his canting arms, to his nephew the horseman as I disguised him in this dream which unfolded in a place whose cadavers, awaiting reanimation, whose modern iron lungs and other apparatuses of survival equipped it as though to make of it, far beyond the vaudeville to which the abundant bed linen would have lent it, the setting for a science fiction intrigue. To the deferred cadaver that I, too, had been, they had applied many of those perfected methods. In the quasi-infantile state in which I found myself, after that type of death, followed by a rebirth, was it very surprising that I should be assailed by distant memories of childhood? Yet it is odd that it should have been those in particular that came back to me, rather than others by which I know I was more marked, and that they should have, in order to knock at the door of my mind, taken the form of that inept story in which a vain ambition for the theater was the only incentive.

The pretensions of this uncle to writing criticism and even to creating actual art (the latter illustrated by the small Impressionist-style pictures he painted, with which he decorated his office at the Ministry of Finance) I had transferred to the nephew, simply changing their object. The uncle, husband and father thrice over, civil servant with the meager salary, had (according to the tittle-tattle) to apply frequently to close relatives in order to pay his bills, and this is why, no doubt, the nephew presented himself in my phantasm in the guise of a petitioner, even though in everyday life he had been one of the supporters of that uncle, who was in fact endowed with enough shrewdness so that his whole circle of friends found more amusing than inopportune his habit of playing the part of the penniless daubster alongside his persona as pen pusher surrounded (as is proper) by green cardboard boxes. Kipouls—one can assume—owed certain of his features to Lutèce, features pushed into a grimace, given my discomfort and the awareness I was gradually acquiring of the singularity of what surrounded me. But, this being so, it still remains to disentangle the reasons why I was obsessed by this Kipouls or, more exactly, by the intrigue of which he was the central figure.

Arms and legs sore, body marked here and there with large purplish-blue deposits, veins hardened by the extractions of blood and various injections, and especially (as a consequence of the tracheotomy) chest racked by that bellows action which seemed to be set in motion when I went to the w.c., amplified in an almost terrifying way in the effort at excretion, and appearing then to involve that whole part of my body between my throat and my bottom, whence the stupefying sensation of having been transformed either into a collapsed accordion or into the pipes and fittings of a mains drainage system, to this being added the oddness of no longer recognizing my sex, which had become to some extent foreign to me, so deformed had it been by the catheter they had inserted without my knowledge and that I had retained while I was biologically reduced to a kind of minimum subsistence—these infirmities, gradually discovered, had given me the feeling that for the time being, I was nothing but a cripple. Was this why, by a detour, the memory of the family gimp became involved, and were there, for my cousin Loulou, in my mind, where a cheerless carnival was taking place, other motives for showing himself than his mandate as substitute for his clubfooted uncle?

I have said that my cousin's constant preoccupation, the obsession that made him so insistent but was in fact only my own insistence in the form of an unending repetition of a single phantasm, that incurable desire which turned him into a pest when in truth what was pestering me must have come from the depths of my own desires, was to succeed in gaining a position as dramatist or, failing that, as theater critic. I have also described—with respect to the real cousin—the attachments he had to the world of the stage, by way of one person at least whom I knew very well and whose memory does not fail to move me: the woman who, for me, was "Aunt Claire" and, for him, his father's second wife. If the unexpected intervention of this cousin, whom I am far from regarding as a nuisance but to whom I have never given more than his due of familial affection, can scarcely be explained except by his role as emissary of someone or something the recollection of which was provoked by my pitiful condition, I believe that the club-foot—even if my infirmity attracted his and I used his failings as a basis for composing a type of would-be artist and petitioner—has less weight here than the singer, and that it is to my aunt, an actual native of Brussels, rather than to the Lutetian so proud of belonging to the circle of "Les Parisiens de Paris" that I must turn, in order to decipher the message that I addressed to myself by inventing the intrigue of which my cousin was the shabby hero.

This half-fictional relative whom I had fashioned the way one creates a character in a novel, mingling features taken from someone else with certain of his real features (the slender figure that seemed expressed by the word "Kipouls," the rich-young-heir aspect to which must have corresponded my choice of a neighborhood such as Passy or La Muette, in which he never lived, as the site of his machinations)—did he not represent at that moment a grotesque or hateful version of those who, where art is concerned, are only dabblers avid to see their names printed in the gazettes? After the elegant British couple placed in a very Lake Poet verdant setting, after the variety star who had burned the boards all her life and even when retired still burned with a holy fire, came this needy amateur wiping his soles on every doormat and maneuvering to place at whatever cost a production so mediocre that it could not interest anyone. Helot at the same time as foil, this absurd abstraction showed me that thing which, for every artist—including the most authentic—is the monster that may one day devour him: a certain thirst for success liable to declare itself even before he has become aware of it, a thirst that will of course be impossible for him ever to slake (one success only increasing the desire for success) and that, once the first bold move has been made, is likely to produce a succession of incredible platitudes even on the part of one who, in this regard, has avoided it for many long years. It illustrated, in other words, what I flatter myself I have not become but, equally, what I was in a fair way to becoming at the time when my nascent intellectual pretensions and my snobbery as petty bourgeois of the sixteenth arrondissement were blending into a single unpleasant amalgam. As he was depicted by the echoes that came back to me, wasn't my cousin, in a sense, another version of me: an apish copy, no doubt, but not without some sort of resemblance, exactly as between monkey and man there is, beyond the imitation that makes one laugh, a real underlayer of original similitude that one must expect to see manifest itself—even if in rare flashes—in the most civilized man? Was it therefore owing to a disquieting analogy of this kind, calculated as though I had been gifted with second sight into the densest of my shadows, that, like a remorse which one cannot shake off, the outrageous puppet wielded his inexhaustible power to harass? Or, through him, was it not the singer who slyly sought to intervene, she who had been, for me as a child, the embodiment of great art, and the memory of whom could scarcely fail to be ensconced in a recess of this intrigue, which not only implicated someone of her immediate circle but seemed to parody the efforts, at once tender and tinged with childish vanity, that her husband (I was told) used to lavish so that she should be recognized as she deserved to be?

With the couple of English writers, I identified so fully that I experienced no difficulty at finding myself divided into the duality of a man and a woman. With the variety actress, with whom I had identified at the beginning in the first person, a distinction had eventually been established. As for the calamitous cousin, we had nothing else in common but this relationship of cousinhood, and if I speak of him today as of an ironic double, it is only hesitantly and upon reflection, long after my stay in the Hôpital Claude-Bernard, mistaken in the very beginning for a hospital in Brussels. From the earliest to the latest of these phantasms one could observe a degradation, as though progressively, as the element of mythic extravagance was eliminated, the artistic life itself—the single thread running through these three illusions—had become for me distant enough to be the object of a judgment and had at the same time been denuded of its too marvelous colors: I belonged, with total satisfaction, to that prestigious pair of literary people that I was; I fostered, as though they had been mine, the glittering memories and present-day concerns of the great actress; now, while the concept of my own identity was not in the least eclipsed, I was haunted by the pitiful little man whose laughable schemes—which reached me only as secondary realities since they were conveyed to me by public rumor—could neither immediately nor remotely be chalked up to my account and irritated me, not so much the way one is irritated by blunders committed by a close relation as because they had been dinned into my ears. At one end, therefore, was a blind acceptance of a metamorphosis absurd but as seductive as a fairy tale; at the other, a refusal to risk myself in wretched incidents that also involved artistic activity but regarded as dirty linen and with a most critical eye. Between this childlike adherence and this disenchanted rejection, there was my captivated interest in the words and deeds of that Sandier or Sanguier, whose name with its taste of blood and fire could have been that of a corsair or leader of a gang, an actress with a talent certainly a little crude but marked by a generosity which the couple moving about with their air of superiority in the highest intellectuality lacked just as much as did the poor conceited specimen of humanity for whom the small theaters where he was trying contemptibly to be performed represented an inaccessible Olympus.

Leading, in the guise of this couple, the almost divine life I have long dreamed of—a life à la Coleridge or Thomas de Quincey as open to the adventurous enchantments of opium as to refined conversations conducted over tea—I had merged with them without the even minimal distance between us that would have been expressed by the fact of giving them a name. On the other hand, I had dubbed with the burlesque pseudonym of "Kipouls" the character with whom I refused to discover the least analogy in myself. Anonymous to the extent that I had projected myself entirely into her image, still softly lit by the limelight, the woman of the theater had been given the handsome name of Sandier or Sanguier at the moment when, without disimpregnating myself of her, I had begun to differentiate myself from her. Having returned from the utopian heights of the time when the poets whom I would have liked to resemble appeared to me as creatures of a different clay, like the dandies, the prophets, or the demigods, yet undefeated by the discouraging profusion of lilliputian Babels that my eyes—as they sharpened—revealed to me little by little in this domain, it seems that with this figure of the actress, soon positioned at a distance as though I had detached her from myself only the better to admire her, I held in equal balance the naïvely superterrestrial effusion and the gaze that reduces to dust everything it evaluates in order to put it back in its place.

An illusion that vanished without my having had to try to escape from it, the couple of English aesthetes had barely occupied me more than twenty-four hours. If my cousin, the failure, proved more tenacious, it was against my wishes. I submitted, on the other hand, with fairly good grace to the incursions, just as indiscreet, of that woman of the theater whose profession, in the marginal way of a prostitute (she, too, devoted to makeup, the night life, and artificial light), was to move an audience and to enclose it for a time within the magic circle of a completely personal seduction. Doesn't one have to deduce from this that if, with the English couple, I had allowed those pure spirits which occupy a place of honor in the transcendence of art to return to their home, and if, by thrusting away the undesirable Kipouls, I was intending to flee the cads who make use of art—gracelessly—as a means of obtaining a certain social consideration, I felt myself on an equal footing with those people of whom the old star performer of Paris—whose acting always sparkled with passion—appeared to me a perfect example? Neither angel nor demon, but fantasy with a fully living form, she had probably been sent—into that hell-like chamber where my dream occupied the royal bed of justice—to offer me, in a striking abridgment, the image of the condition of the artist in what was for me its sharpest truth: a mix of splendors and miseries, of greatness and servitude, that equivocal condition concerning which, despite Baudelaire's fulgurating statement about art considered as a form of prostitution, I was slow to grasp the fact that the gift of the self and the desire to please, sincerity and stagecraft, adjust themselves in it according to the same necessity as the obverse and reverse of a coin, whatever the sovereign may be whose effigy the smelters have struck upon it.

It was an actress whose retirement did not stop her from working for the good of her profession, who had come to me as the embodiment of the type of artist I now hold to be the most moving and whom I would declare exemplary if not for my fear of stupidly laying down laws merely on the basis of something that touches me in a completely personal and perhaps purely circumstantial way: the ardor with which she had always acted had shown that she was ensnared and more or less in love with the gestures she made and the sounds she uttered; it was also a relationship of love that had tied her to her public; yet now it was clear that, beyond the love which, through love of her work, she had for her own person, she loved the theater enough not to think of anything but herself, since the only attachment she had kept to the world was her devotion to those of whom she could say to herself that the stage had consumed them or that, younger, they were bravely preparing themselves to undergo the trial of it. Did I want to prove to myself that if I did not have the same unconditional love for my calling, I was also capable of playing my part with ardor and entering deeply into the skin of my character, when I swallowed the dose of poison that led me in imagination to Brussels, concerning which I have for a long time tried to understand why my delirium chose that city, thinking at first that the choice might have been suggested to me by the fact that my cocktail party hosts had gone there in the days immediately preceding that party, also by the fact that it was in Brussels that I had met for the first time that young woman with whom I had too openly flirted, finally asking myself whether it was not for a more profound and at the same time simpler reason: attached to that city by childhood memories that remain very dear to me, and notably by the memory of my Aunt Claire, whom I saw there in all her brilliance as professional singer, I had perhaps gone back there the way a wounded bull returns to its *querencia* and attempts to take refuge on the small piece of ground it has chosen as its place of asylum?

In that room which, once the illusion of Brussels had dissipated, I still did not manage to situate right away (placing the Hôpital Claude-Bernard first somewhere near the street of that name, in other words in the southern part of the Ecoles quartier, and not in the north of Paris, near the Porte d'Aubervilliers), my cousin took over from the actress every night. It did not occur to me that there might exist a relationship between two characters of such opposite natures and whose succession corresponded to that of two very distinct motifs. From the ex-star to the insipid aspiring playwright, the distance was such that I scarcely noticed that there was a certain similarity of profession between her and him. I was far less aware, even, that they both took me back to the same period of the past, she, with her fame that must have dated back to the first years of the century, he, to the extent that the ill-natured gossip of which he was the object concerned, not the married man I knew best, but the bachelor I met when I myself was a very small boy. With greater reason, I did not notice that in the case of one as of the other, I was setting foot in a very particular sector of my distant past. The old celebrity whose name recalled to certain people so many beautiful evenings was, in fact, a résumé of the celebrities of my earliest youth, and the sparkling wake of that name, which had been on everyone's lips in the tumult of the boulevard, did not cease to reflect certain wonders that Paris had in the old days caused me to experience (like the evening when I had been taken into the vicinity of the Madeleine or the Opéra swarming with promenaders to see the "illuminations" for which a visit, I believe, from the King of Belgium had been the occasion). My cousin, so unfairly changed into a swaggering nobody, came to me, despite his dismal figure, from the same shining and slightly equivocal background, since in him were confusedly assembled that "artistic" line of my mother's family into which it was no doubt not by simple chance that a professional singer had married and of which I knew rather early on that it included in a distant branch the very famous actress Lanthelme (whose pearl necklace contributed to her rather murky renown as a pretty woman and who, almost on the eve of the war of 1914, disappeared mysteriously in the waters of the Rhine when she was sailing in a yacht with the editor of a large Paris newspaper and a few other people).

Unlike the pair of aesthetes, so insubstantial in their ethereal heights that they were like a fragrance emanating from flowers in which one becomes lost but from which one soon separates as the walk continues, the aged actress and the bachelor anxious to make himself known stuck to me with all the weight of the layer of memories which they implied. What they carried thus, like a wealth of contraband, was not the artistic life such as I was able to imagine it when I set my heart on being a poet, but a much more ancient bit of my past life: the one that, beyond the splendors with which the Alexandre III Bridge (as though gilt-edged) and the coach of the Comte de Chambord (as incandescent as the name of its royal owner) had amazed me early on, allowed me to glimpse that world apart which the little word "art" serves to position as a whole, even though incapable of summing up the fantastic diversity of its charms.

Thus named because of its shadowy spaces, whence people and things seem to emerge, whereas it represents (as everyone knows) a scene in broad daylight, Rembrandt's *The Night Watch* happens to have been the first monumental painting that I admired after having been duly informed of its quality as masterpiece. I was eight or nine years old, and my parents had taken us on a trip around Holland on the occasion either of an Easter vacation that began in Brussels—where my Aunt Claire had been living since she was widowed—or of a summer visit to a beach on the North Sea. Besides the "chiaroscuro" that brought out, along with the central character, a background figure that one might think was that of a woman, very small (as was my mother), but which I now know to be that of a little girl in a long dress, I appreciated the historical nature of the picture, and, oddly, the Louis XIII appearance of the male costumes and of the large musketeer-like felt hats, the whole coated with a noble patina and thus misted over in the exact proportion required by the antiquity of the scene. In the course of that trip, I also saw *The Anatomy Lesson* (à propos of which my father pointed out that the cadaver they were dissecting seemed to light up the room in which the picture was hung) and other great examples of Flemish painting, including (if it is in fact there) a *Christ on the Cross* by Van Dyck, the Christ with tawny, lined flesh that my mother, in Holland or elsewhere, found so moving the moment she rested her eyes on it and the pathos of which, conveyed to me by my mother's attitude, struck me too. Our summer vacation the year before had been spent in a place close to Lake Geneva which we had left to make a few excursions, going to Freiburg (where I saw, in an old city setting of which I recall no detail but only the antiquated atmosphere, a gray or tiger cat of a phenomenal size sitting in front of a door), to Berne (of which I remember only the bears), to Zermatt whence we went up a mountain that measures, as I have not forgotten, 3,136 meters in height and is called the Gornergrat. Begun with a night on a train, that trip had been the first that I made across the border, and I have not forgotten how, in the Swiss stations, the sight of the stationmasters in red caps and abundantly ornamented with braid gave me the enchanted feeling of being far from home. I brought back from it several wooden knickknacks representing bears, a few greenish foliated stones collected on mountain paths, and a postcard or other image in color showing the Simplon express going full speed. The number one attraction, which was also the final attraction, had been our ascent of the Gornergrat, where I learned, in the presence of the Matterhorn and Mont Rose (given life and movement by a party of mountain climbers like a line of ants, visible through the telescope), what proud intoxication you experience face to face with the high peaks, even when your belvedere is a spot to which you have been taken by a cable car. It was a revelation of nature in its "eternal snows" aspect, like a first degree of initiation before the one that, the following year, would consist in having a foretaste of the beauties that can be produced by human hands.

Between the discovery of the mountain site where tourists come from far away to contemplate the panorama and that of the masterpiece that seems to have been painted only in order to become, for its part, too, the goal of a pilgrimage, between these two discoveries of wonders of the world that did not operate on the same plane—the first on the level of what I had been taught about the seven days of Creation, the second on the closer but hardly less imposing level of the marvels that certain people have had the gift to achieve—a year at the most had elapsed. But certainly in passing from the excursion to Gornergrat to the visit to the Amsterdam museum, the kid that I was had crossed an important threshold: whereas at Gornergrat the ride on the cable car and the presence of instruments such as the panoramic table and telescope played a large part in my pleasure, in this respect hardly distinct from that which I found among my playthings (except that in this case things were taking place on a large scale and it was well understood that this was not "for fun"), the Amsterdam museum had offered me nothing that was on the order of a game or spectacular play, and the pleasure that I had taken there, if it was not yet that of an art lover, was at least the profound contentment of a boy very proud of having been judged capable of appreciating what one was presenting to him as a shrine of painting.

The heavy dress of the frail creature who seems to have encountered the civil guard by chance, and, in passing, to have turned toward the man who was observing the scene and has now created the picture of it, the jackets barred or belted with silk, the plumed hats, the pointed beards of the two officers one sees walking at the head of the cortège, the gleam of helmets and halberds (or other arms of large complicated iron), the flags, half unfurled, in the background and, in a corner, a drum whose muffled beat one would think one could hear, somewhere a dog that reminds one of an army dog—how can one know exactly what, out of all these details, was recorded by the child of eight or nine years openmouthed before *The Night Watch*, so debased that I now rank it among the works which one eventually doubts having seen, so difficult is it to distinguish between what one has derived from really seeing them and from seeing, many times over, their reproductions! Referring to a dictionary engraving (the most discreet memory aid and because of this fact the most reliable) in order to try to rediscover my first impression while falsifying it as little as possible, I realized right away that this was leading nowhere . . . What reappeared via the engraving was a quantity of *Night Watches* seen at various periods, and the oldest of them—if, of course, my desire to remember is not pushing me to imagine this—was not at all the original (with its warm tonality, dark and golden) contemplated at the time of the visit to the Amsterdam museum, but a print that must have been part of the modest art treasure exhibited on the walls of our 8 rue Michel-Ange. Besides its most important piece, the portrait in charcoal or pencil that the celebrated Munkacsy had drawn before the eyes of my maternal grandfather by copying his own image reflected in a mirror (which was presented to us as a kind of tour de force and which explained, if our educators were to be believed, a certain singularity of gaze), this heteroclite assemblage included, along with a *Rouget de l'Isle Composing "La Marseillaise"* as well as a lithograph by Léandre representing Pierrot and Colombine in company with a black cat whose pale lunula, which it would be indecorous to name, was visible under its raised tail, a medium-sized oil painting signed "Horace de Callias," a submission to the Salon whose career ended, I do not know why, in our home and which depicted the avenue of a public garden, in autumn, I think, with a woman strolling in formal visiting dress presented in profile, there being in addition to this many works of various different techniques and sizes that had scarcely any other meaning than that of family relics: miniatures dating from the great Revolution and depicting three or four of those ancestors who on my mother's side were royalists but on my father's side included a republican listed as a regicide; etchings of my father and his own father, the deportee from Lambessa, by that paternal uncle who, dying too early for me to have known him, had been an engraver by profession; a group of eighteenth-century cupids painted by a deceased relative of my mother's, also a professional, the wings of which embellishing their chubby bodies made for me charming "little angels"; an old canvas, lastly, reproducing the features of one of my great-grandmothers, a woman of middle age, it seemed to me (even though she had to have been still young when she posed thus as Motherhood), coiffed in a vast straw hat with strings and holding asleep in her arms a naked baby—my maternal grandmother—in whose hands the anonymous portraitist had placed a bunch of grapes.

Like everything that our apartment on the third floor of the rue Michel-Ange contained in the way of art objects or knickknacks, these works, painted, drawn, or engraved, and even those that were not connected by the slightest invisible fibril to some sequence of events in the family mythology—the poster with Léandre's white Pierrot, for example, or the public garden painted by Horace de Callias, which were only, in the case of the first, a framed image that my father liked very much, in the case of the other, a picture concerning which I do not know why it was there and which besides said nothing to me—these works attached to the walls within which I breathed were, more than anything else, pieces of the everyday decor and differed scarcely at all from a pious object like the crucifix on a bed of red velvet that my mother preserved up to her last day, nor from the other references with which might be associated what I knew about my parents and those who, living or dead, belonged to our circle. In order to open a first window for me on the species of other world which it is the function of a work of art to create, what was needed was not only an authentic masterpiece, before which I would be expressly invited to go into ecstasies, but also, no doubt, a masterpiece that was out of reach, like *The Night Watch*, and which a trip as considerable as was, for me, the trip to Holland, at the age I was when I made it, would lead me to discover. What I could have seen at the Louvre would, for lack of the proper remove, have participated to some extent in the family memories, as was the case for me with monuments such as the Palais de Versailles or Napoleon's Tomb. More distant, and endowed with extensions into history distinct from those that were more or less familiar to me, *The Night Watch* awed me with all the kilometers that had had to be traveled in order for one to be in a position to look at it and led me to begin to suspect that there existed paintings whose inestimable virtue, beyond their subject, is to show what great painting is.

It was in Holland, then, that I crossed the preliminary threshold, which would be followed by another threshold that I would not cross until I became an adolescent, if not a young man: to be moved by a painting that was not exalted by any fame and that did not owe its attractiveness to any historical or anecdotal feature. It was, I believe, some landscapes by Jongkind—another Flemish painter—that I saw thus by chance in the course of a walk through the Musée du Louvre. I would find it very difficult to date this walk and just as difficult to identify its circumstances. What I am, however, almost certain of is that, standing before these paintings or watercolors by Jongkind, I experienced for the first time something that was neither the slightly formal or ceremonial feeling of admiration that had been inspired in me by *The Night Watch*, its grand-opera types of costumes and accessories contributing to that feeling, nor the still quite childish interest I had had in the elegiac and coquettish expression of motherly love presented by the double portrait in which Mme Vigée-Lebrun (who painted Queen Marie Antoinette) was represented holding her daughter in her lovely arms, which one presumes were very soft, nor the stupefaction before imposing compositions like *Les Noces de Cana* or *Le Sacre de Napoléon*, nor the amused wonderment produced in me by the romantic vivacity of Gustave Doré when I leafed through the books he illustrated (*Roland furieux, Don Quichotte, La Divine Comédie,* La Fontaine's *Fables,* or *Le Capitaine Fracasse*, which happens to have been the first properly literary book that I read and which I understood was, as we said in my house, "well written"). Landscapes that I recall as being stretched out horizontally like the long plains they depicted, with perhaps mills, boats on the water of the river or canal, skies with frayed clouds above the yellow earth, perhaps also thin trees, the works of Jongkind—whatever their precise content may have been—had opened for me astonishing holes in the solemn walls of the museum. That ambiguous state of passionate tenderness and sadness which, much later, my voluntary disappearance into the coma caused by the phenobarbital provoked as though it were its conclusion in the full sense of the word—it seems to me I felt a very distant premonition of it as I stood before those landscapes about which, even today, I am not capable of saying precisely what was the source of their insidious power. As I looked at the light touches of color with which this man with the name of *joncs* [reeds], or jonquils growing thickly in the cold of the North, evoked places that were undoubtedly localized but whose limits they denied, rather than set, I felt fulfilled, but at the same time in some sense aspirated out of myself and projected toward an infinitely receding horizon. A bizarre mingling of distress and exultation similar to that which, afterward, seemed to me expressed by the productions of modern genius that—on a plane very distinct from that of pure painting—touch me the most closely. I might mention, for example, without trying to produce a compendium: Picasso's acrobats and his curtain for the ballet *Parade*; the Cubist canvases in gray and beige scaffoldings syncopated like ragtimes for troops of English chorus girls; certain sequences by Max Jacob and a few other poets in which poetry itself becomes the theme of poetry; the story *L'Enfant polaire* by my friend Limbour (a native of Le Havre); and the strangely denuded music of Satie (born in Honfleur, as we know). In more carefully considered terms: these are things that I love quite apart from any intellectual or aesthetic judgment, and that, in moments which are certainly melancholy but probably better than any others I know of, express with a melodious simplicity what—during the time, at least, that this enchantment lasts—seems to me to be my truth, unintelligible in any other form . . .

From the hospital room that I peopled each night with my dreams, while a few meters from me vegetated a sort of living dead man, one had a view, during the day, over the worksites and warehouses of the Compagnie du Gaz de Paris. After a sunrise of which, getting out of bed in order to look through the window at the sky that was at last illuminated, I could admire the delicate colors while my ear was cheered by the chirping of the birds, a beautiful and sinister landscape took shape, with piles of coal almost as big as slag heaps, a metal walkway of impressive height and length, a surmounted building of steel beams, windows, and wood, the whole very dilapidated. It is only now that I measure to what extent the picture which, until the end of the day, was thus presented to me was kin to that which one sees of the coal-bearing regions of France and Belgium when one makes the train trip from Paris to Brussels. At the time, I limited myself to savoring a spectacle that moved me to the extent that it seemed to me the image of my life's ambiguity: a sky with exquisite rosy tints above a distressing piece of industrial suburb; birdsongs that came to me in a retreat so covered with coal dust (despite the care of the ward maids) that one day when I rubbed the top of my head with a little eau de Cologne, I blackened my cotton pad in an instant, birdsongs similar to those that, in my basement room in the Musée de l'Homme, at the moment when the wound of a bad quarrel was closing, we heard suddenly, I and the woman who, that afternoon, had seemed to me clearly to have been sent to restore some freshness to my life but at the same time to instill a poison into it. If certain aspects of Belgium and Flanders finally became coupled with this fragment of northern suburb, I had to have, for this, an occasion to return to Brussels when I had already been digging for a long time into the magma of daydreams from which I try steadfastly to extract some identifiable substance.

This journey that allowed me to see the pyramids of the mines again, scarcely less beautiful from a distance than the tombs of Giza, was made last year, while an international exhibition was being held in Brussels, as depressing as ordinarily are these sorts of events, which tend in fact to place the products of our arts and industries on the level of inventions for the Concours Lépine and show the little to which our creations are reduced. From lack of time even more than discouragement, I scarcely cast a glance in passing at the monuments or architectural groups (Saint Gudula, for instance, and the Grand Place) the visit to which had been one of the main attractions of the first of those tours that we made in Belgium when I was a small child, and which, followed by Holland and then a stay on the other side of the Channel two or three years after, as though the North attracted us the way it does a magnetized needle, prepared the way for the taste I professed for the nordic regions until the period when my trips as an adult began to teach me that romanticism can find its climate elsewhere than in the mists or snows of the septentrion.

Except for one initial rainy day, it was fairly nice during the long weekend that my wife and I, escorted by a friend, spent there, so that we were out and about a good deal, those who hosted us taking us sometimes to the exhibition, sometimes to other spots in Brussels (whose large commercial streets were abundantly illuminated at night, with, as far as the eye could see, triumphal arches of a sort, made of lightweight strips of electric lightbulbs, like a succession of slender, shining bridges thrown over the roadway), driving us also to Ghent (to pay our respects, of course, to *The Mystic Lamb*), to Bruges (for the museums, the Beguinage, and the motorboat excursion on the canals), to Liège, to Ostende, and even to Waterloo (where the battle is reconstructed within a single room, in a vast and dusty panorama). One ethnographic detail: I observed here and there what (I was told) they call "postures," that is, vases, statuettes, or other shoddy art objects that many people of the petty and middle bourgeoisie display behind the glass of their bow windows, facing the street, which would induce one to make an ironic comment about art as a response to a need for ostentation: isn't a beautiful thing the thing that one likes (or would like) to display—in the case of the collector, what a beautiful diamond is for the one wearing it on his finger; in the case of the author, what his member in its glory is for the exhibitionist? In Ghent, I think, I drank a little of the beverage that some people (as others mention crushed bugs in relation to whiskey) describe as horse piss but of which I am very fond, *gueuze lambic*, with its tart, sour, and at the same time slightly fruity taste, whose beautiful orange color verges on mahogany and which, in a manner more surprising still than the fermented drinks of Africa such as millet beer and palm wine, gives when one swallows it the impression that one is assimilating the plant world itself. In short, despite the disenchanted reflections to which I had been led by the exhibition and its funfair tumult, I had some pleasant days there, with people I like very much, with whom I could forget to some extent the nasty turn politics in France had taken some months before, already, with the war in Algeria dragging on, the army quite determined to do only what it liked, and the total disorientation of most people in the face of the reactionary spirit of certain ones.

I had no desire to see the church of Saint Gudula again; not that a visit to a cathedral arouses in me some anticlerical bile, but because I no longer have the same taste I used to for gothic churches in a very flowery style (those of Rouen and of Reims, for instance, other touristic objectives of certain early Easter vacations), those monuments of which my parents had me admire the "stone lacework" and of which I learned, perhaps a little later, that the soaring of their ogives invites prayer. I would happily have stopped at the Grand Place, on the other hand, for the memory I have of it is that of an ensemble, if not of a high quality, at least picturesque and lively, that I see today as a theater set framing in its garland of sculpted figures a procession of various guilds, in some small town, German, Swiss, or in fact Flemish, of the Middle Ages or the Renaissance, craftsmen and merchants passing in groups with banners and emblems in profusion before the burgomeisters and aldermen, for the finale of a spectacle that would resemble *Hans le joueur de flute*, *William Tell*, and *The Mastersingers of Nuremberg*.

Not far from the Grand Place—which is situated, I think, in the old quarter of the Marolles or close to it—is the rue des Eburons, where my Aunt Claire lived. I confess that despite my attachment, I have not returned to that street since the period when my aunt lived there, sharing the true doll's house that was her minuscule townhouse with a servant of whom I remember that, not very young and of most honest deportment, she bore a first name ending in *a* like an opera buffa soubrette, and that after many years of total abnegation, her head suddenly turned by a lover, she ran off, helping herself to the most precious things the pretty little candy box contained. At the time of this trip, what connected me to that street had grown stronger inside me and touched me through a channel too open for me not to have a frank desire to go there, with the reservation, however, that, though I might wish to take a walk, I felt repugnance at the idea of a pilgrimage. To explain to my friends why I was bent on inserting this visit into a program that was already full, to ask them, if necessary, to guide me there, would have led me to make remarks about my feelings in which I'm quite willing to indulge if I do it in writing, with the greater distance inherent in this mode of expression, but which I could not broach viva voce without experiencing a certain embarrassment, in this case all the stronger because I happened to be engaged in prospecting that very layer of memories, for the work that is, here, finding its formal realization. To instigate a visit that would have recalled a number of things to me at just the right moment—this should not have been done, anyway, on any account, because it would have amounted, in fact, to organizing the collection of documents and impressions that, added to what my memory was already furnishing me on its own, would have filled some gaps, but so mechanically that it would have encumbered the whole thing with a dead weight. I very nearly, therefore, left Brussels without going back to the rue des Eburons, whose name I remembered because of my Aunt Claire, of course, but just as much because of what is odd about it for a child who may view the "Eburons" [Eburones, Germanic people of Belgian Gaul] as tradespeople (*bûcherons* [woodcutters] or *forgerons* [blacksmiths]), as well as the sort of Hurons who were, if names have a meaning, that nation whose membership in our circle is not marked by any natural line of descent like that which connects the *Alamans* [third-century confederation of Germanic tribes] to the Allemands [Germans] and the *Burgondes* [fifth-century Germanic people] to the Bourguignons [Burgundians]. But by chance, the matter was resolved without there being any need of a formal request: passing through the Grand Place in our hostess's car, I asked whether it was not in this vicinity that one could find the rue des Eburons, where a relative of mine had lived who sang in the Théâtre de la Monnaie. No sooner said than done: at a slower speed, we drove up the peaceful street that I had known and that was in fact quite nearby. At an intersection with another street, I had time to see the creamy whiteness of a very small house situated on the corner whose corner ground-floor room, topped with a small terrace, pointed into the intersection of the two streets like the prow of a ship. This was definitely the place I was looking for and, had I examined it more closely, perhaps I would have recognized other details that might have opened up a path for my memories . . . In any case, I contented myself with this quick view, for I did not want—since I would have felt I was doing it too conspicuously had we stopped the car—to assume, with respect to the rediscovered house, the attitude of the painter in arrested motion, his eyes squinting and his pencil already poised, before the site or the slice of life that is no longer for him more than a motif from which he will try to extract all that his skill may permit him to extract.

Apart from its exterior, which I did not think, incidentally, I would remember well enough to recognize it right away, what I recall about this house is reduced to very little: the calm and order that reigned in the parlor, whose candy-box preciosity did not conform very well with the robust beauty of its inhabitant, who was created on the scale of the lyric-theater stages on which she appeared; the presence, in a good spot in this excessively mincing parlor, of a glass-fronted cabinet where my aunt kept objects of which I would be incapable today of drawing up an inventory — even if limited to general categories — but of which I know that several at least related to her life in the theater. Among the bibelots thus kept behind glass, I think that my aunt showed us a small Spanish dancer similar to those we had seen in the second act of *Carmen* when we went to the Monnaie to hear her in that opera; but it is very possible that here I am only transferring into the glass case a memory of the show at which we had been present, and that I am seeing now, shrunk to the proportions of a slender figurine, what was originally a ballerina perceived from the entire distance that separated me from the stage. I recall most distinctly, on the other hand, the slightly intimidated joy I felt when my aunt showed us and allowed us to touch — extracted from this treasure of bibelots, perhaps also taken from a table-top or out of a drawer — the pair of castanets that was the very same one she had used when she sang the role of the cigarette girl who knows how to handle a knife, turn men's heads, roam the mountains helping smugglers, and read the imminence of her death in a combination of cards against which her cunning can do nothing.

That my aunt had learned to wield a pair of castanets in order to give Carmencita all her pungency and local color, seemed to me evidence of a professional conscientiousness worthy of the great artist that she was. But that she should add this talent to her other talents, and precisely this one, was for me a thing as marvelous as if she had demonstrated that the extent of her gifts was unlimited: she, who, if need be, could join to the art of professional singer that of the gypsy — was there any performance or transformation of which she would not be capable, should one of her roles demand it? The pair of castanets which reminded us that in the home of our citizen of Brussels we were also in the home of Carmen had, thus, all the weight of a piece of evidence, and I would not be able to say by which virtue it impressed me more, when my aunt presented it to us as one among others of the objects that made up the setting of her daily life: as theater accessory and—like a fairy's wand that I could touch with my finger—emblem of a magic brought suddenly, in this way, inside the four walls of a parlor, or as formal proof of the multiple capacities of this beautiful and good opera singer whom I had the happiness of coming close to, through the kinship that connected us.

In Brussels, I had seen my Aunt Claire on a theater stage for the first time, and, also for the first time, I had seen her in her private life. We had met her closest family: a sister, I believe, and a brother-in-law of whom I now know that he was the director of a furniture company, whereas I thought until just recently that he owned a glassworks and that we had even visited his factory, an irritating confusion because it forces me to wonder where on earth I could have seen that glassworks, of which, not having a more complete picture, what remains in my memory is one specific image (a worker blowing a bottle or other receptacle before our eyes), and because it obliges me to regard as suspect many childhood memories which, until now, were for me certainties. These people were the parents of a nice little brown-haired girl whom they called "Clairot," a diminutive of Claire, her aunt's first name. *You know, Clairot . . .* , her mother often said to her in a soft and modulated voice, with an accent by which my own parents were constantly amused, like so many French people, sensitive only to what seems to them a deformation of their language, and inclined to smile at inflections that, in certain mouths, nevertheless merely embellish the words with a few flourishes and give them a new flavor.

My aunt certainly did not have a Belgian accent. But that is really all I can remember, negatively, about her everyday voice. When she sang, the richly timbred voice did not seem either to emerge from her throat nor to reach your ears. It was a wave that enveloped you, moved you without your knowing where exactly its power came from: from the dramatic nature of the words that were uttered (and that were illustrated by the singer's face, so easily convulsed), from the character of the melody in which these words were incarnated, or from the substance of the sound alone, as ample as the very body of the woman producing it, of whom it appeared to be, even more than the expression, the irradiation or the transposition into another register. What would that voice do to me if I heard it now? And what precisely did it do to me when the entire volume of air enclosed in my parents' parlor was so penetrated by it that I have the impression, in retrospect, that what we were breathing was this voice itself? The only certainty is that this is how the memory she left me comes back to me, and that, if I listen today to a voice of the same type, what serves me as a touchstone by which to judge the gold of this other voice is what I believe I have retained of her voice.

D'art et d'amour [Of art and of love] . . . Thus begins, in the French language version, the soprano's great aria in the second act of *Tosca*, of which my aunt, who was already known in Belgium, had been the first to sing the role in Paris, as I recently found out from a review I read in an old magazine. Along with the great aria of *Louise*, that of *Samson and Delilah* dedicated to "spring which is beginning," the aria of the Cards from *Carmen* and the Song of the Heart in *La Glu*, this aria was one of the main pieces in her repertoire, at the time when she came to sing at the house and when, too young still to quibble over my pleasure and to trouble myself with frivolous aesthetic discriminations, I allowed myself in all simplicity to be intoxicated by the vocal philter of which, her very nature being straightforward, she possessed as though from birth the secret of creating.

At that period, I had only a very confused notion of Puccini's opera, of which I had heard only the aria in which the singer Floria Tosca pours out her passion and the one in which her lover, on the point of being shot down, says goodbye to life. I scarcely paid any attention to the exact meaning of the words; but, on a level deeper than that of the anecdote, the union of art and love, the union of love and a despairing death, were conveyed not so much by the words as by the melody, as though art, love, and despairing death had been by definition included in that music, whose beauty expressed, by its existence alone, that the high points of human emotion must involve those three. In order to impress this truth upon me, or at least to give me a sort of obscure prescience of it, all that was needed, therefore, was a song, along with these few guiding words: art and love, love and death, links in a single chain or planets in a single system.

As for the voice that thus deployed something analogous to what is called in cartomancy the *great play*—I remember that it was ample, pure, powerful, and velvety. But the memory I have of it, though it allows me to evaluate the treasure that my Aunt Claire possessed, does not correspond to it except in a completely formal way and does not have the necessary sharpness for me to be able, mentally, to hear her sing again. Perhaps this voice touched me so closely because I let myself be permeated by it almost without listening to it? Perhaps it was for me only one of the ways, among others, she had of manifesting herself, this radiant creature whom I cannot now succeed in separating distinctly from the setting in which her epiphanies occurred and whose real presence, also, I more or less confound with the image engraved in me, since then, by her photographs? The mantelpiece of white marble with its two candelabras of twisted bronze, the piano, the chandelier which, when the time of our vacation came, was wrapped in a yellowish and slightly shiny cloth that resembled sticking plaster, the large "lusol" lamp whose light seemed to me to have such brilliance, and that other object often seen in the parlor, which, in our house, was the music room, my brother's violin, of cabinet wood with the undulations of chestnut hair, with its neck, the extremity of which curved back into a lovelock or a bishop's crook and its bow of white horsehair that the violinist, each time he was to play, would rub on a block of rosin (which, if I think of it with some persistence, appears to me of the same half-translucid blond as a myrrh stone)—those things, once inanimate, are an integral part of all that I have retained of my Aunt Claire as visible person: the blackness of her hair and eyebrows, the red of her strongly drawn mouth, the whiteness of her skin, her rather heavy femininity, even more luxuriant than was appropriate in those first years of the century, and the comfortably gaudy dresses that clothed this plump goddess when, kindly and without the least condescension of a star, she came to pay us a visit.

The large plumed hat, the long beribboned cane, and the slightly too labored elegance that mark, in Floria Tosca, a lowering of social position comparable to that which was for a long time evoked for me by the odd qualifier of "demi-mondaine"—it is through a portrait of my aunt produced by the studio of some photographer or other, well known at the time, that I see these features. This portrait of her, in a character whose peculiarities of costume appear natural, since they can be explained by the fact that the person involved here is a woman of the theater, show her to me in her true being, in some sense, since the profession of artist was the most important part of her life and since, of that life, I scarcely knew more than this one aspect. Other portraits—which I have contemplated many times—represent her as both herself and something other than herself: Salomé gazing at the severed head of Yokanaan, Electra dancing with her torch, Leonore dressed as Fidelio (an outfit that did not suit her at all and made her look like an ocean-nymph washerwoman who had been induced by unfortunate illusions about her type of beauty to dress up for some costume ball as a chimney sweep or little marmot-exhibiting Savoyard), a princess of the ancient city of Ys in a voluminous crown, or, in contrast, an old Breton woman in a headdress rolling her tragic eyes, a charming farm girl offering a pitcher of wine with a bright smile, a fresh strapping young woman also from *Les Pêcheurs de Saint-Jean*, her head bearing a huge basket filled with flowers, fruit, fish, or some other sort of victuals. Seen, almost all of them, at Nemours among the great numbers of souvenirs from which my sister has never separated, these other portraits have more reality for me than that one—too distant—of my aunt in finery that evidently situates Tosca, killer of the policeman who is persecuting her lover, midway between the great-hearted courtesan and the beautiful spy. However, the portrait that I would be inclined to say I was infatuated with is that first one, so nebulous that it is cast in doubt and I eventually have to ask myself whether—starting from a photo of my relative in formal visiting dress or from photos of showgirls brilliantly decked out as I used to see them in the pages of programs, and proceeding to a sort of collage such that a figure enriched perhaps artificially with the radiant features of Claire Friché is leaning on a cane that in fact another singer carried in Act I of the drama when I saw it performed a few years ago — I have not, in large part, reconstructed it with the innocent bad faith of a restorer of monuments who believes he is giving a greater impression of authenticity by adding a tower to an old château or a spire to a cathedral.

In the rue des Eburons, at the time of my last visit to Brussels, I had been restrained by a certain fear: that I would appear at once too misty-eyed, in asking that we stop, and too eager to derive a professional advantage from that stop. Yet now I find myself — like a man in love or a scholar examining archival documents — bending over photographs that I am seeking to resurrect in order to rediscover in them the real image of my aunt, at the same time as they provide me, literally, with what in the language of films is called a sequence of scenes. Is this equivocal manipulation of reflections that I put into words more defensible than the action — quite natural, in truth — that I denied myself? I would doubt it, if there were not this difference: it is one thing to contrive things in such a way that I may artificially fatten my stock of memories, another thing to prepare, shape, and set end to end the sentences in which memories I possess already, without having expressly sought them, reassume a little solidity.

Of these photos that I inspect — in my mind — in order to draw closer to someone who had dazzled me, I have none at hand. But it is probably better that they not be documents to which I could lazily refer: thus hidden, they create, between their subject and me, a connection all the more positive because I find myself, in some way, precipitated into the wake of the absent woman by this race to which I am incited by images that must always be grasped again and formed again.

If I can scarcely do more than catalogue these portraits, none of which I have seen again since the pursuit was begun, there is one other that I did not know about but have now complete latitude to contemplate and describe, having cut it out of the women's weekly where it was published more than a year ago, when Italy celebrated Puccini's centenary. Here, my aunt is shown as she was in 1903, at the time of the first French performance of *Tosca*, in other words at a time preceding that of my first memories. Very young, and even more beautiful than I knew her, she is seen in profile, her arms bare (with two large bracelets above her two elbows), her head crowned with a heavy mane of hair restrained by a superb headdress: this was her costume in the middle act of the opera, when Floria Tosca has just sung to the court and goes to the home of Baron Scarpia, whom she finally strikes with a knife snatched up from a table. Her lower lip thick and her eyelids half closed, my aunt has in this photo something of the quality of a very gentle animal, and, in the sensual and fierce melancholy into which she seems to have withdrawn, something also of the quality of an odalisque such as one might conceive of them from Rimsky-Korsakov's *Scheherazade* (whose orientalism, in the past, was a rich pasture for my adolescent imagination). Her hair, which swells out over her forehead and entirely hides her temples and nape, is dressed with a curious harness that, on top, compresses it with two reins joined together at their base (just above the two ears) and in back supports it in a sort of hairnet whose form recalls rather distantly that of a slice of watermelon cut very thick or, better, that of a chin piece of a helmet that is hooked on, on either side of the head, in the same place as the two reins. At the approximately hexagonal attachment shared by this hairnet and those two reins, a pearl or other precious concretion hangs down in the form of a drop of water, on the brown mop of hair covering the ear, on the lobe of which is fixed a rather long pendeloque whose terminal cross seems appropriate to the piety of this Floria, who will take care—after the murder—to arrange two lit torches beside the body of the torturer who has become her victim and to sanctify it by placing on its chest a crucifix.

This photo, the only one that I possess and that I have been able to look at in its smallest details—the arms that thicken markedly where they join the shoulders, the arched black eyebrows, the firmly outlined nose, the tunic with very ample folds under which the two breasts cannot be divined—this photo, which I would wager is a good likeness and in which, even though she is younger, the woman shown probably does not differ very much from the one I heard sing, gives me, in truth, almost nothing. It is not my aunt whom I rediscover in it, and it is not Tosca, either, whom I see in it. It offers me simply the image of the fresh and slightly sibylline creature who was apparently its subject and whom I have great difficulty in identifying as much with the singer whom I admired as with the heroine of the drama in which the torture chamber that was its main property seems so terribly modern now that Baron Scarpias are flourishing among our military (without lace jabots or powdered wigs, but in uniforms spotted like panthers, and that is the only difference). Perhaps the other photos that I have mentioned would have given me nothing more than such themes for sterile reverie, if I had them at hand, as I do this one?

Strangely forgotten while I proceeded with this inventory (doubting its efficacy but finding some satisfaction in drawing it up, as though this procedure itself already included the discovery toward which it is theoretically only a patient advance), another portrait came back to my memory, a photoengraved reproduction that appears in one of the issues of the old magazine *Musica* that my sister gave me, as a high-priced gift, one day when I went to see her at Saint-

Pierre-lès-Nemours. So easy was my access to this document (since all I had to do to reach it was to go, armed with the proper key, into the room called, in my house, the linen room) that to curb my desire to consult it would have been even more artificial than to make use of this memory aid. I therefore drew the incomplete series from the cupboard where it is put away among various revues, books, catalogues, programs, and papers of all sorts, including a heap of letters, postcards, and other notes that I preserve carefully without having done much more than pile them up. Leafing through it from one end to the other, I discovered, to my surprise, that there are in fact a good dozen portraits contained in these rather tattered issues, where I have also been able to read or reread many notices concerning my aunt which demonstrate to me that the beauty of her voice was no more a myth than any of the other gifts that allowed me to recognize in her an authentic creature of the theater.

Vita, from *L'Etranger*. Three photographs show her to me in this role, one of which—the head, in profile—is exactly the image I had recalled, except that I had mistaken the character, attributing to the baker's wife in *L'Enfant roi* (a naturalist work by Alfred Bruneau and Zola that my aunt was the first to perform) the profile which is in reality that of "Vita," the sailor's daughter, in an opera by Vincent d'Indy quite blatant in its mediocre philosophical aims, if I am to judge from the review that was given it by *Musica* and that was illustrated by the most attractive of the three photographs: my aunt standing and seen full face, an earthenware jar on her shoulder (which makes her sway a little) and noticeably more slender than in her other portraits, yet recognizable, her face marked by a mixture of strength, tenderness, and passionate gravity, the sort of face needed, no doubt, to play the part of that young girl whose name means that she is life itself, as the columnist did not fail to stress, for the sake of the naïfs for whom the word "vita" remained—so to speak—Greek. An easy mark, as I often am, I rose to the bait of this symbolic name: one morning, between sleeping and waking, I had the impression that "Vita" signaled to me in clear language what I am trying to rediscover behind the image of my aunt, and I thought that such a key word ought to be represented, in the algebra that I am elaborating here, by a special sign that would consist of a small black equilateral triangle resting either on one of its points (to sum up the word by recalling its initial V) or on one of its sides (to express what is fundamental about it by giving it the firm base of a pyramid). This did not exceed the limits of a brief dream, and it quickly seemed evident to me that I had not benefited from any illumination, but only recognized the obvious, by discovering that through my memory of her, always too imprecise, I am trying to seize what was intensely alive about the woman whom the journalists of not so long ago called "Mademoiselle

Friché," in accordance with proper custom. As for the infinitesimal black sign — concerning which I did not notice that, with its point down, it evokes a woman at the moment when nothing exists beyond her bushy triangle — it soon took on a meaning less associated with Pythagorean philosophy than that which it had as possible typographical mark: fully awake, and several days after that sort of cipher or monogram offered its services to my thoughts, I suddenly saw as obvious the idea that, positioned point upward, it would have some resemblance to that oriental motif in the form of an upside-down heart, the "tree of life," according to what was told me, at the time of our intimacy, by the friend with whom I was still involved well after my emergence from the Hôpital Claude-Bernard and from whom I had wanted to know what the ornament was that I saw, at the level of her shoulder, against the damask whiteness of the material in which she was clothed that morning. Thus, while I, lagging behind the woman from Brussels who was veiled by the muslins of time and who had become a shade flushed with fabulous glimmers, had become taken with a dubious idealism, a subterranean sort of work was taking place, so well hidden that a moment would come when I could imagine myself deflected from the fleshless entity from whom I was seeking asylum, and recalled to burning reality, merely by the almost automatic transition from the too abstract sign I had invented to this emblem whose lanceolate design sums up something I have experienced in the present time of my desire or my embrace, and not in an anachronistic rumination.

Vita, without makeup and her head slightly tipped back (the same portrait from which is extracted the profile reproduced in another issue of *Musica*), the whole of Vita here, in a photomontage occupying a double page of the magazine and assembling, against a forest background that looks like a sacred wood, the most prominent singers of the year 1903 in theater costume, a strange carnival in which all characters and all periods are placed side by side. A beautiful brunette with a resounding laugh — Carmen with mantilla and castanets as I saw her on the stage of the Monnaie in Brussels. Heavy and sad in her folkloric clothing, Senta, the Nordic lover of the Dutchman Volant. The very same photograph that I recall having seen at my sister's house: the basket-carrier of *Pêcheurs de Saint-Jean*. The stupid look and the excessively fat body under the clinging tunic, a hetaira in Camille Erlanger's *Aphrodite*. Eleanor from *Fidelio* (more graceful than when one sees her with her pannier). The Sicilian Santuzza from *Cavalleria Rusticana*, with very large earrings which one can assume are gold. Floria Tosca, less radiant than the version I fashioned from memory, but attesting to the truth of the image about which I had asked myself if, at least in part, I had not invented it. Claire Friché resting her elbows on a piano surrounded by a few other people: her face, with large cheekbones and slanted eyes, looks slightly Mongolian; her hat, of a very boisterous 1900 style, suits her so badly that it resembles something peculiar that might have come from another planet to alight on the top of her head. With this portrait, which supposedly shows the artist in a simpler guise, I am done — I think — with this gallery, so unequal and diverse that it muddles rather than defines the figure whom I would not want to abandon before having deciphered it.

Great art in flesh and blood. Vita. The tree of life. What was intensely alive about Mademoiselle Friché, as about the aforementioned Sandier or Sanguier, who, during my nights as an invalid, alternated with the lamentable Kipouls. The voice that my Aunt Claire so quickly ruined, too proud of proving what a surprising range it had by adopting ordinarily incompatible practices, too happy, also, to lavish it with all her strength every time the occasion presented itself. The sumptuous flesh on which, had she been more of a coquette, she might have prided herself, despite the visible excess of health that made it difficult for her to tackle roles more refined than those of the uninhibited lover or the mother possessed by every passionate feeling inspired in her by the fruit of her womb. Art and life, voice and flesh, in other words what I had been yearning for more intensely than ever, since I thought I was finished as a writer, and since, aware of my aging in its most tangible aspects, I had begun to consider with dismay and disgust the evolution of my physical being.

In my brain — the brain of a survivor, deaf, because of his lack of courage, to all reasons for repeating his error — a revival of the very thing of which I had despaired appeared on the horizon of the twofold dream ironically animated by those two masks of a dance of death: the actress in retirement, whose talent as well as her beauty had become mere memories; and the grotesque creature naïvely expending, for futile purposes of literary vainglory, the little life he had. Art that does not split hairs. Life as an opera, with love inflecting the line of the melody and death giving all its amplitude to the finale. Lyric art, connected to life more directly than any other, if opera is a festivity in whose splendor the players of the game compete with the witnesses of their performances, all either in costume or dressed up, and if there is no work of art offered to the audience thus gathered together that, in one way or another, and in the gravest or most lighthearted tone, is not an appeal for effusion. The adamantine luster of art and the tumultuous nudity of life; fiction and reality; *over-there* and *right-here*, whose conjoining — "for real," and not in allegory or only for a moment — is perhaps my great problem, the only quadrature on which to base myself in order to reconcile myself...

Having started from nothing, or from the slim hypothesis according to which my burlesquely transfigured cousin was merely a delegate from the period in which my Aunt Claire reigned, I soon allowed myself to be invaded by that absent woman whose image, at first excluded, has little by little imposed itself and has ended, if not by becoming entirely real, at least by materializing in photographs. As though, obstinately, I had sought to rejoin this deceased figure, when—shortly after my return from Tuscany—the curtain fell on the living love duet I had been singing with so uncertain a voice, or else to discover behind the features of my relative what was once upon a time Beauty for me, in order to turn it into a law for myself and be no longer so helpless, or even to attach myself to an image the description of which or the very search for which would be in itself beauty, I set about resuscitating her, and it is a long waking dream that for months and months now has taken over from the initial dream. Along the way, certain irresolute ideas have crystallized around this image, which seems to me today to have appeared armed from head to toe as early as on those nights neither of waking nor of dreaming during which I was at the mercy of two indefinitely repeated divagations.

Mired in my various labors, having recovered from the naïveté that for a long time had caused me to believe in the magic of traveling, and no longer even desiring to go anywhere at all, engaged in an adventure that was not a way out, either, since I did not want to, or could not, sever the ties that bind me to my companion or settle into duplicity, I had—almost by accident—consumed the sort of *provision for suicide* that for long months had served me as an emergency supply or viaticum. Having emerged from the coma, and my initial exaltation having subsided, I had said to myself that soon it was all going to start up again, even more difficult than before: it would be impossible, now, to rely on the idea of that provision, which I would not be able to reproduce without expending a good deal of patience and cunning and which, besides, it would be better not to reproduce, if I did not want to become a specialist in failed suicide (knowing that I would never have the courage to make the decisive gesture, the one that would have consisted, for instance, in consuming the poison not at home, but locked in my office at the Musée de l'Homme at an hour when no one could have saved me). Since I did not envisage repeating the act, this time without remission, what remained was for me to rediscover some reasons for living, problematic as that was. In what direction to turn, if not toward the domain concerning which I had the proof that, whether fortunately or not, for me, it was my chosen domain? Having appeared when I was still in total chaos, weren't the English aesthetes, the retired actress, and even that laughable dramaturge (whom the singer would soon eclipse) directional arrows for this, all pointing in the same direction: toward art—but illustrated by these various phantoms as a way of life rather than regarded on its own, as though its insertion into existence had been at the center of my preoccupations?

When I was still a child, those who were for me the "great artists," whom one always mentioned with emotion, were neither writers, nor painters, nor sculptors, nor composers of music—distant celebrities whom no one I knew had even seen—but the great performers, and particularly the actors or singers, who seemed to me very real people, though clothed in the dress of legend because of their vocation itself and the fact that my parents scarcely spoke of them except from the perspective of memory and as people whose transcendent species had more or less disappeared: Adelina Patti or rather "la Patti" (whom my mother, as a girl, had heard at the Théâtre Italien), Sybil Sanderson, the English or American soprano (whose millionaire name is close to that of Sangar, sister of Ivan Ogareff and femme fatale in *Michel Strogoff*), the Wagnerian tenor Van Dyck (who was incomparable in singing the story of the Grail), Coquelin the elder (creator, with unequaled panache, of *Cyrano de Bergerac*), the refined monologist Anna Judic, Sarah Bernhardt in her great period (or some other sacred monster of whom it was told how fans had unharnessed her horses in order to escort her by pulling and pushing her carriage themselves), specialists in melodrama such as Tailhade and the actor who played the roles of traitors in so convincing a way that people would wait for him at the stage door in order to beat him up, others, still, whose names I could cite, names almost forgotten by our contemporaries but always magical when I happen to utter them in my mind.

Not only were creatures of this kind haloed by all the annals of the theater, but I also situated them in a sort of golden age: the great era that my father and mother had known and of which a few very rare artists of my time would allow me, just barely, to form for myself a pale idea. The private lives of some of them—of these days or in earlier times—gave rise to pieces of gossip that added a somewhat coarse note to the mythology: this one had ruined his voice by going to Les Halles too often, to carouse till dawn; that one, who spent lavishly, died in poverty after appearing before audiences of sovereigns; one actress, one evening, had gone on stage dead drunk; another chanced to take home with her a handsome on-duty fireman she had spotted as she was performing a drama or tragedy. By contrast, those whom people liked to cite for their regular life seemed endowed with a true sainthood, without which they would not have been able to face unharmed a career so sown with temptations.

About some, they confined themselves to reporting a picturesque anecdote, suited to inspiring respect, provoking complicitous laughter, or drawing tears: the risks, for example, taken by a certain performer in the role of a robber, when, in order to gather material, he had haunted the worst slums and associated with the dangerous hooligans who were a constant presence there; the experience of that celebrated baritone whose unreliable memory had obliged him, one evening, to sing a good portion of an opera aria without pronouncing the words; the final wretched poverty of those two brothers or friends in whose home someone had afterward found a large banknote slipped between two pages of a program or piece of music by a too discreet patron whose guests had been charmed by their number as duettists. Parallel to the wonders accomplished behind the limelight, these episodes were presented as examples demonstrating that there is something naturally epic about theater people, even if they are neither actors "brought up on the boards" nor the buffeted passengers of a "chariot of Thespis," like that of the traveling actors in *Captain Fracasse*. Isn't an epic halo just what I need when, behind a work that I admire, I want there to stand a "beautiful character"? A natural actor or a fiery virtuoso, a genius exposed to poverty or other sufferings, a pioneer of a heroic epoch, a fire-stealing poet or a revolutionary one, a writer at the tragically conditioned game of torero, a creator rebelling against all compromise—aren't these the avatars of that figure which I have made into my model and which, after many hesitations, I have stripped of its showy adornment and rationalized, but certainly also gentrified, since I had, to a certain degree, to suffer the influence of the age, which impels one to make adjustments by which the gap between oneself and what one has dreamed may be after a fashion reduced? The artist who pays with his person and whose life is tossed about by the same winds as his art: it was he whom, even from my hospital bed, I had rediscovered in his first form, through the intermediary of the old actress with whom I identified. Since I could not begin living again without taking everything back to its beginnings, concerning what remains at the very heart of my interest, did I not have to encounter—scarcely back up out of my abyss—the woman who was (even though safe from all scandal) the "great artist" of my childhood, my aunt, the singer Claire Friché?

Sad odd-jobs man that he was, after the suave aesthetes, and pathetic counterpart of a form that seems to me to illustrate what is most humanly moving about the art of the theater—an art in which everything receives a response there and then, either ovations or catcalls immediately sanctioning merit or demerit, an art that comes into being through living and active people capable of great moments that will be evoked later as historic dates—my cousin offered me an image of my literary ambitions as unpleasant as though it had been reflected back at me by a distorting mirror (one of those that make people laugh and that in Shanghai I heard referred to, in English, as "*ha ha* mirrors" by the interpreters who were escorting us, my companions and me, in our visit to the *Ta Si Kia* or "Great World," a building with Piranesian stairways and terraces, with attractions on the ground floor and upper stories, each including several theaters in which the most different things were being performed simultaneously). I have never asked to have myself published and have undertaken nothing to win myself a public, but that does not prove that, lacking any vanity, I am indifferent to the effect I may produce: an enthusiast of the theater, I have, like an actor, my role that I want to play, paying particular attention only to playing a role that resembles me and does not oblige me, afterward, to disavow it. Histrion of letters, alternating with a feminine figure who was certainly conventional and not without vulgarity but was at least that of a truly artistic nature, my cousin reminded me, on the one hand, of that thing which a writer ought to avoid like the plague, but which the reading of press clippings and the windfall of a literary prize had perhaps given me a taste for: that excessive flattery for which actors are so avid (which is consistent with their way of acting in *direct contact* with a crowd confronted in a sort of close combat), that extreme praise which in the theater forms part of the liturgy but that professionals in the other arts cannot drink in without running the risk of losing their way, those who work in the silence of their rooms or studios and for whom the audience—dispersed in time as in space—is, as a rule, simply the person to whom the artist is sending a message from afar, without seeing or hearing him. Linked to me by certain shared episodes of our past, my cousin, on the other hand, took me back to the portion of my childhood which had been ornamented with this woman, so much admired, whose pure and direct singing had obscurely shown me the half-intoxicated, half-desolate tone of the message I would one day believe I was obliged to deliver. But wasn't the state of physical and mental upheaval in which I found myself favorable to all sorts of regressions, and was it really to that prehistoric phase of my existence, to the exclusion of all other beginnings, that I was inclined to go back when those rumors so strangely located themselves to the right of my bed, the rumors concerning this outrageous fellow, my cousin metamorphosed into an aspiring dramaturge?

I would like to go to Taormina . . . The speaker is a young girl with dark hair, a little plump but with a lively, delicate face. She is wearing (I think) a black dress and is standing next to me, on the balcony of the old middle-class apartment where we have just had lunch. This is taking place in the early nineteen twenties, and probably in the summer, since, having drunk our coffee, we have moved from the closed space of the dining room or living room to this narrow rectangle almost in the open air, to chat and enjoy the spectacle of the street. Our host is my cousin Loulou, who, for quite a long time now, has ceased to be the bachelor I later so absurdly adopted as the central figure of one of my very recent obsessions as hospital patient. His wife is an excellent person, older, and, especially, much taller and stronger than he, which accentuates that appearance of his that I have always observed in him, as a small young man whose smiling but slightly retiring ways (due in part to the screen of the pince-nez required by his extreme myopia), may be the effect as much of a good education as of a natural shyness. Through ramifications of maternal cousinhoods and marriages which, even at the time, I would not have been able to disentangle, the girl who was expressing to me her desire for Greek ruins and sun belonged—very distantly—to the circle of my relations. When he died, her father had left her, along with her two sisters and her mother, harder pressed, by far, than they had been when he was managing his enamel factory in the Paris region. Was it for this reason (I have since asked myself) that the pair of good souls that my cousin and his companion were had had the idea of this luncheon? Three daughters to marry off is a burden for a widow no longer of an age to "start her life over," and it was doing her a kindness to arrange, for at least one of the three, a meeting from which might arise a feeling of fondness capable of taking, afterward, a turn toward marriage. I was far from representing a rich match, but they knew me, and they must have, at the very least, thought me a suitable boy. Wouldn't it have been sensible and friendly to hope for a conjunction between that girl with "artistic" tastes who dreamed of Sicily (a country not so vulgarized at that time) and myself, of whom none of my friends or family was ignorant of the fact that I dreamed about modern art and poetry?

Whether we were invited solely for the joy of bringing us together or for a little more than that, the fact is that there was no sequel to this lunch. Even though I was sensitive to her attractions, I did not try to see the girl I had been talking to again, and there was no way I could know, afterward, whether our several hours of concord signified that a deeper fellow feeling was possible between us. Our hosts, in truth, were familiar with my life only in its most external features, and their calculations—if they really had made any—rested on a poor foundation: from an outing during which the two of us leaned tenderly against the railing of one of the sightseeing boats that went up and down the Seine at that time, like omnibuses ricocheting from one landing stage to the next, was born, without there being any need of the Sicilian sky, an idyll that hardly led us beyond the limits where a passionate friendship stops, but took hold of me body and soul at the moment when her admission concerning Taormina might have incited me to attempt to see that the woman who was formulating it actually went there with me. What was in her body and soul? I would certainly be flattering myself as to my own powers to think that that conversation, if it hadn't been for the other bond that inhibited me, might have resulted in a reciprocal commitment! At a distance of forty years, or almost, and when I could be the father of the woman I am talking about, it is easy for me to say: "It was entirely up to me . . ." Everything levels out, at such a great distance, and that encounter appears, in memory, like one of those happy dreams in which love forms of its own accord and without the slightest obstacle, while the promise it held out remains unaltered, since one never went so far as to try one's chances.

As I see her again, now, the girl with whom I had felt in such immediate sympathy (justified neither by the vague family connection of which I have spoken nor by the fact, uncertain anyway, that I had seen her with her sisters once or twice when we were very small), this girl who had charmed me by the very thing that I lacked, the great ardor for living which was perceptible through her gestures and her words, she is severely dressed in black, on that balcony overhanging, in the Bastille neighborhood, the tranquil boulevard which the name of the dramaturge Beaumarchais designates without qualifying, as is the case for most of the names attributed to the streets of Paris. Did a recent bereavement oblige her to wear that gloomy color or is it I, recalling her as a half orphan, who have clothed her after the fact in the proper dress for the part? Even though I know from experience what mutations the stuff of memories, rarely indifferent, may undergo, I do not think my memory is at fault here, for I'm sure that in my state of mind at the time, this girl would have seemed less fetching to me without that contrast between the relish she obviously had for life and the mourning that seemed indicated by the severity of her attire. But I'm sure, also, that it was not the loss of her father that caused her thus to be dressed in mourning, and that she owed to a more recent misfortune the gloomy envelope in which (I now believe) she appeared somewhat of the same substance as those girls or women of certain poor villages in Mediterranean countries, so often consigned to black because of accumulated deaths, and whose sunny skin surprises us, who are accustomed to associate mourning with pallor. Rather than turning toward the manufacturer, whose manner at once crude and formal I vaguely recollect, it is in the direction of his widow—more gracious—that I should look in order to find the probable addressee of the piece of darkness in which, that day, their daughter was wrapped: the shade honored by this garment had to be, in fact, that of one of her maternal grandparents, both of whom were people of the theater who had won renown in the comic opera and of whom, at the time of our meeting, the survivor had just (I believe) disappeared in his turn into an inferno in no way Offenbachian.

No doubt I have spoken, reclothing in my own way some romantic commonplaces, of my predilection for the countries of the North: the dignity of the cold, the places and the people of too harsh a grain for the postcard effect, a city like Liverpool attractive to the extent that its name puts winter [*l'hiver*] in our bones, the adventure that smoulders deep inside little bars with softened lights in ports fragrant with tar. With my forbidding skies I was far away, certainly, from her azure, but we shared the same desire to travel. What figure could I have cut in her eyes? I don't know. As for me, I attributed to her all the more piquancy because she was the granddaughter of a comic-opera star whose charm and talent I had heard praised many times. The niece also (through her mother) of a well-known actor, she was without a doubt a child brought up on the boards . . . Wasn't there a little coquetry mingled with her quick-witted ways, as though, quite simply, she had decided to play in daily life a role in keeping with the most attractive of what was offered by the branches of her genealogy? This sort of choice, however, can hardly be absolutely premeditated, and I have, after all, no reason to suspect this girl of artificiality considering that her so very pleasantly spontaneous manner had permitted this dialogue in which, when one person said "south," the other, without becoming aloof, could answer "north."

I have known for a little while now that that amiable grandmother (to whom, I would like to think, the mourning of my table companion was dedicated) had created, among other light works, *Les Cloches de Corneville*, an operetta which I cannot think of without mixing in, with the memory of its music, more than three-quarters extinguished, a confused noise of an alarm, having learned at the time of my first stay in Martinique that at the moment of the disastrous eruption of Mount Peleus it was being performed at the theater of Saint-Pierre, a town that in the blink of an eye was to be changed by the catastrophe into a heap of ashes. Even before knowing that (her connection with those *Cloches* [bells] that, one evening, would awaken tragic echoes), I projected onto the figure of the comic-opera star—a figure completely imagined, since all I knew of her were a few poor photographs—a rather boisterous light, which came straight from a lavish production in which she was also the first to perform: *Les Quatre Cents Coups du Diable*, put on at the Châtelet several years before the other war and the text of which I read, when I was very young, in an illustrated periodical that must have been called *Mon Beau Livre*.

I recall it very clearly, the play included a first scene or prologue situated—as the text indicated—"on the banks of the Styx." A rather small reproduction showed, in the center of a rocky setting, the famous comic-opera star dressed up as Satan: in clinging tights, a mephistophelian headdress, and a large coat which, hanging down from her two outstretched arms, gave her something like two vast wings. Next, the devil abandoning its infernal attributes, the star appeared as a man, dressed notably in an elegant modern suit in order to sing (perhaps among the winter residents and the gamblers of Monte Carlo) couplets that I have entirely forgotten, except that the booklet specified that they were sung to the tune of *Big Brass Band*, which—I now assume—must have been a cakewalk or ragtime. There was, close to the beginning, a tableau called "Les Valentins et Valentines," a pretext for a balletic interlude; then another entitled "Alcofribas's laboratory," in which, by means of mechanical contrivances or pure theater, one witnessed various wonders; finally, shortly before the finale, a military scene with fusillade and explosion that took place in "the fortress of the Carpathians." Is it true? Is it false? According to the illustrations and the text itself, I remember soldiers bundled up in large dark greatcoats (and these were, perhaps, children in disguise), a magician in an ample robe and great white beard, young men offering girls Valentine's Day bouquets, a grotto indicated only by the simulacra of rough surfaces that framed the stage, a wild lair in which the spectator was supposed to find himself (like its diabolical inhabitants) and whose entrance gaped on the open air evoked by the backdrop.

However confused my memory of this fairy play may prove to be, in the end—a play that I no doubt read many times but scarcely a few scenes of which had been shown me by the detour of photography—still, it made a strong enough impression on me so that certain details (accurate or distorted) are more vivid in me than some realities that I could describe with less of a margin of approximation. It goes without saying that I was thinking of other things beside reconstructing all this, while, on my cousin's balcony, I chatted with the granddaughter of the deceased actress whom, in small format and without color or depth, I had seen playing the part of Satan. But, almost certainly, I was unconsciously adding, to the granddaughter's natural vivacity, a speck of devilishness taken from the grandmother and that the phrase "banks of the Styx" hovered as a sort of distant resonance deep within my ear when she said "Taormina." Was it the sparkle that enlivened her features as she spoke of that place? The texture of a name that seemed to have been made, like the names "Oloossone" and "Camyre," for a play in Alexandrine verses celebrating the ancient fasti? The blossoming—as I listened to it—of a mirage of a happy place in contrast to the harsh tenor of my own nordic mirage? There is no need (it may appear) to seek elsewhere for the reason why, of all our remarks, the one that suddenly unfurled the whiteness of Taormina is the only one that I have retained. Biased as I was against the Mediterranean with its too facile enchantments, it nevertheless seems to me that whether indifferent or disgusted rather than attracted, I would have—on this point also—been inclined to forget, if everything about this pleasant girl had not given added color to her remark, in which whimsically tinted magic-lantern glimmers interfered with the pure classical light in which the Sicilian village is bathed.

On the boulevard Beaumarchais, at the time of this luncheon, I did not foresee that one day—upon my return from a voyage that, almost without moving from home, I made "to the banks of the Styx"—a curious substitute for my cousin would come daily to visit me. At the time, this series of visits seemed to me an absurd fantasy connected to my deficient state, nothing more (apart from the repetition) than those dreams brought on by fever whose extreme oddness distinguishes them from most other dreams, as though the oneiric world itself were deformed in them as much as the real world is in an ordinary dream. I very soon recognized that this invention had as its basis a myth of the theater, as old as all the distance that separates me from my childhood. But I discovered its true root only after examining all that, in my cousin as he is defined by our places on the family chessboard and the few vivid details offered me by the history of our relations, could predestine him personally to the mandate in the name of which he had intervened with so much insistence.

It was a truly strange excursion that I had imagined, when I thought that after my nocturnal jump to Cannes I had found myself in a Brussels hospital, as though the devil of the Monacan tableau of *Les Quatre Cents Coups* had put into the same bag the shores of the Riviera of which the song speaks and the banks of the Senne mocked by Baudelaire. Such was the disorder that reigned in me as to the cardinal points and as to my own cartography that one may say I had, literally, *lost my compass* [French idiom meaning "gone mad"]: in place of the South of France, which appeared as the goal of a sort of pilgrimage or pardon, was substituted the North, and the town in which lives the artist whom I have admired above all others since I became an adult mutated into the one inhabited by the great artiste of my childhood. After the sort of mortal negation to which my troubles had driven me—an act of which I could only be ashamed in the presence of the indefectible pioneer known as Picasso—a recoil occurred and caused me to retreat into the naïve period in which neither love nor art posed any serious problem for me since the first, at that time, was hardly more than a pretty word and the second, still quite exterior, like a chandelier or mantelpiece ornament, was embodied in a moving and beautiful person whose kindness tempered her too great majesty. A return to my origins, soon to be recaptured in the form of my cousin, whose own duty would be to bring me back—by ways equally indirect—to two distinct levels of time and not to my childhood alone.

Through my mother, through my Aunt Claire, and, more subtly, through the comic-opera star whose shadow floats over that girl to whom I suspect him and his wife of having thought of marrying me, my cousin touched a world that fascinated me, and he had full plenary right of entree into the half-sleep of my hospital night since (symbolically) they are intertwined, the theater and he, in shining thin cords which, above and beyond old age and disenchantment, attach me to two crucial phases of my life: the childish period of the first great admirations; the moment when, the die not yet cast, the beginner seeks his way at the same time as, privately, he prepares to bet on one of the four queens. Could I confess to myself that those innocent preambles to what, afterward, would become so terribly muddled on the level of art as on that of love had become for me a twofold object of nostalgia? If I secretly aspired to draw close to it, I had within my reach an ideal intermediary in the person of my cousin, disguised as much as was required by the clandestine nature of his mission, but clothed in pieces of tawdry finery that revealed the nature of that mission at the same time as they concealed it. Promoted to a helot drunk on dramaturgy—as though at the moment when art offered me a last hope, I had had, in order to set off again on another foot, to heap with scorn the artist that for so long I had dreamed of being—my cousin showed me plainly what I should never cease to guard myself against, and, in sibylline language, which vicinities harbored the cool springs in which I wanted to bathe myself again.

North and South, Brussels and Taormina. It was not while listening to the girl who expressed her ardent desire to visit not Sicily, but the particular spot which probably seemed to her to incarnate Sicily, that I effected my conversion, directing toward the bottom of the map those eyes which had until then been drawn toward the top, and adopting as my preferred lands those countries that were warmed tenderly or harshly by the sun. It was two or three years after this conversation, which remained the only chapter (as I have said), that I changed my plans, when for the first time I went to the Côte d'Azur where, at extremely various times and places, I spent so many hours illuminated by Picasso and where I would return fictively to make my confession, to him who had been witness not only to my life as a writer but also to my married life from its beginnings and who, seeing the thing from that angle still, could have criticized twice over my attempt at desertion. Visiting Antibes in 1925 for my summer vacation, I understood à propos of the South of France what I had only heard à propos of Taormina and I discovered, along with our agreement about the beauty of the South, a deeper understanding with the woman who, before we set off, had reported it to me and who up to now has remained my constant tablemate and interlocutrice despite the setbacks that, through my fault, our union may have encountered. Of Taormina I thought I had a distant view when—going to Egypt at the time of the fit of depression of which I have spoken—I sailed past off the coast of Sicily: it seemed to me I could distinguish several white shafts of columns, similar to what I had glimpsed, not from the bridge of a ship, but with my feet firmly planted on a balcony overlooking the boulevard Beaumarchais. At the same time, or almost, I was shown Etna, whose nature as a volcano did not differentiate it from any other mountain. When, shortly after the last war, I found myself in the frightfully touristic place dreamed of in my presence by the nice brown-haired girl, I encountered nothing which could be recognized as that succession of white columns, and I concluded from this that my imagination had been working hard at the moment when I had known that the steamship *Lamartine* was within sight of Taormina. During the short stay that I made there with my wife, I often went to walk or sit in the remains of the famous theater, but the most interesting image left to me by this period of pleasant idleness was that of another girl with brown hair. In the main street lined with many lace and souvenir shops the saleswomen in which did not hesitate to accost the customers, she stood at all hours of the day on the threshold of her door and smiled at us as soon as we approached, so that I fell into the habit of greeting her with a cordial buon giorno, allowing my gaze to rest on her for an instant as though there were between that stranger and myself a tacit complicity.

A Flemish woman with the pure voice and black eyebrows of Tosca, a brown-haired girl dazzled by what she had heard or read about Taormina, a shopkeeper with dark hair and a welcoming smile—if I have turned my eyes toward these images, too indistinct or too fleetingly imprinted not to be perfectly safe, it is perhaps out of a concern for avoiding the image of the woman so full of life, also raven-haired, who was able, one day, to make me cry when for a long time I had not been able to rediscover that sort of release except figuratively, when I chanced to burst into sobs in one of the increasingly rare dreams I had.

A collapse caused, at the time of our bad quarrel, by words at once harsh and foolish, whose deceptively displayed propriety marked (beyond the actual injury) all the thickness of what separated us, words in the face of which I shamefully measured my weakness, giving in because I could not bury a hope which those words proved, however, that, if fulfilled, would not correspond to my desire. Tears that sprang forth as though from a well which, in the innermost part of me, had reached the level of anguish, tenderness, despair, and irony that consists more or less of what I would like to express but that is also—very probably—unsayable. The sudden afflux of birdsongs when, fine weather having just followed the rain, my eyes were dampening from too much exultation and no longer from sorrow. The chirps that reached my sickroom and, reproducing those that had provided the fanfare for a reconciliation only a few weeks before my gesture of disorderly retreat, also reminded me of the noise that had so intrigued me the first night of my stay in China: notes that I thought at first came from aeolian harps or perhaps (according to some story I no longer remember, real or invented, that I had read) lightweight bamboo pipes the Chinese would attach under the belly or wings of certain birds so that the air would pass through them, notes that in fact were nothing more than the strangely flutelike whistles of locomotives approaching or departing from the Peking station. The great din of winged creatures and insects, the ardor for living and the indomitable melancholy with which the warbling of nature in its abundance seemed charged when, after the Liberation, at the time of the second voyage I made to Africa, I crossed at nightfall, in a Dodge truck, the frontier zone between Côte d'Ivoire and Guinea.

The days of my death throes, whose torments those close to me—and not the zero which I had then become—had suffered. The living dead woman whom I incarnated every night and whose strength was fully equal to that of the man shot during the war with Spain who, during his last vigil in a Barcelona prison, apparently had the courage (but I know none of his compatriots who is surprised at this) to express his ill fortune by singing *coplas*. The pleasantly wild music, performed by those sparrows who could not reasonably be supposed to inhabit the dismal landscape dominated by the gas company, but who scarcely lost any of their mystery when I was informed of the existence of a courtyard garden onto which faced the other side of the wing where the resuscitations were carried out. The precious technique I had been taught, in the first days of my return to consciousness, to stop my voice from being harsh and staccato: to press with my hand, when I spoke, the dressing that I wore on my throat, which obturated my wound and allowed me to breathe normally.

It was a pretty physical therapist who had shown me this procedure, a rather small girl, brown-haired, plump, and cheerful, a native of Toulouse, the same one who revealed—when I was a little better—the enclosure, Edenic for me, represented by the courtyard garden and pointed out to me, guiding me, the route I should take when I wanted to go there for a walk: a few meters of hallway on the left as I came out of my room, then, on my right, a glass-paned door. Between these two lessons, I gave her some tickets I had received for an evening at the Salle Pleyel, where they were showing Chinese films, and, according to what she told me the next day, I believe she liked the event. "Seeing you, I have recovered my taste for life," I declared to her once, not out of vain gallantry but because her entire person positively invited me to see the future from a better angle, as though her freshness had a power similar to that of the three young boys put into the service of Zarastro by the librettist of *The Magic Flute*. It is, however, only in the light of memory that this analogy occurred to me, a very much later counterpart to an impression I received upon emerging from an examination of my wound—not entirely scarred over—in the offices of the ear-nose-and-throat doctors who had operated on me: could I not believe that the suite of underground rooms where they officiated, their foreheads strapped round with fat electric lamps, as though with visors in the form of dogs' muzzles, had changed them into infernal judges before whom I was appearing, in an Egypt with curiously modernized hypogeums rather than in a hospital?

Knowingly I transformed the physical therapist into a kindly spirit helping me to sail around certain capes of a voyage beyond the grave—that young woman to whom I was indebted for a twofold initiation: breathing better when I spoke, taking the air in the courtyard garden. But it was in perfect innocence that, on one of the very first days, I changed the more robust and more mature nurse who was caring for me into an Old Lady Who Lived in a Shoe. That she had twelve children in her charge seemed to me self-evident, and no doubt it was true that, tied to a hospital bed and returned almost to the state of a newborn, since I had to be made to eat and was not allowed to get up by myself, I was inclined to situate her in a context in which child welfare, relief for orphans, the procreation of twins or of record litters would have been mixed in higglety-pigglety with romantic notions about motherhood in the working classes—this woman who, at that moment, was for me what the wet nurse is for the urchin. "My poor monsieur Leiris! What would I do with twelve children? I have two, and that's quite enough . . . ," she said to me, when I thought to express to her my grateful interest by pitying her for the difficulty that such a numerous progeny could not fail to cause her, worn out as she must be already by the obligations of a job that was among the most thankless.

It was at several different levels and in the various branches of a hierarchy as nuanced as a celestial hierarchy that these women were situated, all in white from head to foot but of unequal grace, some passing, others entering to tidy the room, to escort doctors at the hour of their visits, if not to occupy themselves directly with me or, even more often, with the poor companion whom one hoped each day to see return to human life and concerning whom, though I certainly joined in that shared hope, I occasionally began thinking that, thus as discreet as it could be, his presence was probably less burdensome than it would become if he rose to the rank of a neighbor with whom I would have to converse. As I learned a little later, those who worked at housekeeping or, like my very good and very expert nanny, formed the lowest class of the medical staff, because they lacked diplomas, were entitled only to those humble pieces of cloth knotted around their heads like the scarves of gypsy women, whereas the much more elaborate headdresses, of different forms and dimensions, that one observed on certain women were the prerogative of the supervisors and nurses with degrees. Standing out against this multitude, in which the angels wore the veil and the archangels the headdress, as though for a folklore demonstration, the physical therapists sported a sort of small skullcap, more or less hemispherical, a raffish mobcap accentuating the corps-de-ballet aspect of their young and nimble team. Despite the cruel questions that I had the leisure to debate and the strain of uneasiness that found its way into my dreams, certainly my forced retirement, by giving me a respite, assumed something of the appearance of a holiday, won with sufficient difficulty, furthermore, so that I could enjoy it without the slightest remorse. Thus was I disposed to observe as a dilettante, with an eye always curious and readily amused, this world in truth more sinister than picturesque, since illness and death were its cornerstones.

One morning, when I knew already that once my wound was closed I would return home, an event occurred more important than it might seem, for the conversation of a few minutes of which it consisted was very helpful to my inner rehabilitation, without which my rescue would have made no sense. I do not know what I was occupied with when one of the doctors who visited me every day entered, dressed in his white shirt. Perhaps I was in the midst of scratching, with the tip of my pointed pen, a few lines in the notebook that I had very soon asked for, among other objects judged to be highly necessary: a thick notebook, brand new, whose cover bore a rather large glued vignette representing, seen from downstream, the middle of the Pont Neuf and the Square du Vert Galant, with, in characters of very large type, the word LUTÈCE, concerning which I do not know, lacking the requisite chronological facts, whether its presence on the front of the notebook (an encounter that strikes me now) could have had something to do with the intervention of my cousin under a name inspired, as I have said, by the noble and ancient pseudonym that his uncle had adopted? Perhaps I was plunged (as much as I was allowed by a faculty of attention that has never been great) in one or the other of the two books that I had had brought to me: the amazing and preposterous notes of Mallarmé relating to his famous "Book," in the end never written, but which he had made the very goal of his life and which he seems to have conceived as the total work in which the universe is summed up and justified; *L'Afrique ambiguë* by the ethnologist Georges Balandier, in which one sees tradition and modernity confront each other among the men of the black continent, a work that had come to me as a review copy and was related to the other side of my professional activity, the ethnographic side (that of humanist scholarship and commitment), whereas Mallarmé's unpublished work—to the reading of which I devoted much more time and passionate application—had to do with the side that was not even literary but strictly poetic? Then again, perhaps I was not engaged in anything definite, thinking about my difficult endeavor to regain my balance in work as well as in life and shifting about in my head the mental signs of a few desires that were always the same and in themselves fairly simple but of which I was powerless to find the means of achieving in practice the synthesis? However it may have been, the doctor crossed the threshold and came to sit down next to my bed.

The presence of my roommate did not even resemble that of a man entombed in a deep sleep, for in his case no sudden awakening was to be feared. Thus my visitor and I talked as though we were alone together. Not troubling himself with useless circumlocutions, this man with a calm face and a very slight smile that was more wise than cheerful, with a gaze neither too detached nor too inquisitive, with an appearance that was perfectly healthy without any unpleasant excess of prosperity, this rather young but somewhat slow and probably not at all chatty man who, having settled next to me as one of my close friends would have done, seemed to me a creature most punctilious in his duties at the same time as most reasonable, broached almost immediately what had, for him, to be the crux of the matter, or, at least, to lead straight to it: someone had spoken to him (and I thought afterward that it was a police report that had informed him) about my "habits of intemperance," so that he wanted to learn from me exactly what this was all about. I did not absolutely deny anything but, smiling a little, I retorted to him that, if I had happened in fact much too often to drink too much and if that still happened to me sometimes, I had never been a drunk properly speaking and still less an alcoholic; drink was, for me, a means of dealing with the uneasiness of certain circumstances and one which, without my contributing anything, I had frequent occasions, socially, to use; I was quite far from resorting to it as regularly as might have been described. Since he questioned me about my precise occupations, I explained in a few words about my double profession, as writer and ethnographer, and then I confessed more or less everything to him. Very placidly, he then said to me that a man like me should not let himself go as I had. Could I not, with the help of sojourns in the country and sports, lead a more physically active life, which would take care of a lot of things? I rejected such a program, alleging my need to devote my moments of freedom to my literary work, on which I set a very high price; but I answered affirmatively when he asked me whether, among the people I knew, there might not be a psychoanalyst or a psychiatrist to whom I could address myself. I acquiesced to the advice he gave me to undergo a treatment of that sort when I left the hospital, and I agreed, as ardently as one can, to a resolution which, one knows, not only represents a last chance, and which elementary good sense therefore commands one to make, but whose significance, insofar as it is the opposite of a lazy solution, since its execution will not be accomplished without effort, is not merely utilitarian. The interview having, with that, reached its logical end, my visitor did not insist, and I, saying goodbye to him, thanked him warmly for having come to talk to me that way, man to man.

Even before my colloquy with one of the heads of that group of men and women whom I saw expending themselves for their patients as though in the front line of a battle, I had said to myself that next to the dubious works of politics, with effects too often the inverse of what one had had in view, there was one thing whose effective value was, by contrast, beyond all argument: the running of an establishment like the one (so well equipped technically and humanly) in which I had regained consciousness. One could not deem it absurd to devote all one's time to such an enterprise, and the fact that it existed was enough perhaps to rehabilitate life, even in the case where it offered us nothing else defensible.

However convinced I may have been of the beauty of the medical profession, there is hardly any need to add that I did not open myself for an instant to an idea that would have been pure chimera, if only because of my age: to devote myself to this relief-worker activity whose *validity*, at the very least, cannot be contested. But what I retained from the example presented to me—as though to deter me from utopias—by the smooth functioning of a hospital, was that a preference for work well done is a cardinal virtue, and that, without scattering myself as I had formerly in all sorts of stray impulses, I ought above all to resume my real professional task by simply putting into it as much awareness and vision as I could.

Like the "resolutions" that at the time (I believe) of my first communion I inscribed in a notebook reserved for pious uses, literary projects—summarily noted—figure among the rapid and irregular notes composing what was a hold-all rather than the journal of my time of illness. To make a critique of monogamy—this is what would perhaps still have some meaning, and I would employ myself at it in the very next part of this *Rules of the Game*, so that, without departing from lived experience, the book, by being oriented toward a critique of our customs, would lose the too personal character that it had had at the beginning and that had disgusted me. Obedient to Mallarmé's lesson, to give myself as my goal the idea of the total book, and to try, with this series of tales and reflections—already a snake biting its own tail, since the search for its own justification was, fundamentally, its main driving force—to achieve a work that would exist as a closed world, complete and incontestable, such could also be my way of escaping from subjectivism, gaining some height, then, instead of choosing a way out that would issue at ground level. To carry out, in all modesty, a piece of work accepted long before but that had not gone beyond the stage of a promise—to write an article on the evolution of Aimé Césaire's political themes and poetry—was what I was in any case supposed to be putting at the top of my program, as of primary urgency. Almost as cursory as the notes, brief poems were hurled directly or recopied onto certain pages of the "school notebook" that its manufacturers had placed under the patronage of Lutèce.

Like those poems of a few lines that from its beginnings marked my unfolding adventure, they derived their flesh and blood from the very thing they brought to life in their turn: that state of *passionate tenderness and sadness* whose ambiguity, one evening, had been expressed silently and suddenly by my nearly fatal intoxication. It was a sentiment resistant to any illumination through the ordinary paths of discourse, but that each of these lyrical combinations of words caused to shine before me like a crystal thus wrested by main force from my inner darkness.

Reflections on myself and on what had happened to me. Simple personal observations. Poems that, more than songs, were fulgurations issuing sometimes from the heart and sometimes from the brain. Plans having to do with my getting back into the saddle, both by my own efforts—by working—and by medical means: psychoanalysis (quite disheartening, for I could not imagine myself, without a feeling of nausea, once again stretched out on the confessional couch); psychosomatic medicine (which had been attracting me for a long time, with its gleams illuminating the strange match that is played between body and mind until the first drags the second along with it in its downfall); to decide nothing, in any case, without having consulted the friend who throughout the past months had been occupied with restoring the health of my liver and purifying my blood. In the notebook, a few pages of which were thus covered with flyspecks not always very legible, I thus delineated some plans, tried to understand them, and accumulated some lines of verse. On the very day after my failed liquidation a choice had been enacted, almost without my knowledge and without my having had to debate about it: I had simply fastened onto it. How should I live? Live doing *what* and doing it *how*? These two questions were the only burning ones, and if, in the background, coiled another question mark—*why* live?—it was in a manner purely formal and almost ornamental.

When I go back now to that singular period, I note it as happy despite the deplorable physical state in which I found myself, the quasi-reclusion implied by my status as hospital patient, and the anguish that filled me when, instead of envisaging the future from the almost scholarly viewpoint of a program to be determined, I contemplated it without veiling the conflict that had not been resolved by my descent into the abysses. A certain calm had come after the turbulence, supplanting little by little the excitation, unconscious in the very beginning, that had caused them to tie me down, as I have mentioned, and then, when I was freed of the ties, once provoked the rough intervention of two night nurses, who, using a sheet folded several times, strapped me tightly to my bed as though they were preparing to fight me. However, the sort of torrid serenity to which I acceded, that joy *in itself*, if I can call it that—a joy that was completely bare, or, at least, lacking in attributes that were actually pleasant—soon revealed itself to have been only a circumstantial reaction and not the consecration of any wisdom: it was the straining of every fiber of my being toward healing, at the same time as a response to the straightforward devotion of those who had revived me and whose conduct seemed dominated by the idea that human life is worth a struggle to prolong it. What marked the turning point was—at the time when I was acknowledged to be nearly convalescent—my transfer into the "men's gallery," a part of the wing that (like its counterpart, the "women's gallery") was theoretically occupied by patients for whose health one no longer had to fight inch by inch.

Objectively, I had gained by this change of locale: I had at my disposition a room with a single bed, a sort of box whose partitions did not reach the ceiling but formed an adequate separation. Despite the lack of disturbance caused me in the other room by the quasi-absent man who vegetated beside me, my solitude was now, certainly, better: it allowed me a greater freedom with my visitors and, the rest of the time, more peace than in that other room, subject to the comings and goings entailed by the many cares my companion needed. Nonetheless, in fact I experienced this change as a return to the most dismal tedium. Scarcely was I settled in before I felt boredom take the place of the ardor that, in various forms, had animated me up to then. My period of high tension was succeeded by that of a broken charm, as though I had been disillusioned, pulled from a dream or abruptly returned to profane duties after the fervor of some pilgrimage.

A room with only one bed instead of the room with three beds of which one was mine, another a resting place between life and death where an obstinate sleeper lay, the third a piece of furniture that would not have counted had I not been afraid of seeing it occupied one day by God knows what arrival! According to this arithmetic, I should have been delighted with a much improved fate. But to consider only the immediately measurable aspect would be to take a deceptive view of the thing, for in this room, where I was now alone, and relieved of too frequent intrusions, I found I was, on the other hand, at the mercy of all that might filter in through partitions whose opacity was not duplicated, unfortunately, by anything equivalent with respect to what might beleaguer my eardrums.

There were radios regularly tuned to the worst drivel in the way of programs, and remarks exchanged by my neighbors, who sometimes joked like soldiers the night before they are demobilized, sometimes bantered piteously about the state of their throats after the tracheotomies they too had undergone (for most were tetanus victims cured by the method that consists of provoking a coma by injection with curare, then "reviving")—all this came to me through the partitions as though, morning and night, a malign Providence had given me an anthology of idiotic quotations to listen to, in order to wash my brain of any inclination toward optimism I might have had. Given what I was hearing, was I not in fact led to say to myself that this hospital work, despite its apparent "validity," was no less aberrant than any other, since it turned out, in the last analysis, to represent a great deal of intelligence, heart, and energy expended with the sole aim of increasing the longevity of a collection of sinister cretins (almost all of them having been proved such, except for a North African whom I spotted a little later through a set of open doors and whose difference of origin or ignorance of French preserved him from the distressing colloquy)? Thus, like a believer who cannot tolerate the crumbling of his faith, I would soon accept, as a truth whose obviousness became glaringly apparent at the very moment one reached the lowest point, the following idea, calculated to recompose the drop of hope that had too quickly evaporated: even if it might be true that a doctor—likewise, also, an artist or soldier—wastes his forces for the benefit of a disgustingly mediocre public, and even if one could, at best, belong to an *active elite* stirring up the emptiness to which (in the main) the passive masses are reduced, this would not discredit such efforts and would only show the urgency of connecting them to the education of these masses, which one could not say were doomed by fate to a constant futility. A rather dopey philosophy but one that, at the time, was likely to be welcome, since by liberating me from a logical despair it would silence my scruples concerning my lack of courage to repeat, this time without any possibility of failure, my attempt to put an end to it all.

Removed from that line of fire, as it were, the rooms of the gravely ill, one of which I had shared with a half-dead man whom they worked unceasingly at keeping alive while waiting for him to wake up, I felt like an evacuated soldier who is dragging his gloom around the hospitals behind the combat zone. There was no trace, here, of the heroic atmosphere of my former sector: for the amazons, often flushed, who relieved one another in a relentless battle against the forces of death, more anodyne creatures seemed to have been substituted, either because the convalescents no longer needed to be assisted by the very finest, or because the fact that they were out of danger led to a home-guard sort of relaxation on the part of women as valiant, when necessary, as those of the shock troop. But whether it was a matter of the people or simply of circumstances, certainly less vigilance and more detached behavior combined to give me the impression that around me, colorless cleaning women—neutral and anonymous—had taken over.

During one of my walks from hallway to hallway (I took them even at night, going to the bathroom being then my alibi), I encountered the indefatigable caregiver who, during the first few days, had seemed to me so maternal and so capable of attending to everything that I thought of course she must have had, at home, to spend herself body and soul on the needs of a burdensome brood. I liked her very much, this woman whose efficient devotion—so profound, no doubt, that it was quite unconscious—did not prevent either from putting you in your place nor from vituperating as though at that very instant she was going to give it all up. Thus, wanting to say something nice to her, I expressed to her my boredom at being a patient in the men's gallery now, and how much better I liked it in the sector that she looked after. Yes . . . *It's livelier where we are!* she declared, laughing, without my being able to tell whether that laughter corresponded to her pure, heartfelt agreement or to a perception of the strangeness of such a judgment about the series of workshops where skillful technicians endeavored to repair creatures who, of their humanity, retained the form only.

Having moved from that place where death flew overhead to one where everything seemed calculated to make me deplore having come back among men, I had—dismaying as it was—progressed at least on one point: there was no more question, henceforth, of calmly enjoying the respite that my withdrawal had brought me; to stay even a single day longer than strictly necessary would have been to linger cravenly in the midst of a degrading stupidity. The decision to leave as soon as possible and to confront, without delay, a future concerning which I had for a moment wondered whether everything did not risk being resolved, in simple disgust, more quickly than I would have believed—such was my almost immediate reaction to these depressing surroundings. I therefore accepted, at last without deferments, the peril of returning to my life of a short time before. Would I have made this choice so easily if I had not had the virtue of hope as an intimate part of my being, despite what I might have thought at other times?

Until then I had been waiting for my wound to heal and for them to decide that I was ready to return home. However, the friend who was assisting me as my attending physician had said to me that by doing this I ran the risk of being kept there for quite a long time: what I had to do was ask for my release; they would surely grant it, because the treatments that my wound still required could be given elsewhere than in the hospital. My unhappy discovery in the men's gallery quickly put an end to any hesitation; I expressed my desire to leave. They immediately signed me up for the next otorhinolaryngological consultation; I would present myself there during the morning on Saturday and depart in the afternoon.

Equipped with a "large curette," the big boss ear-nose-and-throat man had removed some small excrescences that had formed on the edges of my wound, still partially open. This had hurt quite a bit and, back in my room, after leaving the subterranean lair where the consultation was held, I had lain down on my bed in order to recuperate. Then a nurse had come to apply a last dressing, and I had lunched on cakes and fruits. It was very hot, which did not help matters after the almost sleepless night I had had. My slender luggage prepared, all that remained was for me to rest until the moment when my wife would arrive to take me back to the quai des Grands Augustins, along with one of our closest friends, the very same one I have chosen (because he is appreciably younger than I) as posthumous executor of my last wishes and who, perhaps, will have to occupy himself with publishing, arranged as he will find them, the unused slips of paper for *The Rules of the Game*, that work which for a long time now I have been afraid of not being able to finish, for lack of time, and which this fear, by making me tense, prevents me still further from finishing quickly.

My wait was long and all the more irritating because, my goodbyes having been said, and the break effected, I would have liked to decamp at once. To sleep there yet another night, if the too tardy arrival of my escort made it unfortunately impossible for me to go through the formalities of leaving—I could not envisage this without anguish. Two or three times I even went to the duty nurses' office to find out whether some telephone communication had not come, informing me of some hitch or modification added to the protocol envisaged. The nurses reassured me and sent me back to my room, where, too fidgety to read, write, or do anything at all, I could only begin fretting again, asking myself if I had not misunderstood what my wife had said to me the day before. Arising less from reflection than from a mad impatience, my worry was groundless, and I was able, before the afternoon was very advanced, to settle myself in my pajamas and bathrobe in the saloon car that our friend, in order to spare me a few steps too many, had taken it upon himself to bring into the small courtyard close by, where the doctors' cars were parked.

In the intense heat of that June, the ride was tiring. A little on edge, I opened my eyes wide to a summer apparently full of violence, whose outbreak, secluded as I was (for the space of two weeks that were too full to correspond to their measurement on the calendar), I had not suspected, even when I took the air in the Eden that a cheerful physical therapist had revealed to me. The Avenue d'Aubervilliers and the street of the same name, struck by a sun I had so forgotten that it appeared to me of an extreme harshness, extended on either side of the windows, and I looked at them as I would have the arteries of an unfamiliar pattern in an exotic city that would at once have surprised and vaguely frightened me. The splendor of a light on the verge (one could believe) of exploding endowed with a marvelous brilliance this neighborhood of ill repute where, here and there, a café-bar astonished me by its glowing color and the cutthroat appearance it owed to its very tranquility. Among the rare people who walked about or stood on the sidewalks, I noticed a few men—North Africans or others—to whom I attributed, no doubt rather quickly, the profession of pimps, and I especially noted, encamped like fishwives or tragic actresses, women in cheap summer dresses that did not cover them more than dressing gowns, and which, venal or not, they seemed ready to shed in an instant for the lovemaking to which one was incited by this day so radiant that in itself it made one want to be naked. More densely populated, the Faubourg Saint-Denis presented to me, under full sail, to my left and right, its panoply of female thieves scarcely appetizing as a group and, sometimes, hideous enough to send cold shivers down one's spine.

Having been delivered back home, I climbed my four flights of stairs without stopping, even though my breath was short and my legs had hardly any energy. Fearing the reunion with what had been, symbolically, the setting of my last day, I wanted to linger as little as possible on the threshold and plunge, as one throws oneself into the water, toward the meeting that I dreaded. This tactic, in truth, was of no use to me, and even though in the same impetus I went all the way into the study where the chest of drawers stood, from the top drawer of which I had taken my tubes of phenobarbital in order to stuff myself with their contents, I felt a great shock when, stretched out on the couch and trying to catch my breath, I allowed my eyes to alight on that chest of drawers, the other furniture, and the various ornaments of a place that had been the setting for a crisis the likes of which I had never before experienced.

Lying on my back, I faced the ceiling above me with the corner stucco figures and the other moldings of its old-fashioned decoration, whose central motif is an ellipse scarcely less long and less broad than the rectangle formed by the tops of the cornices that surmount the four walls. As is customary, the bowl of the lighting fixture—a cup of frosted glass held up by a disk of steel screwed to the lower end of a vertical axis that is not visible—included the median point of the ceiling in that protuberance, in the form of a well-rounded and discreetly bulging breast, that I sometimes like to compare to a sort of omphalos or navel of the world. But that was not what compelled my attention. Scarcely had I lain down before I perceived, with an acuity that made me almost ill, the singular relief of the ellipse, banal though it was and integrated so perfectly with my daily surroundings that in ordinary times it had, for me, almost ceased to exist. Scoured by the completely new vision I had of it, this modest product of Second Empire bourgeois style swelled with a power of fascination so precise that there undoubtedly exists no masterpiece that could have rivaled it, during the long and agitated interval that I spent there while they prepared the small bedroom which I would leave only when my return to nights of normal sleep marked the end of my convalescence.

During the last war, I once had the good fortune to drink some real coffee, and this beverage, which we had been deprived of for a long time, had almost the same effect on me, I think, as if I had taken some hashish; in a metro filled with people, all (it seemed) astonishingly picturesque, I admired the modeling of the most vulgar sort of nose like a painter in ecstasy before a poor shanty on which the rays of the sun are playing; an antique dealer whom I know thought I was drunk, I showed such pleasure as I observed the way in which lines and colors endowed the African velvets in his collection with a vivid and constantly changing depth; that evening, in a concert hall, it seemed to me that the sounds issuing from the instruments were passing through my whole body, and, the entire time I listened to it, this music, which had turned into my own resonance, provoked in me fantastic bursts of emotion. Without the help of any excitant, it was a sensation similar to these, that the sight of the elliptical motif gave me, while I rested on the couch.

As I viewed it, the room in which I was lying was of an implacable objectivity, which, toward the back, was heavily imposed by the projection of the chest of drawers and, at the top, was affirmed in a more abstract way in the shadows and lights of the moldings that, considered as a whole, appeared to portray a map of a universe extremely simplified and reduced. But crudely as these elements of furniture or ornament made me feel their presence, both were complicated with significations more or less distant, as though at the same time that they were self-contained realities, they were also aides-mémoire placed there to orient my reverie. With all its threatening cubic capacity, the chest of drawers oppressed me, and its volume was the spatial expression of the great gust of passion and despair with which my lungs had filled the last time I had contemplated it. The moldings of the ceiling, and especially what I could see, in their frozen exuberance, of the elaborate figures (mute tempests moving at zero speed) that masked the trihedral angles formed at the four corners of the room by the meeting of the ceiling with the walls—those Napoleon III stuccos of a type probably present in the rue de Rome at the home of the organizer of the illustrious Tuesdays: it was toward the poetry of Mallarmé that they guided me and toward that *Book* which, beginning in the hospital, had been a great help to me by opening prospects of work through its example. All the sumptuousness of eroticism was also condensed there: those bedroom marvels created by the commerce in love, and of which mirrors, consoles, sconces, credenzas, and other ingredients of Mallarméan sonnets are, for me, the purest expression. The terrible fixity of death, too, was proclaimed by the petrified rhetoric of those fiorituras older than we (since they date from our grandparents' time) and at the same time younger (since they will survive us and will perhaps witness our biological collapse).

Whereas vast surfaces (a plain extending to infinity, or a broad, high wall rising vertically) captivated my gaze in those open-air dreams in which an abrupt cliff was the shared feature, what now became embedded in my eyes and forced me into a sort of waking dream was the well-delimited rectangle of a ceiling in a room, closely confined, of a bourgeois apartment. With the geometrical severity of its design and the cruel precision of its reliefs, the ellipse appeared to me not as the persistent sign of a truth that a little ingenuity and patience would have allowed me to discover, but as a *presence* so extraordinarily pronounced that its intensity seemed out of proportion as much with the testimony of my eyes as with that which my hands would have been able to furnish me if those tiny plaster swellings had been within their reach. More than real, to the very extent that it partook of the nature of a hallucination, I experienced this presence simply as presence with dizzying intensity, and, as I endured it, curious things they had described to me at the hospital came back to my memory: the sort of shift or disorientation in their visual perceptions experienced by tetanus sufferers who have been treated with curare and who (like that woman, a convalescent, both angular and bizarrely graceful, whom I encountered sometimes during my strolls in the hallways) remain for a certain time automatons of a sort, with irregular motions, or demons whose infernal masters have shifted their symmetry, without this necessarily making them ugly, since—I had noted it with my own eyes—a charm a trifle simian may cling to their skewed appearance.

The person who, saying to me in substance: *You think you're looking over here and what you see is over there,* had told me about this trouble, of which I was immediately reminded by the disturbing acuity of the ellipse, was a sort of twenty-three-year-old miracle case, slender, pale under her makeup, with brown hair, whose name was Monique. Rather pretty and touching in her illness, this little saint, little fairy, and more certainly little queen in the guise of a dressmaker's assistant or a shorthand typist (which she was) was regarded as a star at the Pavillon Lassen: having recovered after being at death's door, thanks to the treatment using curare, she had been exhibited to a delegation of Soviet doctors, and it had amused her very much, she said, to find herself facing this group of men who were looking upon her as a phenomenon. One of my nurses had often talked to me about her, and, without knowing her, I had had the opportunity of a friendly gesture toward her. The friend who drove me back home—a great connoisseur on the subject of modern art, and, in addition, a discriminating gastronome—had sent me a basket of fruits so magnificent that it would have been indecent to eat it by myself. I therefore tasted some of them,

I offered some to my nurses, and, since there still remained a great many, I sent this woman Monique, so popular, a small basket of strawberries that seemed perfectly prepared to be separated from the large basket. Unable to move, but wanting to thank me otherwise than through an intermediary, the recipient sent me word that she would be happy to have a visit, which—of course!—I hastened to pay her. It was thus that we had a rather long conversation, she half lying down and coquettishly dressed in lounging pajamas, I seated and draped in the Scottish plaid bathrobe that was at the time my formal outfit as well as that of every day. The grace of the girl, the sort of aureole with which she was embellished, her position as lady of the court receiving visitors in her alcove or Violetta dying in the last act of *La Traviata*, made a great impression on me. To the figure of the pretty physical therapist was thus added that of another pleasant person, as though their refreshing apparitions had been planned so that, despite its macabre outfitting and the disgust that seized me at the end, the Hôpital Claude-Bernard was inscribed in my memory in colors more pink than black. Like all sufferers from tetanus restored to health by curare, young Monique had to learn to walk again, and, the morning on which, without support, she risked a few steps surrounded by nurses and physical therapists ready to prevent any possible fall, I was eager to be there to congratulate her and at the same time to say goodbye, for my leaving was by then imminent. It seems to me now that this ill woman, so coddled, will perhaps thus have experienced, despite all the anguish she recounted to me, the finest period of her life: the one that will leave her with the memory of a time when she was the object of the same attentions and almost of the same homages as a prima donna.

Having returned home very much thinner, my nerves fragile and my sleep disordered, I was of course obliged to rest, but this did not imply a total seclusion. I was supposed to become reaccustomed to things, not to sink into an immobility in every respect harmful, and I was advised to go out a little each day, even before my wound was completely closed. I was amenable, naturally, to this prescription, and, if anything, all too amenable, because this way I could go see my friend, for I had not renounced my love for her. Strengthened by the right that I believed I had won by my severe penitence, I profited candidly from our meetings, and, romantically, I derived an increase of felicity from the very efforts that I had to expend each time in order to separate myself from my fatigue. Those hours, which correspond to the period in which my condition as convalescent had been transformed into pure freedom, number—I believe this firmly—among the best that we spent together.

The penitence, after all, was still far from over. Almost as soon as I returned, I was subjected to a police interrogation. Summoned to my neighborhood police station (from which they had pursued me after a first communication that my wife had received and that I had ignored), I had to give an explanation for my "suicide attempt," reported by the administration at the Hôpital Claude-Bernard. At the time of my transfer, my wife, shrinking from revealing the sad truth, had spoken of an accident and the deputy inspector saw a contradiction here that called for a clarification. I assured him that there had in fact been a "suicide attempt" but an almost accidental one, seeing as, without the effect of alcohol, I would not have attempted anything. The deputy inspector wanted to know the reason for it and was annoyed when I told him that, simply depressed, I had acted without a precise motive (which, in the journalistic style of our dialogue, meant that one had to eliminate any idea of marital disagreement, a troubled intimate relationship, or financial distress). To allege depression alone was to lie; but—even if I had had the time and the patience to lay the thing out from A to Z and show it in all its complexity—was I going to make my general confession to this policeman? My interlocutor refused to understand that one can commit suicide *without a reason*. Exasperated, I asked him if he knew what "neurasthenia" was. In uttering this word, which falsified everything still more than before, since it turned me into a purely medical case, I had been quite inspired: the possibility thus provided to the investigator of putting the condemned act away in a compartment he was familiar with appeased him immediately and at the same time brought the interview to an end. Did I have children? That was the question which he asked me next and which was not followed by any other when I had answered it in the negative.

My statement was read back to me, as written down and typed up by a secretary. What I had said, already rather remote from reality, was not even exactly reproduced in it. As though I had wanted to play the hypocrite, they had noted in it, for example, that "libations" were "inhabitual" to me and that my attitude would have been "altogether different" without the excess of drink in which I had indulged. In fact, I had declared that I was not properly speaking a drunk, even though I occasionally overdid it, and I had added that that night, my depression alone would not have been enough to lead me to swallow the poison. I did not care at all about this piece of paper destined to be lost in some vague file, and I therefore signed it without demanding any changes. The secretary, a hail-fellow-well-met type, reminded me of the outdoors and the practice of sports, thus joining others like him, in my mind, my counselor at the Pavillon Lassen and another doctor who had taken care of me a few years before. I have since then undergone two police interrogations and one by an examining magistrate, at the time of the affair of the *Declaration on the right of insubordination in the Algerian War*, which the press immediately dubbed "The Manifesto of the 121," as though the exact number of the first signatories were something that would attract one's attention. How difficult the truth is to determine, even if one goes at it with the best will in the world—this was what those conversations of a rather particular sort managed to convince me.

During the period of happy freedom of which I have spoken, my happiness (if it really was that) had depended on those outings won by sheer force over fatigue and other discomforts with which I was afflicted to the point of feeling crippled: an impression of frost and numbness in the tip of my tongue (because they had, it appears, kept this organ squeezed between the arms of a forceps before the tracheotomy allowed me to breathe more easily); an inflammation of the gums that made me think for a while that I had a toothache and suggested to me that, decidedly, my whole mouth had deteriorated; an infirmity, lastly, that proved more tenacious, the difficulties I experienced in using my lungs, especially when I was lying down, and, also, in clearing my throat of its mucosities (having to draw my breath slowly, deeply and noisily, having persistently to clear my trachea in long fits of coughing without succeeding in completely freeing it). For a long time it also seemed to me that my voice was not the same anymore: older, and as though the emission of each sound cost me an effort; flatter, and so demusicalized as to be incapable of moving (even for a few seconds) from simple speech to song or declamation. In truth, this was scarcely a deprivation, since I had never tried my skills at singing, except in fun, and today, as formerly, my way of life very rarely involves my using a sustained diction to recite or read something. But for a year, more or less, I felt injured and in some sense mutilated by this alteration, which I saw—wrongly or rightly—as a humiliating aftereffect of my operation. To be stricken in my voice was to be wounded in the deepest way, assaulted in what is the living vehicle of language—of that language which always appears to me to represent in fact the *sacred* portion given to the bipeds that we are, no doubt because it is the instrument of communication—and thus of communion—par excellence.

The dressing that bulged out under my Adam's apple, reduced though it was, and the fear of chafing that might affect the state of my wound led me, at least in the first days, to go out without buttoning the collar of my shirt. Much as that fear constrained me, I concealed the wads of gauze and the adhesive tapes that I would have been embarrassed to exhibit in the street with an ample linen handkerchief, more comfortable than a silk scarf because it could be knotted smaller and it stayed tight better. For my first outing, I recall taking one of a solid pink, which not only was the right size and had in its favor its absence of gaudiness but went perfectly with the suit of thin grayish cloth that I had decided was the most appropriate for the heat of that day (a garment of very inexpensive manufacture which in the course of my last, or last but one, summer vacation I had bought in Venice, in a shop in the Marzarie quarter, the "Wiener Mode"). A little too big for me, this casual outfit could be worn without a tie more easily than another and, under the circumstances, was therefore as appropriate to my horror of slovenliness as it was to the temperature. A manner of dressing that was enjoined on me, without a doubt, by a concern for my comfort and for a minimum of correctness but which (I have to admit) corresponded only too well to a certain dramatic layout of the situation: the man saved from drowning, still marked by the claw of death, who throws whatever is at hand on his back to run, panting, to his amorous colloquy.

With this cheap suit, so vaguely my size that one might have thought it was a borrowed outfit (too long and oddly narrow, at the same time too ample in places), with this handkerchief whose pink—especially provocative since it contrasted with my gaunt face—had slightly the air of the pederast or bum, my toilette may have been more or less improvised, but the fact is that it flattered my coquettishness more than any premeditated arrangement. As though by chance, it gave me, in fact, an appearance conforming to the spirit of that type of character I had long been attracted to: the person who, without being a bohemian any more than an outcast, remains in the margins because he is not closely tied to things and—like Hamlet, always at the junction of the ordinary world and another—resides in the equivocal area where the fantastic comes into being; in accordance with a completely modern alchemy, someone who, saturated day and night with an exquisite and consuming drug (poetry, love, eroticism, alcohol, any one of them), exalts his irregular life to the point of endowing it, beyond its high points and low points, with a supreme though (obviously) derisory splendor.

Below or above the world rather than at the actual level of it, and straining to an extreme to overcome my weakness, I was in the skin of the role without having to compose my character. If there was playacting going on in this, I did it innocently, carried along by complicitous circumstances: an outfit that was almost fortuitous, complementing the effects of my physical state. Nevertheless, with its romanticism, this momentary complaisance seems to me now to have been in the same vein (despite the half-century that had elapsed, and my efforts toward rigor) as a real playacting I once indulged in, well before the age at which one likes to see all things—beginning with oneself—in expressly romantic colors. That day, it was with the help of a sip of wine (perhaps champagne) and, I believe, a red Mephistopheles cap—a paper carnival novelty I had on my head—that I endeavored to incarnate a character who, obscurely, appeared to me that of a débauché. It is probably the diabolical note introduced by the cap that induces me to connect this image, through the intermediary of memories that I wish were more certain, to the figure of the woman who created the role of Satan in *Les Quatre Cents Coups*: I wonder, in fact, whether it was not at that Christmas fête—or some other children's afternoon party given at 8 rue Michel-Ange by my parents—that I met the three granddaughters of the star and if the oldest (a redhead?) was not disguised as a gypsy. But it is quite possible that, having said this, I am bringing together scattered elements and merging them into a single masked ball, a brilliant theater scene of which the child in the red headdress—heralding the man in the pink scarf—was the protagonist.

Neither the inconveniences that I have enumerated nor my disordered sleep seriously detracted from my euphoria of the first days, troubled only (at the hour of low tide) by the certainty of its short duration: that forced idleness, a relaxed enough situation so that I could enjoy my freedom without alibis, and that immunity which I had apparently won but which could not possibly continue once I had returned completely to this side of the world, were the temporary conditions of a very precarious happiness! Why did I not grasp the fact that after the unfurling of the wave, the situation, for one moment turned upside down, would prove to be the same as it had been when I had tried to do away with myself? I could even assume that it would be still worse, soon, when my friend left Paris, as she did each year when summer came. Either I would suffer bitterly from her absence; or our adventure would fade into unreality, and I would have nothing left between my fingers but emptiness. If we remained together, though physically separated, I would have to make plans, invoke some completely transparent excuses to go join her, which would earn me, from a companion opposed to all falsehood and cruelly affected by what I had done, an intolerable condemnation, if indeed our new conflict remained latent. Of course, I was sensitive to the seductiveness of my friend; not for a second was I bored with her, and I was moved to feel her so *feminine* from head to toe. But however great her power of enchantment seemed, the idea of an exclusive devotion hardly entered my mind, and I questioned myself constantly about the authenticity of this love: perhaps it was, on my part, the final outburst of an aging man, and, on her own part, the simple conceited satisfaction she enjoyed in the attention I paid her. A drop of poison had, moreover, infiltrated very early into our relationship: something older that I happened to know about her, something she might have wanted to tell me about, but about which, always, she had kept silent; which was not enough to make me blame her, but enough to create some mistrust.

As in a balancing play of opposing forces, these thoughts became more preoccupying as I improved physically, and I eventually said to myself that given my failed gesture—completely absurd, since I was still there, facing the same dilemma, and since all I had done was to display the overwhelming extent of my egocentricity—it would be a nice hell that I was preparing for my wife and for me.

Forced to censor myself (as happens whenever a total revelation would risk resembling too closely the act of informing against another person), I can give only a general view of the end of this episode, instead of entering into the heart of it, as I would have license to do had I chosen to express myself under the disguise of a novel. Without saying any more about that, I will describe the few other sunny days, as light as a schoolboy's escapade, that were—in the very height of the summer—the crowning piece of the fireworks display. And I will add (not without regret) that this crowning piece, in accordance with the norm, was at once a high point and a conclusion.

From Montecatini Terme, where I went to take the cure and where my wife and I had our shared room in the *Grand Hôtel e la Pace* [Peace] (a luxury Peace less exciting than the one, *mir* in Russian, pursued at the Vienna Congress of 1952 by the international pilgrims among whom I was included), I wrote—hiding this, more or less—many letters that received tender replies. Then there was the diversion of a brief stay in Florence, where, restored by the cure, I rediscovered the beautiful life of "summer vacation," which I have always loved but from which my cantankerous humor had closed me off for a long time. Back in Paris, I had to realize that despite a few rough patches, this trip to Italy had represented, for the lover that I believed I was, an easing of the situation at least as much as a privation, so that the imminent return of my friend—an event whose prospect ought to have delighted me—was a thing feared rather than desired by me, since I could measure more coldly than before what a sum of hush-hush mysteries and other unpleasant gymnastics (to say nothing of all the time consumed or frankly squandered) it would cost me to resume our meetings. Thus when my correspondent, noting the change, took it upon herself to break things off at that point, writing that we would have to give up our meetings, I felt less bitterness over this, even, than relief. Whereas the first flame dated from scarcely a few months back, it was in this way, through this epistolary commerce and everything it elicited in the way of written confidences, of avowals glimpsed between the lines and also of misunderstandings, that the end was reached—without a fuss, but never to be resumed—of an intrigue that had so fevered me that it nearly killed me.

At Montecatini, a small town where there is almost nothing unrelated to the thermal baths, the protocol of the cure had inspired amusement in me much more than boredom. What, elsewhere than in Italy, would have seemed to me a depressing routine became under the Tuscan skies a comical ceremonial to which I submitted, my graduated glass of 250 cubic centimeters in my hand, with the same seriousness as an habitué of the great horseraces, his binoculars hanging from his shoulder, or a subscriber to the old Opéra, his opera hat under his arm. Knowing that Giuseppe Verdi had frequented this spa, I had come to terms with its lack even of picturesqueness well before discovering that one of its main roads is dedicated to the musician, who was also one of the symbols of Italian Independence, and well before having deciphered the plaque that, affixed to the façade of the hotel where Verdi was a guest, points out that it was in the waters of Montecatini that he found "the secret of longevity and youth" not only for himself but for his creative genius. My obligations, which occupied me all morning with sometimes a day of rest, were of two sorts: absorption of the waters coming from different sources (Regina, Tettuccio), whose names, like those of two other sources alien to my regimen (Tamerici, Toretta), charmed me as much as the rigorous meticulousness of the prescriptions, presented for each phase of my three weeks of residence on a chart that indicated in what quantities, in what rhythm, according to which alternation and in which form (cold or warm) I ought to drink these waters; applications of volcanic mud on certain locations on my abdomen and back, marked with a few strokes by the doctor on the doubled figure embellishing another printed sheet (a person entirely naked, without hair and with a smooth skull, his arms slightly away from his body and his palms turned forward, a sort of microcosm-man drawn in two versions, one from the front, the other from the back).

These applications, in which I was wrapped in a thick corset of warm, sticky earth, could be dispensed only by one establishment: the Terme Leopoldine, a sturdy, undistinguished building of a completely Roman severity, on the pediment of which was engraved the inscription "Aesculapio et Saluti." But for the other part (the more important) of my treatment, several options were possible. Among the establishments where one consumes the water from various springs, it was the Excelsior that I chose in the very beginning, because it was the closest to my hotel. However, to this fairly discreet building, whose builder had permitted himself only a loggia in the style of Brunelleschi, in the end I preferred the Stabilimento Tettuccio, a grandiose complex with the look of an ancient temple, corrected and augmented by some Victor Emmanuel. Included in the same area as the hall where enormous volumes of water are delivered daily, and of which imposing ranks of sanitary facilities are the necessary counterpart, are counters for tobacco, newspapers and books, a change bureau, a tourist agency (all of these assembled in a sort of waiting room), post, telegraph, and telephones, multiple dependencies such as a bandstand, a café, a dressmaker's shop, and other stores (including a jewelry business and an art gallery), making this monument, embellished with porticoes, courtyards, and vast gardens, a sort of city whose bronze fountain, from which the water of the Tettuccio spring gushes forth from a jumble of crocodiles and other scaly monsters, is the symbolic heart. More modest in Verdi's time (as is shown, among other postcards that I acquired that year and during a second stay, by two photographs representing the maestro with his somewhat Garibaldian white beard, his large peasant felt hat, a black or dark suit, leaving the old Tettuccio: in one, he is getting into a horse-drawn carriage whose canopy and canvases for protection against the sun make it strangely resemble a hearse; in the other, on foot and solitary, he sets out, sheltering under a parasol, to cross the square at the far end of which rises the establishment), that pump room, so large and sumptuous that it took me a certain time to discover that such was its intended purpose, reminded me, because of its excess, of the most spacious and profusely decorated stations of the Moscow subway. Once my imagination was set in motion, this superabundant architectural group also seemed to me to evoke what pleasure towns like Herculaneum and Pompeii must have been like before their destruction by the rain of fire and lava.

The water was handed out in a long gallery, on the left side of the central courtyard. Coiffed with little caps, equipped with aprons and wearing dresses with circles of light blue and white (which made one think of 1900 bathers, even of those in the films of Mack Sennett), a line of young women behind an immense marble counter occupied themselves with serving it. Activating invisible pedals, they caused the water—either warm or cool according to the prescription—to flow from the spring to which they were assigned, and those taking the cure collected it, from the mouths of curved pipes, in their graduated glasses with handles. On the entire length of the wall behind these women extended a series of broad, high panels in ceramic: Childhood (showing a mother with generous curves giving suck surrounded by small children who were pouring water or drinking it, and a few of whom were urinating), Adolescence (with girls and boys carrying pitchers or drinking, and, at the bottom, a group of three or four young discus throwers), Beauty, Fountainhead, Strength, Maturity, Old Age—panels whose common theme was the beneficence of these waters, a true elixir of Youth that imparts vigor and health to anyone willing to drink deep of it. Conceived so that anyone drinking, even the most decrepit, could take comfort in it, this pagan glorification of life extended, in the form of precise allusions to erotic activity, into the large café room where a crowd of people, once they had consumed their water, came to eat copious breakfasts: innocent

Italian landscapes of an archaic sort decorated its walls, but on the ceiling were painted cupids, a few life-sized naked women in poses of courtesans who were restrained by neither modesty nor fear in the divulgation of their attributes, and several love scenes, idylls from Ancient Times or the Renaissance whose female characters appeared to be endowed with a perverse languor à la Sarah Bernhardt. Did these artistic visions simply give the clientele in general an assurance that beauty could be retained or recovered? Or were those of the male fraction who felt they had been dispossessed of the most intimate power of all intimate powers of their flesh supposed to read in these images the announcement of a sort of Risorgimento of which the ithyphallus would be merely the emblem? As far as I myself was concerned, this guarantee of the remission of one of my worst torments was what I wanted to find in this apologia for sensuality.

Lulled by opera or light music melodies emanating from the bandstand—to the right of the central courtyard, a rotunda with a cupola ornamented on the interior by three compositions no less academic though a touch more modern than those of the café (an outdoor concert, chamber music, a salon recital) alternating with three trompe-l'oeil balconies lined with male and female spectators wearing our fashions or close to it—I remained there long enough to drink my five glasses of water. With the obligatory pauses, this took me almost an hour. Neglecting the book I was carrying with me, *War and Peace*, valuable at the time of the siesta that followed the manipulations of the Terme Leopoldine but here more cumbersome than anything else, I observed the cosmopolitan crowd of bathers who chatted or listened to the orchestra, sometimes walking about with glass in hand as serious as in the accomplishment of a ritual, sometimes seated on metal chairs with their glasses, full or empty, always within their reach. I played then at imagining I had arrived, after the ineluctable setbacks, in the palace of some Zarastro whose followers, in groups whose comings and goings were regulated by the celestial harmony, would dispute the loftiest problems as they consumed the beverage of immortality.

This twofold cure—water and mud—that occupied me almost every morning and is the subject of several pages of notes (in the tone of a report rather than a private journal) in my notebook, bound in red boards, from the Hôpital Claude-Bernard; the afternoons and days of full holiday spent in other spots in Tuscany to which friends—Rose and André Masson, who had come purely as tourists—drove us almost daily (*André Masson who, in the evening of a life whose beginnings were stormy, has been able to find serenity,* I wrote in my notebook shortly after my return to Paris, as though to encourage myself with the precedent offered by the evolution of that great painter); trips up to the old town (for there did in fact exist one, Montecatini Alto, served by a road and by a funicular); our lounging as dilettantes more curious than ironic on the terrace of the cabaret Gambrinus; certain walks in the sensibly laid-out parks or as far as a place pointed out by many road signs and posters, Le Panteraie (a swimming pool–restaurant–dance hall of a false elegance situated on a rather pretty hill planted with pines); the baroque note introduced at the hotel as much by the bons vivants avid to embrace too much, since they wanted both to lose weight and to continue to gorge themselves, as by the appearance, one evening in the dining room, of that statue of the Commandant in bourgeois dress, Giorgio de Chirico (white, as spectral as his pictures, his expression sly, like a small court poisoner of the sixteenth century); the occasional use of a tablet of equanil (knowing, however, that the calm procured by "tranquilizers" is not necessarily preferable to its opposite and that, in any case, one cannot dream of relying one's entire life on such a recourse); all this—the restoration of a worn-out liver, the muting of shrill nerves, or the simple distractions—helped me to climb back up the slope. Of course, I still could not see a way out of my situation: how to put back together a life not only cut in two concerning my love (the cramped union on one side, vertigo on the other) but subject to yet another sort of division since the very work I am doing here—which was lagging more obviously than ever behind events as they occurred, without my having either the strength or the lucidity needed to tackle right away the most urgent of my current activities—appeared to me a thing frankly anachronistic and, so to speak, foreign? Sad as these considerations were, I nevertheless know that they no longer affected me as much as had, not long ago, reflections of the same order.

In Florence, where, freed of the cure, I felt the reins slacken, I profited almost without reservation from the beauties of a town that turned out to be a *great city* whereas for years I had been loath to stop there, attributing to it merely on the strength of stories and readings all that is irksome implied by the notion of an *art town*. In better health, I was able to give myself up lightheartedly to the pains and joys of the life of a tourist: work hours involving visits (more or less jostled) to churches, museums, monuments, and other curiosities, reached on foot through streets often narrow and with inadequate sidewalks where, in addition to the menace of the imposing stone structures with their cyclopean look and their fortresslike opacity, there is also the less imaginary danger created by an anarchic traffic of scooters; hours of *farniente*, sometimes spent on meals in the most Tuscan of the restaurants or on purchases in the elegant boutiques, sometimes at a table in the main café of the place de la République (more welcoming than the superb but too frequented place de la Seigneurie) to listen to the arias that alternated with radio-style songs, looking out of the corner of an eye at the façade of the Savoy Hotel ornamented with falsely ancient statues enclosed in niches illuminated in the evening, sometimes on the balcony of our room—when the sun was setting or when the moon was shining—contemplating the Arno and the whole south bank (where, walking on the wooded hills, one sees sumptuous villas standing cheek by jowl with completely rustic spots rich in vines and haystacks). I, who have always been very bad at orienting myself, became accustomed very quickly to finding my way around in this city, Florence, which must derive from what was the financial power of the Medicis that slight air of a southern London, thanks to which, perhaps, the English there seem so much at home. Had I paradoxically acquired what they call a "sense of direction" at the very moment when, in my private life, I was most disoriented? Or, more simply, was it not sympathy that sharpened my attention and thus made Florence more familiar to me than any other town among those where I made only brief stays?

In Paris, where I returned before my friend herself was back, the emotional conflict that had so preoccupied me was resolved (as I said) much more simply than I had assumed it would be. Once again I had behaved, throughout this affair, like a cork floating at the whim of the currents: good fortune had come and then had withdrawn without my having made any real decision and, if I differed from the cork, it was only in that it would not have thought of causing itself to drift. Up to now I still have on my neck—as though an animal, all fangs, had attacked it and been encysted there—the scar left by the tracheotomy: a vertical stroke barred by three shorter horizontal strokes today almost invisible (the one on the bottom especially), a pale rather irregular figure that reminds me of those designs so widespread in Africa in the form, notably, of graffiti schematizing various animals themselves emblematic: saurians such as the crocodile, the monitor (often confused with the iguana and commonly called a *gueule-tapée* [plugged-face]), the lizard, and the salamander; an insect such as the julus (vulgarly known as the centipede). This is another sort of "tree of life," which I bear imprinted on my skin and which, in the first days, I compared (with the satisfaction of a dandy as much as of an ethnographer) to the scarification marking the face of an initiate. It is the mark of my candidature for the act that, more than any other, by changing death into tragedy, makes of it a conclusion and not merely an end. It is a notch recalling the time spent in a high place of the same sort as the cliff of my dreams and whence, as from a balcony, I had embraced my fate with a single glance. It is a rip that closed without having had to be sewn up, but that leaves a signature on my throat through a sort of crude mending, as though the other tear, thus materialized, could not be repaired except imperfectly and by means of an artifice.

Tranquilizers and later a "de-irritant," relaxation exercises (inspired by the

Asians' yoga but which, at first, seem so easy-as-pie that one is surprised afterward by the extent of their effects), a farewell to what they had mistakenly called my "intemperate habits," a zeal brought to the task, despite prudent advice to put it aside, of making up for my slowness in the present book (which, even if it does not exhaust my conflicts with that *I* with which I have been playing for so long and which is never done being spewed out, will perhaps earn a certificate of "work hero" for the lazybones that I have always felt myself to be), these various medicines—of which the last, however, might have derived from a furious desire for a knife in the wound—worked together effectively. I regained the necessary equilibrium to make me a livable companion, and my life went on as though it had never jumped the rails. However, it appears to me more and more that despite the indisputable *happy end* that resulted from my own prohibition as well as from the treatment to which I consented, deep inside me something has been destroyed that I cannot hope to see reconstituted: old age, which has always frightened me so, has finally settled in, and the crisis, as quickly quelled as it had roughly seized me, will turn out to have been the rearguard battle or the gallant *last stand* that I waged against it—every day I am more convinced that this is so.

I have penetrated some sort of wall of sound. I am the only one who heard the explosion. Under the imprecise date of November 1959, these lines, written shortly after a second and last cure at Montecatini, appear in my notebook bound in red boards. I proposed not to note down a discovery, but to express—in view of the present account—what I had been feeling for a long time already and whose most manifest aspect was a certain indifference toward my work as a writer, as though, having pushed too far my effort at lucidity, I had crossed a threshold after which, all my ardor having been stifled, nothing was left for me but the dry industry of a good pupil. The idea of having gone beyond the limit and of being punished for it certainly made me rather proud (or at least it was thus that, in order to avoid a state of prostration, I tried to represent the thing to myself). But what I experienced, in truth, was the equivalent—in a very different domain—of an impression noted earlier and connected to the reflections inspired in me by that country so distant and at the same time so close where so many women had moved me by their seriousness, their tranquil grace, and their affectionate and exquisite manners, forming an image that toppled from its throne, in me, the image of the African woman conceived as an emanation of nature, a sort of satyress or dryad: *A day comes when there is no longer any magic in being naked; no longer a means of converting oneself imaginatively into something like the young sorceress who, her robe removed, awaits her flight toward the demoniacal ball after rubbing her whole body with ointment. Perhaps it is at that moment that one is ripe for tasting the sweet austerity of the girls of new China in masculine-looking dress?* And from that note I go back to another, much older, which seems to express by anticipation—before I really believed it and, consequently, with enough detachment to talk about it without evasions—the state whose essence is named when one uses in this connection the word "state" (one of the most neutral and down-to-earth in the whole dictionary), the state of languor and withdrawal in which some will perhaps see a kind of wisdom but which I recognize for that of old age: *Incapacity to become excited, once old age has come, because one has measured one's limits. The ceiling now solid, there is no longer any way of staving it in. When it has become necessary to make some reductions in the idea that one was forming of oneself, poetry's time is over.* This is therefore not new, and it was well before old age that I suffered these sorts of assault. The difference is that the bad patches of earlier times, which corresponded to periods of depression, are what I am now, it seems to me, living permanently.

Crisis in Laos. Attempt at a counterrevolutionary landing in Cuba. Military putsch in Algeria, fortunately aborted after the threat that it would extend to France. These events, which shook me as they did millions of other people, will have accompanied, with their noise of church organs, the recording of a sinister finding, prepared long in advance but today sanctioned by chronology, since the one who had so prematurely formulated it has just turned sixty. My disgust at the feverishness with which a certain *gang* which is willing to doom the West, under the guise of maintaining it in the first place, to material disasters and to the negation of its own slogans of liberty, has thus been joined by discouragement at feeling I have been caught unprepared and excluded by the workings of time, which leaves me, now, a very narrow margin, some better days from which one may hope, without being foolish, for a final blossoming. "The East Is Red" was one of the songs I heard most often during the national festival at Peking. But even if I believed blindly in what such a dawn proclaims, the chances would remain nil that it would ever come to shed light on me, and when, in the eyes of the living, I am over on the other side—on the verso of a page that for me will not even have been visibly turned—I will have taken (at best) a few indecisive steps toward the opening of these "new ways," the Vie Nuove of which, at Palermo, I had wondered what exactly they were, not knowing then that it was by this name that a large Italian communist weekly chose to call itself. If I grow old, however, and if I die, this is as much as, but not more than, anyone else; I know it perhaps a little better, I am less apt than many others to distract myself from it, but there is no other difference. Despite my strong propensity to take events (large or small) for the vicissitudes of a kingdom that is my own, I cannot ignore the fact that every thinking being is, like me, the center of the world. Now, since such royalty turns out to be shared in this way, it follows that even though a drama or any other sort of adventure may never be experienced except in the first person, it would be clownish to act as though one were the only attraction on the program. Enough, therefore, of imitating those drunks who stroll about expatiating into empty space and beating the air with their arms. Two of the visits that, for medical procedures, I made to the Hôpital Claude-Bernard after leaving it allowed me to perceive with a troubling precision what a small thing it is, even beyond its vulnerability to the blade of death—that first person so fully ours and on which the universe appears to us to rest.

I had been back at home barely twenty days when I returned there, as had been agreed during an earlier visit, to submit to an X-ray inspection of the state of my throat. It was a woman who did it, and once the photos had been taken, she congratulated me, saying in a friendly way that it was a pleasure to see me as I was now. I was surprised at this, for I did not know her at all. But it turned out that I was known to her without my ever having seen her, for it was she who had X-rayed me when I was in the coma. As logical and simple as the explanation was, to be known in such a way by someone who was completely unknown to me appeared to me very strange, and it was not without uneasiness that I realized that, for a certain time, I had been literally a *body without a soul*, a mannequin whose form alone, almost, is all that differentiates him from a piece of furniture. In the same sense, I recalled a little later the cordial signs addressed to me by male and female nurses when they passed in front of the open door of the room I lived in with a creature who persisted, in his case, in living only in the third person: these men and women, who said hello to me as to an old acquaintance, had seen me—perhaps even handled me—while the poisoning had reduced me to no more than a thing, and it was to this latter, now capable in its turn of looking at them, that were addressed the marks of a friendship the beginnings of which, even though I had been the one most directly affected, I had not witnessed.

A year later, or nearly, I went to the Pavillon Lassen one more time, summoned by one of the doctors who was anxious to make sure I was not suffering from any aftereffects of the tracheotomy. When I saw this doctor, I realized with a certain vexation that he was not the one I was expecting: confusing the two names, I had thought that person who had sent the letter was one of his colleagues, whom I remembered much better and with whom I would no doubt have felt to a lesser degree that I was the practically anonymous subject of an observation. The head duty nurse, for her part, recognized me perfectly and, to a question I asked her, told me that the man who had once been my roommate had simply stopped living, without ever having been brought out of the condition of object into which a brain tumor (as they discovered) had precipitated him. "Such a nice man!" a nurse had once said to me, adding: "You can see it in his face . . ." when I asked her how, in the absence of the slightest word or sign she might have received from him, she could know that. In the hallways I met various members of the subordinate staff whose faces were still familiar to me; but I was the one who had to go to those of them I wanted to greet, for—was it forgetfulness or discretion?—they did not pay me any more attention than if I had been a complete stranger. Finding myself face to face with these people, whom I recognized without its being reciprocal, and who, after having lavished attention or encouragement on the rag I was a year earlier, did not even appear to notice my presence, it seemed to me I had returned to this hospital like a ghost, so insubstantial that I offered nothing for the light to rest on, and, a star in bygone days, I experienced the disappointing impression of having become less alive in the eyes of all these people than when I was half dead.

III

I must have been fourteen or fifteen years old when I saw, at the Alhambra in Paris, the following act.

Dressed in a dark suit of very correct cut, a man in the prime of life—announced as a magician and having, it seems to me, a Dutch name—came onto the stage with a hurried step. Speaking volubly and moving incessantly from opposite-prompter to prompt-side and vice versa, he unfurled handkerchiefs or other pieces of material, manipulated utensils picked up from occasional tables or taken out of suitcases. Then he invited one, and soon many, spectators to come up onto the boards, volunteer collaborators or colleagues such as often take part in conjuring acts. Once there, in a sarabande punctuated by numerous incidents and even by a pistol shot, he had them spin like teetotums, assigned them duties that one could think were useful, encumbered them with a quantity of props, and put into the arms of some of them the most unexpected burdens (giving one, for example, an enormous block of ice brought from the wings). After a good quarter of an hour of this game, the stage being now crowded with people and strewn with heteroclite objects, he would break off in the middle. The curtain would drop, and one would realize then—confirming a suspicion that had only just dawned—that from beginning to end of his performance he had done absolutely nothing, not even the most innocent sleight of hand.

With this book, into which I have thrown, almost unsorted, descriptions, evocations of people, accounts of dreams and real events, notations of the condition of my soul, and very diverse perceptions, the whole accumulating without great profit in a baroque profusion, haven't I done to some extent what that professional hustler did, or rather what, humorously, he contrived not to do? Since my own goal is not to keep the company amused and to mystify by creating a pointless imbroglio, it is time for me to get to the end of it . . .

One or two kilometers, as the crow flies, from my house in Saint Hilaire, on a wooded eminence which one can climb effortlessly along paths scarcely cleared, for (unlike the cliff of which I have dreamed so many times) it is neither very high nor very steep, there is a small ruined tower that one can see, to the left, from the road that leads from Châlo-Saint-Mars to Boutervilliers and that, after a level crossing, runs alongside, for a time, a single-track railroad to the right, on which, on weekdays, a short freight train with an electric engine passes going in one direction in the morning and coming back in the other in the evening. A little farther along on the road, and also on the left hand, before passing under a bridge whose only purpose seems to be to connect two sections of the same vast property dominated by a building that one takes, from a distance, to be a château (a massive structure with walls striped horizontally white and red, in faded and dirtied tones, on the edge of a terrace perceptibly more elevated than the top of the tower), one finds a curious monument composed of an obviously imitation dolmen and a great wooden cross. At the foot of this assemblage, on a tablet wedged between the crude blocks of a small stone wall, is engraved the following text, the end of which, worn away, is unfortunately not decipherable: *Man succeeds in conquering the earth. Humanity is approaching its great end. This country was once Gaul, with druidism, and is now France, with Catholicism.*

Closed by a door with a large latch that has now fallen down, probably under the blows of some adult or childish depredator, the tower is covered with graffiti on the inside—dates, first names, and other inscriptions—left there by visitors a good number of whom, at least, Sunday walkers, must have been couples in love. "Chocolat from Bevoie," "Mémé from Belleville," "Mimile" (from where, I don't remember) are a trio of names that I have read on the wood of the door, now that, laid almost horizontal, it covers a good part of the small round space circumscribed by the stone wall, itself clothed in an underbrush of letters and numbers from which, as far as I know, the inquisitive can sift out nothing that is not perfectly decent or, at the very most, banally romantic. If this small-scale donjon, with perhaps quite a brief past (for nothing attests to its medieval authenticity), was the setting for love affairs that took place in the open air at the same time as behind closed doors, there remains, certainly, no other trace of it than this abstract tangle of signs that are not, after all, the formal proof of any embrace. If some have used it, alone or not, as a secluded spot where the organism can free itself of its more or less nauseating products, each time I have gone there I have not found the least mark of that, either. A few shards of bottles, a weekly ticket for trips on the bus, several pieces of crumpled paper, that is all the detritus my last visit allowed me to observe.

To this ruin with its romantic look, slightly gallowslike to anyone who makes his way inside, I went in the company of my dog Dine three or four times, in the course of walks that had another goal than this one, which is too close to home and admissible only as the pretext for a brief detour from a longer circuit. The last time, the dog needed a great deal of coaxing to enter. I always keep her on a leash, because otherwise she would go off hunting, would risk getting caught in a trap, and would in any case come back only the devil knows when. Thus, pulling stoutly on her studded collar through the interposition of the leather strap, I managed to drag her in after me. But it was as though she were restrained by a frank repugnance, which could hardly be explained by the sordid state of the place, since a boxer dog, and a rustic one like her, is not so fastidious. Capable, by nature, of indulging in romantic constructions, I did not fail to notice that in returning to the tower I was making a pilgrimage to the very spot that I had thought of choosing as the last receptacle of my living body, at the time when I was cherishing a plan to commit suicide. Going off, as I do fairly regularly, to take a walk with the animal, I would have carried along in my pocket my provision of phenobarbital, and it would be there that I would go to withdraw for the fatal picnic, at once far from all help and in a place such that the eventual discovery of my remains would be (it seemed to me) less macabre there than elsewhere, given the hooky-playing sort of aspect that—thus conceived—the whole scenario would assume. Tempting as such an explanation may be (the mysterious antennae supposedly possessed by my friend Dine that would keep her away from a spot which her master had thought of as the most desirable setting for his death), common sense keeps me from subscribing to it: this recent walk was not the first time I had made the pilgrimage, and the dog's refusal would therefore already have had an occasion to manifest itself, if it had been motivated by the funereal signification that the tower has retained for me. Yet the fact is that when—two years after my recovery—I had been taken by the desire to go back to the scene (no more than symbolic) of a crime that, even if successful, would not have been really criminal since it would have stricken only its author, my black-muzzled companion had entered along with me, without resisting by trying to anchor herself in the ground with her four large, strong paws. Pulling the door (then still in place) after me and trying vainly to close it by pushing the inner latch, I noted simply that the tip of the latter met the wall a little lower than the cavity intended to receive it and that consequently I could not make it work. The idea came to me then that if, when I dreamed of it, I had wanted to carry out my sinister plan, the fact of not being able to close myself in—an unexpected circumstance, a grain of sand that stopped the functioning of the mechanism—would probably have dissuaded me from it.

A body perhaps half rotted that would have been discovered in that ruin, had I actually chosen it as my final ivory tower. A body cut to bits that we could imagine, my companions and I, at the foot of the Mountain of the West, when, as we were visiting its Taoist temple, we were told about the suicide of the man who had sculpted its most precious and most loftily situated chapel, habitation of two seated, bearded figures framing a gilded god who, with his right foot, is standing on a water dragon and, on the sole of his left foot, apparently lifted in running position, bears a fruit tree. According to our guide—the president of the local section of the Association of the Chinese People's Cultural Relations with Foreigners—the conch or horn of plenty that the statue holds in his left hand is a piece of money, and a paintbrush the object that it holds in its right. The gilded personage is not a god but a man, who, after the illness and death of the woman he loved, felt that life no longer had any meaning for him and decided to devote himself exclusively to artistic work. This was why he executed the figures and other ornaments in the chapel, then threw himself from the top of the escarpment, not finding in his work sufficient consolation. Afterward, a paintbrush had been put in the right hand of the statue leaping so curiously, an emblem recalling the very man who had fashioned it and whom (they told us) it represented.

However confused may have been the overall effect of the explanations that were given us (uncertain in the mind of our guide, imperfectly translated by our interpreter, or ill understood by ourselves, whence some oddnesses if not improbabilities, such as the identification as self-portrait assigned to one obviously divine figuration), what I retain from this account, which was at least imprecise, and perhaps altered by the translation, is the idea that love, art, and death appear in it intimately mingled.

The splendor of the golden personage (surprised, one would have said, as he was dashing forward simply in order to dash forward, and not in order to overcome some prey), the peace that reigned supreme inside the chapel (animated, not by a host of things upon each of which in succession the eye would have been able to alight, but by the sole and extraordinary presence of the three figures), the harshness of the mountainside chosen by the devotees of Tao as a place in which to nest their vertiginous constructions, compensated for the poverty of a narrative produced by a man who, here making use of an obvious commonplace, had first said that this chapel—scarcely more than a century old, but belonging to the old China—attested to the "high cultural level" of those who had built it. If that astonishing setting had not made me sensitive to it, surely the three key words of the story (those words not uttered, but paraphrased, by the anecdote) would not have presented themselves, in my memory, with such prominence: "love," "art," and "death," which designate realities that I believe are closely conjoined, since between art and love there is the link of beauty and since both—the first in that it goes beyond what is given by nature and creates a simulacrum of eternity, the second in that it explodes the *self* by precipitating it into the *other*—take us into a boundless terrain that can no more be charted than the immense plain of death.

The man with a complexion the color of brown bread, in a gray uniform with the collar closed under his chin (wearing a sailor-style cap of the same material and the same color), the civil servant—or something approaching it— somewhat surly, unlike most of the Chinese we had met up to then, the lusterless president of the local section of the organization whose guests we were, could not have been telling the entire truth, or, if he was correct in what he said, had transmitted to us a message that must have been distorted at one or several points along the way from him to the interpreter Wang Sien and from Wang Sien to us. To the same extent as seemed believable—in its guise as legend— the touching anecdote he had told us about the young buffalo whose statue we had seen during our climb (that little buffalo which, in tears, had begged the butcher to spare it, and, hiding under its belly the tool for cutting its throat, had so deeply moved its executioner that the latter, realizing that animals, too, have feelings, had given up his cruel profession and retired to the mountain to become a bonze), the story of the suicide was suspect, without one being able to tax with ignorance or bad faith an informant whose cultural functions did not empower him, for all that, to inform us about the folklore relating to the various constructions of the temple. Perhaps it went without saying that the unfortunate lover did not discover in himself a vocation as an artist except through that of monk, and that it was only within the framework of pious contemplation that his work was, temporarily, meaningful to him? When he threw himself to the bottom of the mountain, was it really as a man disabused, who sees that art cannot heal sorrow, or as a mystic who is pushing his asceticism to an extreme and flees life after having given up his ordinary ways, as though it was not possible to achieve fullness except through the extreme gesture in which the individual denies himself forever? In other words, had this act been the quasi-accidental result of a disappointment or the culminating point that the monk artist had already obscurely determined for himself when he had undertaken to decorate the chapel? If the object placed in the right hand of the statue is really a paintbrush that was not included originally, to see it as an offering to the god who is represented here, or as one of his attributes added belatedly, appears more sensible than to make of it what our guide did: a commemorative sign identifying the work as a self-portrait of the sculptor. The story of the suicide of the Mountain of the West, as I have set it down, thus presents many disputable points and no doubt many gaps. It is not, however, for this purely logical reason that I cannot be satisfied with it, but because the very appearance of the statue—the central part of the whole story—incites me to rethink the melodrama: whatever the dead man's fate may have been exactly, his work is in no way that of the pitiful victim of despair over love.

I had not noticed it immediately, but there was a glaring discrepancy between that sad story of the unconsoled widower and the exuberant passion of the figure whose author he was. Supported by his right foot alone, the personage seemed to have been captured in midbound toward a goal that was unknown, perhaps nonexistent, and not distinct from the pure joy of bounding forward in that way, his whole being tense with the animation of an excess of life. His radiance would have made one think he was invulnerable, were it not for the instability of his pose, which, in itself, evoked a danger. But the radiance would not have gone beyond what it was—a vulgar gilding on a sculpture without great style, a little taller than life-sized—if there had not been this impetuous movement, with its inherent risk (so it seemed) for the very one who was abandoning himself to it. Someone expert in the subject of Oriental religions and philosophies would perhaps have identified the personage—god or sage—right away from the marine monster on which he was standing, from the shrub that sprang up from his left foot, from the supposed money, more conch or horn of plenty, and from the problematic paintbrush. But I, forced to confine myself to what I had before my eyes and what was hardly illuminated by the remarks of our guide, was sensitive only to the unbridled ardor that emanated from that creature apparently devoted solely to the intoxication of living and of spending himself.

Taken to an extreme, such a rage to live does not differ from the rage to destroy oneself: the moth fuddled by a source of light and consumed by it is a common symbol of that fusion of opposites also conveyed, in familiar language, by the expression *to burn the candle at both ends*, applied to the person who shortens his days by abandoning himself excessively to his thirst for pleasure. In a realm apparently less deleterious, can we not regard as the composition of a coat of arms of suffering and death those classical emblems of romantic enthusiasm: fires and flames, lightning bolts, an arrow piercing a heart, verbal or graphic accessories of which the last, when one carves it in bark, is nevertheless equivalent to a tree of life? And if, most often, *to die of love, to love till we die* are only pious hyperboles, do they fail, for all that, to indicate what a sinister vanishing point old-fashioned lovers, when they reach the height of exultation, give to the perspective of their paradise? From the pleasure seeker who seeks only to "live his life," but does so without stinting, to the legendary hero of the type of Tristan or Liang Chan-po, who dies love (so to speak) rather than lives it, certainly the distance is great. Still, in one as in the other, the great impetus is a desire that consumes and that finally acts as a summons to death.

The vertigo of love, experienced physically when a man takes a woman in his arms in order to forget, to deny the disturbance—in some way chemical—caused by the almost tactile sensation of her presence and when to cling to this animate pillar seems the only means of reestablishing his disrupted equilibrium. The vertigo of death, or more exactly of the notion of death, hardly less dizzying than the view of an abyss, of which the horror itself that one has of it is doubled by the temptation to throw oneself into it to cut short the uneasiness it engenders. The vertigo of art, peculiar to that thing which is neither game nor religion but discovery and exhibition of indecipherable realities which can only be brought out by giving them a form, so that, at once powder in the eyes and revelation, illusion and truth, it is a tightrope walk for anyone who devotes himself to it without too much naïveté. To palliate the effects of a presence by increasing its proximity, to flee the fear of a fall by falling on purpose, to change into a categorical instability the accidental lack of a stable position (evident in the artist, and especially in the poet, for, in a life in which everything should cohere, how can one detach oneself from things and transcend them), these motions can only betray the existence of certain fundamental ambiguities, unless they arise from vulgar foolishness or display the talon of the famous *demon of perversity*, which, in many a case, malignly changes the desire to escape a feeling of anguish into a desire to enter its ways (a demon whom, from the point of view of current history, one could easily take for an éminence grise of Western politics, prodigal in bad farces of this sort: the proponents of an ultra-French Algeria acting in such a way as to deepen still further the gulf between Algerians and French, or the American anticommunists throwing Cuba into the arms of the Soviet Union, to cite only those two examples—to laugh at or to cry over—of apparently deliberately swapping a false menace for the very thing one was dreading).

Each generating its own vertigo (or perhaps the same vertigo, since the embrace is not only a refuge but also a whirlpool in which one believes one can annihilate oneself, and because aesthetic creation, that funambulist's trick, puts one in touch with a world beyond, where the laws of nature are abolished), love, art, and death seem linked by a delicate web of reciprocal demands: the fact that we must die increases our need to love (either in order to find oblivion, or so that something may still happen before we disappear) but the lovers' fever is expressed by many in the vow to die together (in order to attain the impossible fusion or because they cannot accept a future in which one survives the other); sharpening a thirst that it slakes only metaphorically, art induces us to seek its satisfaction in passion, which in turn opens out onto art because passion must, we believe, be surrounded by enchantments and because, in its beautiful castle (also, and just as much, a thatched cottage), etiquette would have us express ourselves otherwise than in a profane language (as witness, besides the flowers and gifts, so much talk and so many love letters, even the most awkward of which are works of poetry); lastly, if art presupposes a refusal of the mortal condition (denying the erosion of time, suffering and the final checkmate by escaping from the current world, or, more greedily, producing something a little less transitory than a human life), in practice it may experience crises and—in the same way as drunkenness, eroticism and other common ways of *escaping oneself*—divert one toward a simulacrum of death. I felt this strongly in earlier times when, seeing the poetic state as a sort of fury (a notion that seemed to me to correspond better to the very basis of the surrealist spirit than that of revolt, already too ideological), I was, when I wanted to write, seized by a desire for a trance that would be accompanied by violent outward signs—scratching on the walls or jumping up to the ceiling, tipping over backward—as though I felt that the gesticulations of a man suffering from some kind of epilepsy could trigger its mental equivalent and cause me to move onto a plane, if not exterior to life, at least such that my limits there would be obliterated.

Not without difficulty, I am trying to rationalize what was given me, as pure feeling, in a single mass instead of coming to me by way of reflection: starting in my childhood (as I have already said), love, art, and death were presented to me in one cluster by everything I knew about the great arias of opera, for me summits of art, and which hardly spoke to me about anything else but love and death. In variable forms, this mythology, which says, in sum, that true beauty is tragic in its essence, has not ceased to impress me, and when, about fifteen years ago, I gave up bullfights, seeing them only occasionally, whereas my afición (far from fading) was transferred to Italian opera, this was in fact a return to the source, because I rediscovered there, in its first freshness, the absolutely dionysiac philter which, as a young child, I had been permitted to taste. However, if I now prefer, to the bloody reality of the taurine tragedy, the fictive tragedy of opera, it is not simply because of the fact that my age, and the atrocious turn taken by events, with this latest war, which has not yet subsided, have made me more sensitive to the sight of death and have increased my attachment to the period when my consciousness was still awakening; it is also because it has become apparent to me that one experiences at the theater—in the presence of its flagrant trompe-l'oeil—an emotion paradoxically more authentic (given the smaller degree of ambiguity) than in the plaza de toros, where one so readily believes oneself on the same level as the tragedy that one is experiencing when it is others who are experiencing it. Rejecting this comfortable illusion, and turning, a little ironically, toward a dilettantism that is no longer of our century, did not distance me from the splendors of tragedy: one evening, I hurled myself into it, thoughtlessly, in order to escape, of course, problems that I felt powerless to resolve, but especially (I am now persuaded) because art and love—poetry and its most direct illustration, the twofold object of my covetousness even before I became a writer—were, in me, the source of an exaltation too tender and too piercing not to be confused with the desire to die from it. Crammed with what I had drunk like a gluttonous child, and with the drug apt to make me literally dead drunk, I lay down between the sheets that would have been my tragedian's peplum, if not my gisant's robe, and was engulfed in them without thinking that it is also in the whiteness of the bed that, in adolescence, one feverishly experiences those mysteries of which, later, I wanted the occupation of poet to restore to me at least a distant glimmer: the heavy sorrows in which one loves to become lost, plunging one's face in the pillow, the fleeting joys crowning the carnal enchantments that, in a hallucinated delirium, one gives to oneself alone, as much in order to drive away the fear of the night, open as it is to a parade of nightmares and apparitions of all sorts, as for the pleasure itself.

The sky has detained its guests, said the president of the association courteously, observing at the time of the final goodbyes the rainy weather that called for (he explained) the use of this dictum and of which his gray uniform, as well as the boredom emanating from his whole person, seemed the accompaniment required by the celestial protocol. The fires of the sun, in that region which had been overtaken by a wave of cold temperatures, had perhaps condensed in the golden statue which, beyond rain and fair weather, pursued without moving its inexorable course and gave quite a different lesson from the mediocre apologue for which it had been the pretext. The fact that it was endowed with such brilliance and such movement makes it impossible for me, at a distance, to see its author as someone whom adversity had finally crushed. Much rather, it bears witness to the resources of art to fuse good and ill fortune in a single entity and admit death as one of the dimensions of life. Thus, neglecting to seek out its positive meaning—what man or what god?—and retaining only its tacit response to the question that worries me, I have in the end classified it in my personal pantheon, as a sublime male counterpart of the heroines to whom my aunt the singer lent her voice and the richnesses of her physique: Carmen who attacks with a knife and later appears to run straight to the fatal blow of the *navaja*, Salome in ecstasy before the severed head and even beneath the soldiers' shields, Tosca who kills, believes she is saving, then with a great maenad cry hurls herself from the top of the ramparts, and finally, those women who are led by a passionate devotion to throw themselves into the waves, the lover of the Flying Dutchman and her epigone Vita.

All the sorrow of the world in a single cup of wine. The despairs one ruminates on with one's face buried in the childish pillow. The Latin maxim *Est quaedam flere voluptas* (translated by one of our humorists as *There are ladies one sniffs with most sensual pleasure*). To see Naples and die. To listen on one's deathbed to Bellini's *Casta diva* (as Chopin or some other famous romantic wished to do, and as I too would formulate the desire to do, if I had to fill out a questionnaire about preferences). That fury which, in the mid–nineteen twenties, I held to be a necessary condition—was it the more masculine form which I wanted to give to a depth of sadness that dates back to my earliest youth and represents the ancient foundation on which all that I do is built? An unconditional sadness, which could not simply be thrust away, and to which, from the outset, I was connected by the times—full of disturbance, it seems to me, and sweetness—when, before sleeping, I dampened my pillow with tears and pressed it with my mouth, open as though to bite. A sort of *original sorrow*, perhaps as determining for me as, on the universal scale, was the first sin, according to the Scriptures and many other mythologies.

Whether the rain was a hospitable gesture of the sky or (as I would more readily believe) a sign of its ill humor, our excursion to the Mountain of the West was not at all spoiled by it. But the fact is that we had a vision of Kounming that in no way corresponded to the promises of Wang Yuen-chen: the city of eternal springtime where our interpreter was born appeared to us—in the image of his first name, *Cloud color of pearl*—bathed in a damp grayness and I retain a memory of it as murky as was the atmosphere itself. If it were not for the testimony of my notebooks, I might ask myself if it was really there that we were presented, because of a chance encounter in the street, with a spectacle by which I was charmed, despite my little taste for things military: in one of the main thoroughfares, a group of soldiers without weapons proceeding, as is proper, in ranks; all identical, except that certain ones—mixed in among the others and walking with the same slow pace—wore the double pigtail, a difference that nothing allowed one to assume before one saw them from the back. These soldiers, men and women, were on their way, we were told, to a lecture (which one could guess to be Marxist-Leninist), and this no doubt explained their look of well-behaved schoolchildren. The martial appearance, which I hardly appreciate in the representatives of the stronger sex, seems to me still less admissible in those of the weaker sex, and as for women soldiers (carrying rifles or simple auxiliaries like the "gray mice" of the Occupation), they remind me, almost all of them, of a scene of the 1914 mobilization that shocked me by its disorderly crudeness, even though I was at the time too young to find the war in itself repugnant: near me, in the boulevard Suchet, where there was a barracks, a regiment parading "flowers in their rifles" flanked by a woman, probably drunk, whose chauvinistic excitation and, perhaps, her condition as soldiers' girl had led to wear gaily on her head a policeman's cap. There was nothing reminiscent of a farce among the young infantrywomen I saw in Kounming; except for the color, close to khaki, their uniform differed little from the overall-style dress so widespread for both sexes in the new China and, above all, they seemed to assume their role with a perfect naturalness, as though this was only one duty among their ordinary duties: work in the fields or in the factory, political education, tasks more militant or less, family occupations. These, we were told, were women who had remained in the army since the Liberation or were soldiers' wives employed at functions such as nursing. That women should change so gently into soldiers — even if only as simple menders of the war force — may seem worse than when a carnivalesque note, by showing them disguised rather than metamorphosed, attests to the incongruity of their militarization. But this apparently outrageous affront to femininity on the part of the Chinese is justified by the framework in which it is inscribed: the great movement that animates the whole life of their country and that would not be a truly *popular* emancipation if certain activities remained, as with us, the almost exclusive prerogative of the men.

From the Mountain of the West we were taken to spend the night at the Hot Springs, formerly frequented by the French of Indochina, who came to Kounming to rest, not too far from their home port, in a climate cooled by the altitude. The hotel was still outfitted as a thermal establishment, so that in the early morning I could, like someone taking the cure, bathe in warm water coming directly from the springs. To do this, I had only to go down several stairways and corridors, and then, having taken possession of a room including, along with the bathroom and the alcove for the shower, a vestibule equipped with more than one needed in the way of furniture for resting, linen for drying oneself, and pairs of slippers, to descend again a fairly large number of steps and, having reached catacomb-like depths, to descend still farther by immersing myself in the rectangular tank provided with a slatted bottom and with two round seats entirely submerged.

The farthest stage of my tour through the provinces of the southwest, the Hot Springs represents, along with Kounming, the southernmost point of China that I reached. The humidity there resulted for me in a disappointment concerning the convenience of shirts made of synthetic cloth on excursions during which one does not have time to send clothes to be washed: if ordinarily they dry quickly, it is not the same in a place where dampness prevails and, when we left the Hot Springs, I had to put back on, damp, the nylon shirt that I had innocently washed before going to bed. This tropical impression contrasted with the really quite Nordic impression I had had of the first town in Manchuria where we stopped: Changchun, whose forbidding appearance reminded me of Charleville (where I have never been, but which, through the prism of Rimbaud, I imagine to be the most disagreeable of cities). Crisscrossed by tramways with very sonorous horns and plowed by carts drawn by robust little white horses with short-cropped manes, this town of houses without any picturesqueness seemed to me inhabited by people with quilted jackets, their hands snugly thrust into their sleeves as though into muffs, and some of them wore fur caps on their heads with the ear flaps, designed to protect them against the chill, hanging down. As I was suffering from a bad cold and my abdomen was affected by a disorder even more bothersome (the consequences of a European-style lunch accepted two days before at the Peking Hotel, contrary to my habit of eating only Chinese-style, for which I had always felt all the better), I was peremptorily subjected to a medical examination. Scarcely an hour after our arrival, the kind Wang Yuen-chen entered my room escorted by two women, one of whom was a lady doctor wearing two braids and the other a nurse in the classic costume of her profession. Wang Yuen-chen seated herself familiarly on the arm of the easy chair I was occupying, facing my two healers, and it was through her as intermediary that the questioning took place. I was very much afraid that too zealous a concern for my health would lead the lady doctor to send me to the hospital, which would have been in itself an interesting experience and no doubt an occasion for pampering, but would have deprived me of quite a few touristic joys. The thermometer they placed in my armpit indicated a normal temperature, and I could, furthermore, declare in all good faith that my other troubles seemed to be over. This was why the gentle and serious lady doctor confined herself to giving me some medicines for the cough and allowed me to continue on my way through the region, where the autumn was proving less sunny than that of Peking.

The little girl of sugar candy, with braids of licorice, takes our hand to lead us to the butterflies club, a Marxist-Leninist Monelle. In Shanghai, whose streets swarm with a crowd more turbulent than that of the capital and where what was once the neighborhood of the foreign concessions presents an example of perhaps the most distressing products of Western architecture, I saw, on the site of the English racecourse, now the People's Park, and its outbuildings, troupes of children who were apparently participating with the same enthusiasm in outdoor exercises and lecture-walks: dances and processions on the grounds where gambling and the spectacle of the races must, in their time, have attracted sporting people of both races; murmuring files of schoolboys and schoolgirls, under the tutelage of young women or girls, passing through the Historical Museum, whose rooms occupy two stories in the buildings adjoining the old grandstands. I admired the fact that they had spared these buildings, and it seemed to me I had here a proof of the practical sense and goodwill of the Chinese revolutionaries, who had changed into an instrument of education what others (without one being able, in this precise case, to tax them with vandalism) would probably have burned down or degraded in some manner, seeing them only as a scandalous symbol of foreign ascendancy and the corruption inherent in capitalism. Once night fell, when an account of the day came to feed my logbook as usual, I noted what had most struck me among the two thousand or so objects that were displayed in this museum, already rich even though still embryonic. Arranged chronologically, the collections included—without mentioning the generally not very encouraging products of modern handicrafts—many very beautiful things of bronze, jade, ceramic, porcelain, stone, clay, and wood, some paintings (notably from the Song period) and other evidence of the past that, quite beyond any aesthetic consideration, one could not look at without emotion, such as some documents relating to writing (a large tortoise shell and a bovine humerus engraved with ancient characters, many secular manuscripts, as well as old specimens of printing on paper, that Chinese invention), such as, also, tools found in Zhoukoudian, where the illustrious prehominid lived and died whom modern schoolbooks present as the first great man in the history of China.

A single thread that has never been broken, from Sinanthropus Pekinensis to comrade Mao Tse-tung. Contemplating, from the top of the twelve skillfully piled stories of a pagoda broad at the base but narrower at the top, a superb river spectacle (in the setting sun and under a sky fairly cloudy in the direction of the mountain, the progress of a line of eight pairs of delicately colored junks pulled by a tug over the shimmering water, while a train crossed the metal bridge spanning the broad elbow of the estuary they call "Chou" at this point because of its snaking form), several of us, at the close of our visit to Hangzhou and its environs, dreamed of a new Prayer on the Acropolis: no Greek miracle, in this case, but the miracle of China, a country where an amazing harmony reigns between past and present, monuments and living beings, a country, too, whose gardens share with those created by the Arabs the honor of being "places of real spiritual comfort." This last observation we had made that same morning, one of my companions and I, in the course of an excursion out onto a lake during which our group had been taken to an island crowded with summer houses by a flotilla of light craft propelled some by boatmen, some by boatwomen.

The exemplary power supposedly possessed by Negroes—like all those who are called "savages"—to abandon themselves without reticence to the pulsations of life (as their gift for rhythm would suffice to attest), the serene gravity of the people of the Far East, whose mysterious cast of features is purportedly explained by their friendly relations with death, are simplistic notions, if not fallacious ones; but the fact is that they exert on me the seductiveness of the great utopias. For the Westerner that I am, they represent two poles, each of which would indicate a possible truth, and I believe I have aimed at both these two goals, one after the other, beyond my immediate motivations: the first when, still young, I devoted twenty-one months to crossing Africa, the second when, a quarter of a century later, I spent five weeks in China, a trip whose ridiculous brevity suited me, in that, under the twofold weight of age and a gradually regularized life, I had become more covetous of my time and less available in a practical sense. Tropics loaded with "involuntary poetry," a Far East wise and courteous as one no longer can be, the industrialization of countries whose exoticism had charmed us, so that we have trouble accepting the idea that they are gradually losing it, daydreams based on their past (at least the past one imagined), hopes justified by what one sees of their present—these form the background of a dream that I had in China and that, for me, would still be lost in total oblivion if it had not been recalled to me, long after our return, by one of my comrades to whom I had described it because he was the hero of it: just as, in Polynesia, beautiful islanders give travelers large collars of flowers that each will wear around his neck as though he were the Fatted Calf, young Chinese girls in new-style jackets and pants offer bicycle tires or inner tubes to that companion of mine, who, for the film he was to entitle *A Sunday in Peking*, at that time took his camera with him everywhere.

Easter in Kumasi. Underlined with a wavy stroke, these words—which remind me of colors harsher than the delicate nuances of *Sunday at Peking*—appear at the head of four of my slips of paper, a copy of an extract from the notebook that I kept during my tour through the Ivory Coast and through the Gold Coast, which now no longer bears a name that also alluded to the era of trade. That Sunday, April 1, 1945, having been in residence for several days in the large market town that is the Ashanti capital, I had gone to the cathedral to enjoy the spectacle of the high mass, a ceremony in which the priest—a White, of what nationality I do not know—officiated in person, assisted by two Dutch Fathers. It was here that I experienced not my *Easter in New York*, like the poet and *globetrotter* Blaise Cendrars, but that African Easter that I would later call my *Easter in Kumasi*.

When I entered, the church was completely swarming with a Negro crowd in which the women in printed calico and madras, the men in loincloths draped so that one shoulder was left bare, were far more numerous than the people dressed in European style. It was the end of eight o'clock mass, they were handing out the communion, and an enormous number of the faithful were filing up to receive it. I mingled at first with the marvelously motley crowd that filled the nave and I felt good there, experiencing that impression of peace, or immemorial understanding with nature, that, utopianly, I have always sought among Blacks. I would not have dreamed of extricating myself from this crowd if several women had not made me understand by signs that my proper place was in the choir. Docile, I walked in the direction of the main altar and sat down, in the right part of the choir, on the first seat I saw available. However, it was soon evident to me that by thus installing myself I had committed another blunder: this side of the area occupied by Whites was not that of the Europeans, who were all gathered in the left part of the choir, but the side of the Levantine tradesmen. No one, this time, signaled to me to move. Thus I did not pursue any further my concern to conform to the correct rule, as the dumb show of the ladies in madras had engaged me to do.

Right away, I had recognized one of the two servers of the mass as the bearded ecclesiastic whom I had met the day before, when I cast a first glance inside the frightful cathedral, and with whom I had talked about the investigation in which I was participating. It included, among other points, the clarification of the motives for which, each year, workers poured into the Gold Coast surreptitiously from the French territories to work in the mines or on the plantations, whereas our administration wondered how, after the suppression of forced labor, it would cope with the shortage of manpower from which the south of the Ivory Coast suffered endemically. The motives were in truth quite simple, and amounted more or less to this: among the English they were paid in *cash*, they had more freedom in the way they lived, and the Kumasi market abounded in Manchester cotton goods and other handsome articles which upon their return they could present to their relatives, they themselves dressed with ostentation and covered with pride for having gotten lucky in a City of Light no less rich in pleasures than in manufactured products. Such was, at least, the mirage that attracted the immigrants, for a good number of them remained without work, and, not daring to go back after such a failure, only swelled the city's mob. If one was to believe the good Father, the Kumasi prison was packed with those unemployed who had become delinquents, and as for the luckier ones, what they gained from the attraction that had been exerted on their imagination by what was said about the Ashanti Babylon was to bring back home, besides sleeping sickness, ailments of venereal origin.

Inhabitants, in heteroclite costumes, of a Babylon or a merchant city like Alexandria — this was how I saw the people of all ages, sexes, and other categories with which the cathedral was full to bursting. In the back, black soldiers in uniforms of khaki drill enhanced, in the case of the musicians, by a sort of bright red vest. At the organ, a choir of young men in long crimson tunics gathered at the waist. Almost everywhere, packs of children and adolescents dressed in various ways. Not only was there a great troop of little Negro boys in the surplices of choirboys, as well as a significant group of little Negro girls clothed in little white dresses with sky-blue edges and coiffed with a sort of American sailor cap, also white and edged in sky blue, but a fairly numerous gang of brats sat on the ground, in the center space, and more had to be chased from behind the high altar because they were blocking the aisle. These young people did not always display the proper composure, and I saw one small boy—one of the occupants of the passageway—entertain himself during the entire ceremony with the cord that he must usually have worn around his neck but that, in the circumstance, served him as an instrument for those string games so appreciated by ethnographers because the figures obtained by the variable crisscrossings determined by the positions and movements of the fingers of the two hands placed opposite each other seem to correspond to very ancient symbolic systems.

The mass was said, and the server I knew read in English some sort of pastoral letter or pious text that was translated into Ashanti by a black man of about fifty, a lean man with a small mustache whose clothing was that of a perfect gentleman. Then the priest, miter on his head and crozier in his hand, sitting with his back to the altar, delivered a sermon that the same interpreter translated a little at a time, during the pauses the priest allowed for this purpose. Despite the difficulties that a foreign language presents to me more than anyone else (even English, though I have studied it and fairly often have the opportunity to speak it), I understood that one of the themes of the sermon was the story of Jonas, because of the several scraps of the priest's remarks that I understood, and especially because of the frequent repetition of the name, easily identifiable, of the man in the whale. This story, despite my lack of belief, touches me in a very special way, and it is not without good reason that a certain philosopher—in one of the books he has devoted to what he calls the material imagination—attributes to the "Jonas complex" one of the most spontaneous pieces I have ever written, a half oneiric expression of a profound desire: to descend into the thickness of the organic night and thus return to the original matrix, like the prophet swallowed by the marine monster that is a refuge for him at the same time as a jail. Even though this episode is linked, I believe, to the promise of a resurrection and it is therefore normal for one to refer to it in a paschal sermon, the priest's recalling of it struck me as much as if it had been meant for me personally, by virtue of some decree of fate.

It all ended with a *Hallelujah!* to the strong beat of the soldiers' bass drum and snares. Preceded by the cross and traveling with slow steps the entire length of the central nave, the prelate effected a theatrical exit which, as soon as he was outside, turned into a procession. First came two lines of beautiful, robust young black girls in long dresses of a strong blue edged in white (probably Children of Mary), bareheaded with their frizzy hair cut very short, so that one could admire in all its purity the shape of the skull. Escorting the cross and the bishop, next came the young men of the choir, in their crimson tunics. As for the soldiers, they went off in their own direction, in a double phalanx: the drums on one side, the brasses much farther away. Perhaps these were the same musicians whom, toward the end of the preceding day, I had seen enliven the revels of a parade of ordinary folk led by two clowns in disguises that looked medieval, their faces masked with cowls of a sort painted pink like European faces? In the end, the festival at which a curiosity more frivolous than scholarly had induced me to be present—that turbulent and colorful Easter whose accompaniment, both instrumental and vocal, moved me to the same extent as the *negro spirituals* that I apparently heard in the middle of the cotton fields, somewhere in the region of Louisiana—appeared to me one of those events that, after the fact, give the impression not merely of being valuable in themselves but of having been produced because we were the only ones completely capable of experiencing them. Since then, I have now and then thought that if I did not return to Catholicism that day (as it seemed to me I was invited to do by that Negro crowd and that sermon, whose translation by fragments conferred more solemnity on it, and a poetry that probably was not present in it), it was because, decidedly, my childhood beliefs have truly abandoned me!

A Sunday more Sunday than the real Sundays, in Peking, the great day of the Chinese national festival, which was the pretext for the trip in a delegation, in which the filmmaker Chris Marker had taken part, like me. A Sunday officially Sunday and perhaps the only authentic one for the whole of Christianity, that Easter Sunday which, after my earliest youth, had lost for me all its brilliance, but momentarily recovered it as I saw it celebrated in one of the ugliest colonial buildings that existed in Kumasi. On the Gold Coast and in China, I had enjoyed a spectacle that, in both cases (despite the smaller size of the African festival), were presented somewhat as a Last Judgment in which all— each in the position assigned to him—would find themselves gathered in hope rather than in terror: the Ashanti Easter, with its various cohorts of angels and the strict order that placed, opposite the more numerous, shifting and colorful crowd with which the nave was filled, to the right of the bearer of the good word the Europeans with their formal manner, and to his left, the Levantines whom only after a certain time I had been able to distinguish from the former; the commemorative festival in which all of Chinese life had appeared to me to be summarized in a single procession, at the foot of an edifice that goes back to the Ming era, the "Gate of Heavenly Peace," today transformed into a grandstand for the people of influence and the most prominent guests of the People's Republic. However, it is certain that in Kumasi I had followed as at the theater (allowing myself to be moved but remaining at a distance) the service that I nevertheless would have readily believed to be ordered quite expressly to open me to Grace, whereas in Peking, being present at that parade with respect to which I was no more than a small particle, I had taken part in a ceremony in which, actor as much as spectator, I assumed a modest but precise function: that of a member of one of the groups whose coming from western Europe was in itself a gesture of friendship toward the Revolution. If (to judge from my own reaction and what I was able to grasp of my companions') the Peking festival was essentially just as religious as the Kumasi festival, there was this difference between the two demonstrations: one corresponded to a pure mythology, Christianity with its ideas of God made man, the immortal soul, and resurrection; the other to a hope that cannot fail to be a myth as well (for one can only dream of humanity being mistress of its destiny), but a myth that, nevertheless, contains a reality—the possibility of social transformations such that the subman may no longer be more than a pathological case—and that invites one to a form of action whose prospects, in no way supernatural, though excessive in relation to the limits of a single individual's life, do not exceed those of the merely terrestrial adventure of the species to which we belong.

On one side, the old dream of perpetuity; on the other, the preparation of a more just future. I have been convinced for a long time now that what Marxism-Leninism opposes to the mystiques of the past is another mystique, for a doctrine of pure reason is without motivating power, like a machine lacking a combustible or other source of energy. But this new religion, which does not allow itself to be one and cynically accords more importance to the economic factor than the nobler factors of the evolution of societies, requires a positive knowledge of the contradictory world that one cannot validly reform except by starting from its very tensions and discords. This is why, being a science as well as a form of messianism, it has the special property of being paradoxically a *true religion*, both a means of pulling life out of the mud and also the revelation of natural processes. Whence this law of primary importance, which in my opinion all militants—and sympathizers, among whom I rank myself—ought to regard as absolutely imperative: to avoid the situation in which the usual practice of resorting too quickly to lies, which the demands of the struggle may appear to justify, places the whole enterprise decisively within the control of mythology and, all rigor abolished, so disorients it as to make it miss its goal, which is to end the exploitation of man by man, real only when there are no longer either mystifiers or mystified.

These perceptions are too abstract and, certainly, quite cloudy, in this day and age when our vocabulary is spangled with borrowed words that are striking in their brutal dryness (*putsch, clash, twist, jet*, which would seem to have emerged from the same mold, even though the last two are fairly innocent, one designating only a dance with vehement hip-wiggling, the other those aerial craft that in six or seven hours by the clock hurl Parisians to New York and vice versa), in this day and age when terms formerly completely anodyne are tinted with sinister gleams: "sigle" [set of initials], of rare usage a few years ago but in current use now in the dailies and essentially evoking the man with legs spread and chest crossed by a rifle SS-fashion whom one imagines, flanked by an imbecilically rounded eye and a snake about to release its saliva or venom, at the center of the inscription O.A.S. [Organisation Armée Secrète, or Organization of the Secret Army, opposing Algerian independence from France]; "*arts plastiques*" [plastic arts], which one cannot read or utter without the adjective [*plastiques*] changing to the singular, detaching itself and becoming a substantive [*plastique*], no longer colored with a touch of eroticism through the forms it designates in the feminine, but weighted, in the masculine [plastic explosive], with the effective substance which the fascists, in France as in Algeria, use in their assaults. Perceptions which—now that what is known as "decolonization" is provoking such unrest and bloody convulsions—are merely pale generalities, ill attuned to the great striking of the gong, so deep and so muffled that, at the time, many had not heard it: *Bandung*, otherwise known as the conference that was held between Africans and Asians rebelling against the supremacy of the West, a primacy especially dubious since in spreading its culture it has, materially, delivered up a part of its arms and, spiritually, lost the monopoly it pleaded in order to claim the right to have the upper hand.

Whether the flood of events pushes me to a semblance of action or whether an ebb returns me to the thread of my musings, at each instant I remain torn between two sorts of affinities that are opposed in the manner of two factions, of which one continues its schemings while the other holds the power. Sensitive to this image, as to the plates of an old atlas whose maps are embellished with figures representing men of various races, animals fierce or pleasantly odd, dolphins, sirens, and monsters of other species, I have baptized them—a pastiche in debatable taste—my "Mao Tse-tung's way" and my "Kumasi way," thinking I can better define them thus than by the coldness of a formal exposition. On the one hand, the wish to acquire—in order to be truly a man—the practical intelligence and courage of which the builders of the new world set the example; on the other hand, the desire for a recovered freshness that my Ashanti Easter satisfied doubly, since that yearning carries me just as much toward the far reaches of memory as toward the far reaches, period. In sum, two ways for which two festivals in which I mingled with an end-of-time crowd provided me with the references, two ways that correspond approximately to the poles of the dream in which, after a walk on the mountain, I found myself in a house with garden: a house that was the site of an intrigue having to do with politics, since there I harbored Césaire the tribune and since I saw it invaded, no doubt in an electoral period, by people whom I found both agreeable and a little wearisome, experiencing with respect to them a feeling as mixed as that which I feel toward militant activity (one is not manly unless one takes sides, but what tedium and what constraints when one has taken sides); a garden in which nothing happened and which—indistinct, beyond its tangle of underbrush—was there like a simple reminder of other gardens, as much of the day as of the night, gardens that concealed times of amazement, fear, or throbbing pain. A house without mystery, where the presence of these Antilleans—not to mention the relic of my first trip to Africa, the laced boots—introduced, nevertheless, a little *elsewhere* or *in other times*, as though there were between the house and the garden (strangely diffuse though very close) a little more than the link that organically joins the architectural part and the terran part of a single country property. And the fact is that if I turn my back on the anachronistic glamour of Kumasi and look toward the actuality of the communists of Peking, the enchantments that have emanated from remote countries or ages are not unrelated to this conversion. In order for me to take a few steps down a path upon which a consideration of wretchedness close at hand had been powerless to engage me, have I not had to be shown the need for a wholesale transformation in countries which, including China, gave me an ample measure of enchantments of that sort?

More and more headlong, the course of events around me in which I take part as an individual bobbing about among thousands of others has the effect of retarding, if not blocking, the course I am following here. Not only do I become worried and waste my leisure time listening to the news (the radio set being supplemented by the diabolical *transistor*, which is always within hand's reach and which one can, almost without moving, turn on as easily upon awakening as at the moment of going to sleep), not only have I, like a miser, transferred into our country house—a precaution against those present-day risks, explosive plastic and police searches—the notes and the notebooks that are respectively the bases of my work and the receptacles for its results (so that I am physically cut off from it, and only the intermission of the weekend allows me a real contact with this book, woven of my life and having become my life itself, not so much because it contains the story of it and because I spend the greater part of my time fabricating it, but because it is at once what I remember and the memory that I want to leave, a substitute for my strength, which will die without ever having truly existed, and the tomb I am building for myself), it is certain, furthermore, that a threat like the fascist one, with the prospect of a massive descent into stupidity and cruelty opened by this exacerbation, half delusional, half coordinated, of group feeling at its most archaic, makes me doubt more than ever the validity of an effort as compartmentalized as mine. Between the self that I am and the self that I write, a twofold gap therefore appears: with these pages that jam and get stuck in one place, a crazy advance that, over the eternal laggard that is the narrated *I*, is made by the narrating *I*, drawn along by the course of events today even more rapid than yesterday; the loss of interest that distances me from this self-portrait, diminished in value as much as its model is reduced to insignificance when everything tells me that I am only a wisp of straw tossed about by the great wind of the Algerian affair, itself a mere detail in the vast movement that is shaking our familiar world to its foundations.

Supposing we possessed—like a Tibetan ascetic—the art of seeing ourselves from outside as though we were not ourselves, then to compose our written portrait would remain an illusion, if by that we mean to paint in his interiority the one who at that moment is holding the pen and not another whom, already, one knows only from memory when he is outlined on the paper. Because of the fact that, even before the transcription is finished, the thing to be transcribed has changed, this radical impossibility has, in truth, no practical consequence from which one should seriously protect oneself: if one has changed, it is not to such a point that the image thus traced resembles us as little as the reflection sent back by a distorting mirror; on the other hand, a portrait of this sort does not have to imitate the photographic snapshot, since one is aiming for a sort of timelessness rather than timeliness when one tries (as I am doing here) to define one's own features by attaching oneself to the circumstantial in order to extract from it what it contains that is constant. However, despite these reassuring reasonings, the inevitable disjunction between the moment in which one describes and the moment that one describes can become a harsh dissonance for one who, like me, does not know how to go otherwise than more slowly when it is a question of taking his bearings within himself, of drawing up an account of the events in relation to which he situates himself, even of establishing any sort of statement in which lyrical effusion would be unsuitable. What I am writing in the present being only too often from the past long passed by, I see myself (not without uneasiness) divided between two sorts of duration, the time of my life itself and the time of the book, which I almost never manage—even approximately—to make coincide.

That I am conforming to two different clockworks, each going its own speed—this is to some extent what I am feeling. It is a position all the more uncomfortable since in addition to the disharmony there is the irregularity of these movements: life that sometimes drags and sometimes gallops, despite the calendar imperturbably keeping time, the book that is suddenly blocked when it seemed sufficiently well launched to arrive rapidly at its end. This would still be nothing if the time of the book were not itself divided into two durations: the time of the author, very long when a page costs me many hours (even days) of work, shorter when, by chance, the writing is not too difficult; the time of the reader, for whom the flow of the lines is as uniform as that of sand in an hourglass, so that at each moment he finds himself misaligned with respect to me, who would like to be grasped in the present—a true present and not one of convention—in all parts of this book that do not deal expressly with old things. A specific example will make it easier to understand me and will show to what absurdity I may be led by these *flashes* having to do with the context of practical life that it seems to me in certain cases I cannot leave in the shadow.

Several weeks ago, I wrote that as a precautionary measure I had transported to the country my notes in immediate use and my fair copy notebooks; however, about two weeks ago, as the threat became less distinct, I brought back to Paris all those papers whose absence, by removing from me the possibility of handling them daily, prevented the sort of hypnosis by which I might become one with my task, and without which I am as disarmed before it as before a schoolmaster's assignment of a written paper presenting a reasoned argument. Thus at the moment when I spoke about the transfer (effected already some time ago), I was about to make the opposite decision, and I am bothered by this, as though, reporting it as though it were the *latest news*, I had been in bad faith, since I was contemplating going back on my first decision at the very same time that I was mulling over the sentences that would describe that decision. What is more, the few weeks in question, leaped over here in a few lines, occupy—measured by the eye as it reads—a space whose slenderness corresponds neither to the cataract of events (provoking dumbfounding collisions of hope, rage, and disgust) nor to my own tergiversations. This is, certainly, a fine result: confusion and discord falsifying a passage which, in principle, should enhance the truthfulness of my remarks by indicating what their surroundings are.

So as not to neglect anything I will mention, although the thing is obvious, another trick that time can play on me, even in the short term: everything happens so fast these days that several of my allusions to circumstances (allusions capricious and often indirect, for it is only by fits and starts and almost furtively that I mingle an element altogether journalistic with a piece of writing whose point of view is very different) will perhaps have become strangely sibylline by the time of publication or will refer only to realities obliterated by other realities that will prove historically more prominent but to which I will not have paid any attention, either because another theme then in the works did not leave me the freedom, or because I felt repugnance at seeing strictly informative sentences multiply in my text. Corrections made within the proper interval would in part remedy this disadvantage. However, owing not only to such cuts, additions or substitutions but also to the purely compositional couplings that such changes would impose, the book would lose some of its authenticity (or, to put it better, would lose all of it, for in such an area there is no middle term). And this remedy, worse than the ill, would be all the less justified given that my purpose is not that of a memorialist, since I would like, rather than to reconstruct my life by following it step by step, to gain mastery over it by embracing it with a single glance (a glance situated in time but already outside of time, comparable to the glance attributed to a drowning man who sees once again, in the blink of an eye, his entire life unfolding).

Now this glance in which everything ought suddenly to be condensed and assume the fixedness of a panorama—I cast it over these *Scratches*, these *Scraps*, these *Fibrils* that I am writing not simply in time (in this epoch that is mine and furnishes me my language), but, I may say, with time, since I need long intervals to adjust these materials I have fished from all parts of my life and to link reflections each one of which, far from offering itself in a solid block, is a movement that can be decomposed into several phases. To expect from a discursive, prosaic method the impression of absolute presence and total captivation that can be given only by poetry, in its apparently rootless upwelling, is—of course—to hope for the impossible ... But if the word "expect" [*attendre*, also "wait for"] relates here to a vain expectation, reading it over many times at the head of that sentence which it begins and whose negative content I ran up against (so that I kept coming back to it in order to discover in it the link that would allow me to continue), I have finally connected it to something more concrete: the continual waiting [*l'attente*] to which I am consigned by a process so slow that it almost always makes me miss my appointments with myself—the latest implication of a word that I had used almost by chance without foreseeing that an effect of double meaning would lead it to betray, in an indirect way analogous to that of an involuntary slip, the flaw in my method.

These notes that I keep in a box, waiting to use them, and whose content, when I return to them, has lost its freshness. The elements of my conclusion which I have already noted down—in advance, therefore, of the evolution of this series of writings—but that I leave waiting as a bureaucrat leaves dormant an unworkable portfolio as long as it is incomplete. A patience masking, perhaps, a sort of laziness or the desire to elude the hour of truth, a tactic after the fashion of Fabius (that cunctator whose story the *De Viris* during my first year of lycée had told me, at the same time that it taught me what it was to temporize), the wait for the ripening of some phrases that, coming in lightning succession, ought to culminate like the embrace with regard to which what has gone before will represent, at the very most, skilled approaches. On the very verge of my work, a wait that was closely and directly related to the century itself, since it was at the beginning of the Occupation that I set to my task, thinking—all projects in suspense—I could not better employ than in an extended tour of the inner horizon the time that would elapse before our emergence from the tunnel, this without seeing that I was entering another tunnel: this book that would soon aim at the invention of a rule of life based—taking into account my weaknesses—on my most real desires, but which is turning out to be too complicated to materialize within a useful time and because of which, perhaps, worn out more than helped by the constant sifting that it demands, I will have nearly died before fate undertakes to eliminate me. Tired of waiting to reach my goal, I condemn any waiting that, from the beginning, may have played a part in the drafting of these pages. A certain position taken that nevertheless allows me to arrive at this: to establish the main headings, to let things come, to plan an investigation to be conducted in stages and for which one soberly takes notes, is to put off until later the attainment of what must, if writing is other than a vulgar tool, be realized at each instant and without any deferment. Nothing in common between the due date prepared by these approaches and the eternal noon or midnight sovereignly decreed by poetic creation. And if I thus shake in my dice box rubble from my past, clots of the living present and grains of the gestating future, instead of provoking the throw of the dice by which rotations round the clock face and horizons would at last be dominated, I flounder about in a time that one could call *unsettled* if one were talking about meteorology.

Saturation? Growing doubt—as I approach the last bend—about my capacity to conclude and even about the advantage of concluding, since the rule that I would like to formulate in a few phrases of the same kind as were offered by the oracles would be, in truth, a clumsy system impossible to build without specious reasonings? Fear of having gone astray, when what had at first been a florilegium of singular facts, and their restitution even more than their study, turned into the thoughtful inventory of what matters most to me and the attempt to deduce from it the law in which would be summed up for me both a savoir-vivre and an art of poetry? Consciousness—and bad conscience [*conscience*: both "conscience" and "consciousness"]—of having applied this more severe program without rigor and of having too readily confused what I liked to tell with something from which a lesson should be drawn? Disturbance, even thinking of this change of direction, proving as it does (even if it remained purely theoretical) how vulnerable all this work is to time, since its aim, altering along the way instead of preserving a sort of ideal intemporality, has itself proved to be the plaything of the passing years? All these reasons that I may have for marking time, none of which excludes another, are brocaded onto a background of defiance but also of discomfiture, and I rediscover in each the stigmata of that subjection to time from which, by writing, I was trying to escape. Whether too languid an effort leads me to disgust, or whether, greedy for a truth with instantaneous fulgurations, I reject in advance a patiently structured doctrine, or whether, the habit having been acquired, I remain attached to ways of proceeding that I know to be no longer valid, or whether I am disappointed by a project about which I note that it has undergone fluctuations over time, it is the latter that always appears as the tyrant or the nuisance whose intrigues I contrive, without managing to do better than feel their weight a little more, to elude!

An adventure whose setting, during the "phony war," was South Oran provided me with the occasion for a portrait: the Algerian Khadidja in whom I admired—a moral beauty almost as much as a physical one—her long goatherd's strides, a vestige (I liked to think) of a nomad ancestry from whom this recluse with her lowly profession might have derived a part of her nobility. It was on the eve of my departure for China that the story of our meeting appeared; the sixteen years that had elapsed had no doubt marked my companion of the Béni Ounif *bousbir* enough to alter perceptibly her resemblance to the portrait, already retrospective, that was contained in my notebooks. In order to find her again as I knew her, in the splendor and misery of the twenty-three years attributed to her by her prostitute's card, it is not to this lovingly drawn image that I must refer, anyway, but to the simple word "Sarrasins" [Saracens; also, Saracen corn or buckwheat], which recalls to me—because of the grain and because of the rhyme—one of the treats of my childhood, those round raisin buns [*petits pains au raisin*] whose crumb, of the same color as that of rye bread, was speckled with black grains, also the treat offered to me, in unclothing herself, by the Clorinda without helmet or breastplate who was my friend, with a demeanor of a completely Saracen boldness, with swarthy flesh darker where the two grapes of her breasts thrust out, and whose slightly sour or spicy aroma she disdained to mask by steeping it in the vulgar bazaar perfumes that were all she would have had available to her.

Now that the "phony war," which soon changed into a real war, has been succeeded by conflicts—in Vietnam and North Africa—in which it was the turn of the French to be the oppressors determined to break a popular resistance, the adventure that I have told appears to me in a less innocent light, for it seems to me I displayed one of the forms of the colonial spirit most difficult to extirpate (because it is interpreted as merely a sign of subtle receptiveness), by seeing only those aspects of Algeria likely to attract me, in a sublime misunderstanding of the problems that were already tormenting it. Ignoring everything else, was I not sensitive only to the purely picturesque, rendered tangible in that idyll that was so terribly *Butterfly*, if not *Petite Tonkinoise*, worthy—if one considers only the hard facts—of the sailor or soldier who, back in his country, will acknowledge, with a tear in his eye, the good qualities of the woman overseas (mousmée, congaie, *mousso*, vahine, or *fatma*) whom he turned into his plaything or his wild animal pet, without ever granting her a wholehearted love, or even, as in my case, conceding her only niggardly material profits? Here too, in the contest I am waging against it, time has the last word. Perhaps the description I wrote fixed for me—in an indelible way—Khadidja as she was at twenty-three and embedded itself to the point of making me forget that in this year 1962, which has seen the struggles in Algeria come to an end, its model has double the age which I remember and is no doubt an old woman (for women of her country and her condition fade quickly). But time keeps no less within its power the character one encounters in the book, whose twenty-three years ought to elude all change: to have been depicted as though for eternity has not protected Khadidja—even as heroine of a fairy tale—from the action of the years with its thousand resources, since the perspective that recent events have imposed on me endows this story, so naïvely experienced, with a signification that singularly depreciates the one I gave it in describing my marvelous commerce with that girl at once so servile and so proud whom I will henceforth no longer be able to regard with exactly the same eyes.

Often, naturally, I imagined Khadidja playing a role consistent with the idea I had formed—from the press, the radio, or simply hearsay—of one of the phases of that Algerian war from which France emerged soiled up to the haunches, with its Phrygian cap badly rumpled: the prostitute patriotically refusing her favors to Europeans or, the opposite, removing her veils during the comedy of fraternization that followed the all-too-famous May 13; or a veiled militant carrying a flag of the F.L.N. (in which I rediscover, along with the blood from her ears, which were wounded one evening, the white robe and green turban she had put on as ceremonial dress the morning we took leave of each other); or an already mature woman standing on a terrace still warm from the day's sun and encouraging with her *youyous* [ululations] the demonstrators in the Casbah. These, however, were only fleeting thoughts, and even if—the likely sign of a respect that has not diminished—I affixed the traditional veil to her face, which I always knew uncovered, it was the Khadidja of former times, almost intact, who was integrated into these tableaux and not what I could have divined of the Khadidja that in these last few years she must have become, unless a premature death definitively thrust her back into the immutable world of images.

Before inserting her thus, as I might have done in a dream, in scenes whose fabric was furnished by Algeria in revolt, I had asked myself what might have become of Khadidja in another revolution whose fate I take particularly to heart: that of present-day China, which has made the emancipation of women one of its primary objectives. Within the confines of Mongolia, in a long landscape of undulating plain in the far background like a line of Camelidae (one of those landscapes the extent of which the song "The East Is Red" suffices to reveal to me in my thoughts), would she be employed in a pastoral activity, in keeping with the vocation that seemed indicated by her physique of goatherd? Wearing as a veil the little white mask that protects the mouth and nose from dust, would she have worked in a cotton mill, like one I visited in Peking whose workforce was almost entirely female? Or, faithful to herself and rebelling against the reclassification suffered by her peers, would she have emigrated to Hong Kong in order to be free to continue practicing her lifelong profession, in the opiated mildness and the cosmopolitanism of that port, which represents for me an immense Asiatic Kumasi? In these suppositions, modeled and remodeled according to caprice alone, I had, however, a twofold reason to indulge myself: my interest in the reforms accomplished in China and the secret desire to associate with them a figure to whom I remain profoundly attached, in order to connect to the universe of my passions what, despite everything, they retain for me that is abstract; the need to dilute in these apparently serious reflections the shame that I felt toward Khadidja and her people, also toward the Chinese men and women I knew in the course of my trip (this time without any myth of love or adventure), who remain "comrades" with respect to whom the opinion they might have of me influences my behavior—the belated shame that overcame me when the severity of the struggle in which Algeria was engaged led me to think that, full of bourgeois dilettantism as I was, I had seen from the narrow point of view of a comic-opera intrigue a country most of whose inhabitants were, each in his own way, humiliated and insulted.

The image that I wanted to preserve by enclosing it within a book has, then, been frozen there without escaping from the always active flow of time. If its projection on paper had made it intangible, this intangibility would be that of a sort of Judith or Rachel, a cold figure circulating through successive combinations in which, though identical to itself, it assumes a new meaning each time, as in the deployment of the *full deck* by a fortune-teller as she groups, in mosaics with unforeseeable and moving patterns, the cardboard rectangles about which I learn—verifying in a dictionary whether the two queens with biblical names are in fact both red, the only color assignable to Khadidja—that an old Italian text situates their origin in the "country of the Saracens," a discovery that strengthens my parallel between a queen of hearts or diamonds and the image of the friend of whom I have said that, in order to recover a little of her presence, despite the wall interposed by time, "Saracens" is an open-sesame more effective than all my sentences so patiently elaborated.

What passes, today, from that Saracen woman, through some hypotheses issuing from my mood, as well as through some conjunctions, and what could not, even while persisting in its being, stop moving as long as I myself still move, turns out to be, in the end, as conventional as a tarot card or a playing card, and certainly as thin. In order for that image to have substance, which its written formulation is not enough to endow it with, wouldn't it be necessary, in the first place, that the person involved be able to recognize herself as in a mirror where she would discover herself *as into herself at last*? Yet supposing Khadidja were able to read me, the story that I have told and the way in which she is shown in it would remain impenetrable to her or, if it were otherwise, would no doubt make her laugh, as much to see such importance attached to ordinary relations between supplier and customer as to find herself promoted from the despised rank of whore to that of magician, midlife infatuation, or angel of death. Thus not shared, and merely subjective, this image—an idol whose constancy will not prevent its signification from being lost—lies in the domain of oneirism for the same reasons as do the reveries to which I abandon myself in connection with it. But would one imagine calling a painted portrait chimerical because the original did not feel it was a good likeness, or because the future viewer would have a different view of it than the contemporary? The negativity in which I end up may derive solely from the absurdity of this requirement: to demand from literature what it is not able to supply, a truth independent of epochs and environments.

To resign myself. To admit that writing, subject as it is to time, cannot be a means of domesticating it, either before or after the term of our life. To practice literature as such, in full awareness of its limits, or else to withdraw from the game, imitating the Abbé de Bucquoy, of whom Nerval relates (in the very fictionalized account that *Les Illuminés* gives of his adventures) that he apparently gave up the frock because he realized that the ascetic discipline had not made him capable of performing miracles. One of these two solutions—to finish this book as an artisan purely and simply executing his task, or to lower the curtain—ought to be what I arrive at, if it were possible, that is, to give up a game that logically I know is lost but for whose outcome, like the gambler who can't be stopped from trying his luck again by anything except complete ruin, I hope there will occur providentially the winning toss; if I did not think also that where art is concerned (in that place where mathematical reasoning no longer prevails), an experiment begun is always worth pursuing, even if one must finally topple into what, according to that same reasoning, cannot be taken for anything but a piece of nonsense; if I did not suspect, lastly, that I am raising difficulties a little like a negotiator who questions everything again on the very eve of signing the agreements, or like a woman whose modesty or coquettishness impels her to find an imperious reason for refusing when she has already decided to succumb. Besides, is it fair to liken to an artisan's work any literature practiced without illusions? *Art for art's sake* certainly amounts to something of this sort, but one can, even though writing without deluding oneself, go beyond pure confection. When by means of that writing I tried to derive my laws and my idées-forces, the objective I was pursuing was not superhuman, but merely difficult to attain. And if I faltered, it was when—as the book extended to the point where the parts I had already drafted were melting behind me into a confused mass and my goal was becoming indistinct—it seemed to me that I must expressly bring the present into that divagation, too long not to require the insertion of temporal markers, before the terminal effort, which would consist of attempting to condense into a single block that could be grasped all at once the essential part of what I want to say, beyond all the kinds of changes and events that have supervened at the mercy of the years. It was, in the end, because of a slowness such that my thoughts seemed to crumble away instead of becoming stronger that the idea of time began to occupy me to the point of obsession, while my mad exactingness became firmer with regard to writing, now enjoined to defeat time. I know very well, after all, that a certain taste for the baroque incites me to accumulate embellishments and digressions (as though they participated directly in my research), instead of walking straight to the goal, a way of proceeding that thwarts my desire to finish rapidly. But I know just as well that I could not give it up without distancing myself from my purpose, since that taste represents (whether I want it to or not) one of my tendencies where aesthetics is concerned and since my quest for a truth too tangible not to be inextricably mingled with beauty must go by way of what, in life, moves me or captivates me and by way of what, on a literary level, an invincible attraction leads me to introduce into the game.

To this taste, which includes my often-expressed predilection for Verdi's operas (baroque in the sense that, in them, a volcanic ardor is miraculously associated with a somewhat academic architecture), must respond, at least partially, not only my way of writing, but more than one of my ways of doing things, and even what I believe belongs to me in my own right within the events that, dazzled and dismayed (as I was in my dream, confronted with a cliff sculpted with multiple figures terribly tall and beautiful), I have been able to consider high points in my life. A taste, certainly, that fluctuates (as demanded by its very object), for if, in Verdi precisely, I love the rich musculature and the distinctly articulated diversity of the commentary brought to the peripetiae of the drama, I also love—and perhaps above all—the dazzling lacerations with which this luxuriance, echoed by the gilding and molding of the hall, even the imagery of the trompe-l'oeil settings, is pierced when the impetuosity of the music (apparently hurled into a panting race to reach a present that is immediately concealed by the fluidity of time) resolves into one of those very plainly lyrical phrases that are great and pure outpourings surging up in the same way as does, out of ornamentation whose abundance jostles the harsh geometry of a building, a certain statue that seems to reproduce the sinuosities of life itself, rather than those of a living body, and captivates the eye all the more because this assemblage of lines with apparently uncontrolled wanderings seems to be the almost peaceful result of the tumult in which the rest is plunged. A taste, therefore, that it would be useless to try to confine within a rigid definition, but which, I am firmly convinced, has its own coherence and is the single source of a number of my behaviors, at first sight disparate: that I direct this book as though a greater or lesser amount of overworking—a superfluity, I could say—were indispensable to me, whatever irritation I might feel about it, in order to avoid a dryness that would be even more repugnant to me than the delays thus caused; that, instead of organizing in traditional ways those of my publications that have to do with pure science, I proceed by "successive explosions of thought," as was observed, close to thirty years ago now, by an expert in Islam assigned to judge my first Africanist memoir, whose articulation was baroque to the highest degree, the placement of details described with prolixity being substituted for any sort of real plan; that I attach myself in an exaggerated way to the forms of what, in life, is likely to exalt us, and that I act, in love, for instance, in the manner—modernized—of a *précieux* for whom passion—an essentially romantic affair—is modeled on the rock garden of the Map of Love rather than obeying impulses issuing directly from the heart and the senses; far from considering the totality of an action in which I am involved, that I retain an isolated element of it, an emotional or merely picturesque scene, and that I grant, finally, less importance to the general development than to this dramatic motif; that I elect, in order therein to rediscover my childhood and try to see clearly into my lifelong emotions, a figure not only connected to what was bizarre about the interiors of environments of 1900 but baroque in itself, as was my Aunt Claire, a caryatid, all curves, whose radiant face was so capable (when necessary) of convulsing into tragic mascarons; that in the course of my trip to China I became infatuated with the adventitious and treated as though they represented what was most essential flowers in railway stations or around policemen, bewitching modulations of voices in town as well as on the stage, ingenious architectural combinations, inventions like the vibrating bronze tub and the convex mirror in which the mountain was reflected (piquant fancies like those in certain of our churches, dating back two or three centuries, that cause the leg of an angel to pass over the corniche or a part executed in the round to complete a personage the rest of whom is done flat), all things that are merely rococo trifles which, not surprisingly, were not able to provide me the wherewithal to give a consistent account of the country I had traveled as fascinated visitor; in many cases, lastly, that I am sensitive to something indirectly by way of an irony (preferring, for example, to any other residence a place anachronistic in itself or in certain, at least, of the characteristics of its furnishings, appreciating a certain song or piece of music whose excess of sentimentality amuses me, or, on the contrary, whose gay and simple manner of presenting itself would, nearly, wring tears from me, prizing, more than other lofty gastronomical venues, localities with good plain Third Republic cooking, liking, in a work of art, that such surprising profit should be derived from very anodyne elements or, on the contrary, that there be manifested in it a sudden contempt for all moderation, which means that the great aria of *Rigoletto*, where, along with the invectives and supplications of the rebuffed buffoon, vehemence and sweetness enjoy themselves to the full, will be par excellence the aria that I would like to be able to sing, but that, in Mallarmé, I will admire the fact that a whole metaphysics springs from a knickknack or a few puffs of tobacco and, in Proust, that he shows as clearly as Freud, though from another point of view, what a world of revelations can be contained in mere nothings).

For very different reasons, doesn't all this indicate at the very least my antipathy toward the regularity of the straight line, a feeling perhaps of the same kind as that of the woman, who was, after all, intelligent and discriminating, who worked for a long time in our house at Saint-Hilaire and who (no doubt believing that parallel or perpendicular arrangements and pleasing arrangements are not compatible) systematically replaced in oblique positions the objects she had displaced to wipe the top of a piece of furniture? In many areas, I myself react as though, disheartened by the *shortest distance between two points*, I look with special favor on the roundabout schoolboys' route, more personal, with its arabesques, zigzags, and deviations, and its rhythm broken by the sudden stop or about-face of a dog invaded by some unknowable idea or attracted by something or other he has smelled or seen. But isn't it the case that to choose a path other than the most direct, or expressly to put askew what would be normal to put straight, is a property of art, which only really begins when one is allowed to add a surplus or to give a few twists to the forms demanded by the needs of a technique or a ritual (a sophistication which at a more advanced stage the baroque illustrates in an exemplary manner since it shows at once the rule and what violates it, the straight line and the curved or broken lines that tend to be substituted for it)? If this is so, and if art—like eroticism, too—responds to this need to complicate things uselessly, by which man stands out from the other animals, I betray myself when, out of a desire to justify myself, I reduce to the level of reasonable means of inquiry what I ought to take, on the contrary, in all its living gratuitousness.

Mao Tse-tung's way, namely (according to my conventions) that of morality and knowledge. The Kumasi way, to which I am attracted by sentiment and gratuitous preferences. Those two domains which I would like to be as little separated as, in the theater, *stage left* and *stage right*—one of my blunders is to have believed sometimes that I was joining them in what I was writing whereas I was mixing them at the wrong time, subjecting material that had completely to do with sensibility to a gloomy regime of reason, or broaching by way of an emotional reaction, or even by way of the picturesque, the thorny problems that are continually posed by the course of political events. I could, of course, make the opposite choice: give up these amalgams and follow my whim, try to save what is indispensable from the realm of poetry and abandon the other realm, by far the more disagreeable. But that would not resolve anything, for to eliminate themes that preoccupy me solely in order not to be constricted any longer would shame me, and that shame would obstruct me more than anything else. It is not the first time I have found myself in this sort of difficulty, but I have always set off along my path again, after a shorter or longer abeyance. Yet it seems to me that if the same question, in various guises, periodically comes along to stop me, it is because I have never been able to ask it with enough frankness and distinctness to be able, at the very least, to reject it as a question which one knows will remain without an answer.

For a long time now—it must be said without hedging—I have no longer hoped to attain what, hesitantly extracted, had gradually affirmed itself as the ultimate goal and raison d'être of a piece of writing which, in the beginning, I did not suspect would become, at least, a trilogy: to unite the two sides between which I feel I am divided, to formulate a golden rule that would at the same time be an art of poetry and of knowing how to live, to discover a means of making the *over-there* coincide with the *right-here,* of being in the myth without turning my back on the real, of creating instants each of which would be an eternity. To want that was to obey a natural impulse: the desire for a complete and perfect life is the reason why most men have a god, in one form or another (even if that of a leader around whom is created a "cult of personality"). But as for me, I cannot rely on anything like that, knowing that a god supplies too well what we lack not to have been invented quite expressly. Thus my demand went beyond the allowed limits: when one does not admit of any deus ex machina of that kind, the astounding marriage of the carp and the rabbit which is what my intention amounted to is doubly untenable. Yet this naïveté is not my only mistake.

Seeking what would be *my* truth, I started from my own examination, and I was threatened by a danger from which I did not, moreover, guard myself very well: to allow myself to be captivated by the portrait I would make, and no longer attach myself to anything but it. On the other hand, the truth of a single person being no more than a dream, it was necessary that others be able, if not to adopt mine (perforce distinct from theirs), at least to recognize the value of its bases. Whence the urgency of enlarging the perspective and the necessity for presenting my arguments. This is why, as I went along, I initiated—if not in so many words, at least between the lines, even during the intermissions—what amounted to debates, general ones, however particular the pretext may have been. But rather than to preside over a trial, what I wanted, even while it seemed to me I was calling everything into question again, was to support or to be quite clear about a choice I had made in the very beginning, since if it had been different, I would not have been primarily interested in the mysteries of language, the raw material of poetry. My gross mistake—worse than the one that consisted in asking for the moon—was to have misunderstood that (or refused to realize it) and to have lingered over false problems that my need for philosophizing led me all the more easily to pose because I sometimes found in them an occasion for shaking myself awake, at the same time as a terrain from which to take off again. Tending to proceed by alternatives (for my convenience and because contrasts have always enchanted me), I would bring face to face—on paper or in my head—two apparently equivalent terms which I believed to be such but which, in fact, were not. It is toward poetry, the *over-there,* and myth that my preferences indubitably go, and the second direction—that of morality and knowledge—is not a counterpart of the first: the myth that one knows to be mythical no longer has anything exalting about it, the *over-there* that one loves one must have right here, the true poet can be neither a swine nor an idiot—this was my thought before it was dressed up in its Sunday best, myth, *over-there,* and poetry being for me the axes of reference and the other term—reality, undeniable presence, acute awareness of what is and of what must be done—having only a secondary role, as a condition that must be fulfilled and not as the object of my possible covetousness.

Except for a very small part of it, what I am saying here is not new: the recollection of ideas expressed along the way, and the deduction that is called for. It is curious, certainly, that I was able to stray from my path to such a point that returning to it gives me, almost, an impression of discovery. But if I deviated thus, was it not because I got it into my head I ought to demonstrate, and not merely show? With the ceremony called for by the need to find reasons for myself, I distanced myself, in fact, both from poetry and from lived realities in order to manipulate mere notions, that is to say, shadows whose forms and dimensions varied according to the lighting, so that there was a moment when, among those silhouettes all equally without flesh and only the more deceptive because of that, I wandered as in a carnival where those very people you know best have become strangers to you. A charade whose dupe, now, I could no longer naïvely be, since I know which false maneuver makes me responsible for it: having rigged the weights without fully realizing it, when, for example, holding the scales to be equal between Kumasi and Peking, I presented as two poles whose attractions I experienced symmetrically that thing to which I have always been attached, I may say without great exaggeration, and that other thing toward which I am borne along, in the absence of a truly militant fervor, by fleeting impulses to which the goads of self-love are surely not alien, the situation being such, today, that one could not fail, except through total renunciation, to be politically "engaged." My mistake, in short, is to have envisaged a conclusion that would answer everything (none of my concerns as a twentieth-century European being set aside) and that, with whatever incisive or subtly periphrastic formulation it might be adorned, could not help being dogmatic, a serious error for two reasons: I could not succeed in this except through a cycle of reasonings, a mode of linking thoughts that is less akin to the flight of an eagle than to the plodding of a beast of burden, and this meant—a fault even worse—obliging myself, in the guise of judging fairly, to pose too abstractly the questions I had to debate for the truth not to suffer. It is patent that, originally, my program was more modest and that, when I thought I had to go farther, I did not know what an abyss there was between the desire to condense into an immediately prehensible block the essential part of what I am and what I value, and the ambition (ineluctably that of a logician) to articulate a system that would be proved equitable and the only one appropriate to my aspirations as well as my possibilities. *To make the magical world of adventures in language coincide with the naked and shocking world of the bird fallen from the nest*—this was expressly my final view at the period, already remote now, when, on the same slip of paper, I noted, first, my belief in the *need to make the frivolous play that takes place between words coincide with something of a vital seriousness*, then expressed my wish to *derive from this attitude toward words a more intense way of life and a rule for living*, a reflection with which a morality is explicitly affirmed, but which no less explicitly subordinates morality to poetry, since it is in a certain *attitude toward words* that I intend to find the indication of a manner of behaving, at the same time as the source of an enrichment of life. *Morality = a rule of the game, that is, that without which there would not even be a game*, I remarked also, playing at seeing in the game—in other words in what seems, in essence, the most contrary to the serious—a justification for ethics, since, in the absence of a demarcation, quite unremarkable anyway, between deeds permitted and deeds forbidden, life would be no more than an almost automatic montage of scenes spaced out from birth to death, and not that contest that can impassion us by reason of the very difficulty one finds in conducting it without moral lapses.

Kumasi and Peking, tender love and constraint, intersections of the imagination and cruxes of reason. If it is clearly in the direction of the imaginary that my scales tips, and if, like those for whom the practice of an art, whatever it may be, is the activity of choice, I give myself up to a game that leads me to neglect many duties, I am, at least, far from being unaware that there can be no game without rules and that failing, consequently, to respect prescriptions that are foreign to what I love above all else, it is to directives implied by the game itself that I must submit. I thus arrive at the idea (glimpsed for a long time now) that, since blind acceptance disqualifies one just as much as the negation of all principles, a *professional morality*—more disengaged from theology than a morality with a capital *M*—is alone capable of constituting the rudimentary code which I cannot do without. All things considered, now that this troubling question (after so many others) has been exposed, my desire to arrive at something more alive than a theoretical insight is not a reason that can excuse me from giving a sketch of one here. In other words: to indicate what laws I am obliged to conform to in order to "play the game" in the framework that I have chosen for myself, the few laws that in a practical sense I cannot infringe, under pain of seeing my work lose all value in my eyes, and perhaps, finally, all virtue (if one admits that the words of a cheat, soon noticed, quickly lose, in the eyes of another person, the capacity to convince, move, or transfigure that they might unduly have had). Of course, the games of beauty would not be able to bend to external injunctions without failing in their essential role of surpassing all, but if this authorizes one to take them as sovereignly immoral, the artist must still pay for the right to devote himself to the immorality of beauty, by being pitilessly rigorous in his observance of the "rules of the game."

A list of prohibited acts, a statement of certain refusals—such has always been this code, starting from its old states of being and continuing right up to the present clarification (anachronistic, for it has revealed itself to be more dubious as I gave it form):

> not to lie;
> not to promise anything that one is not sure of carrying out;
> not to pay with words or pay oneself with words (things that the writer above all must regard as too precious to turn into joking substitutes for real money);
> not to talk lightly, and to distrust ill-natured gossip as well as the thoughtlessness that produces gaffes (grotesque sins against speech, in the same way as there are sins against the spirit);
> not merely to respect the envelope, which does not need to be sealed with red for its violation to be a bloody offense, but to give proof in all circumstances of that basic discretion;
> to exclude the intellectual cowardice that would lead one to pad one's talk with locutions in the style of the day, and also the affectation that would be represented by the opposite, the use of language either too scholarly or too pure;
> to hold one's tongue to the extent of being able to suffer without bestially giving way to crying, and if necessary to keep a secret despite torture or risk of death;
> finally, to forbid oneself, more severely than might anyone else when one practices the literary art, that which in real life is a crime of injury against language, and to succeed in being not merely master of one's words and perfect confederate of speech, but a "man of his word" as the current sense of that expression may require.

One can adopt these taboos—or that *morality of speech* which, ideally, the person cannot contravene without the work being thereby degraded—as foundation for a poetic art (in the very broad sense in which I mean it), as well as for a savoir-vivre:

> not to lie, and therefore to scorn the artful dodges likely to deceive the reader, who—if he must be seduced—must be so in other ways than by maneuvers aiming at effect alone and comparable (minus the heroic flame) to those of the legendary *burlador* of Seville, condemned much less for having been a corrupter than for having been a glib talker whose false oath was one of his principal weapons;
> no empty promises, and consequently to reject, in favor of the most exact

expression, all verbal inflation, the poet being, anyway, his own first dupe if he takes himself for a seer, no writer being excused from forgetting that the earth continues to turn while he indulges in his games;

to treat words as something other than wind and, hence, to proscribe pieces of bravura for the same reason as redundancies, embellishments, and filler words;

not to talk thoughtlessly, whence the incongruity of making literature into an art of the dilettante Jack-of-all-trades;

no sacrilegious attack on the thinking of another person, and thus not to alter a text in the least through reshaping, prudish pruning, tendentious quotation, or deceptive interpretation;

to avoid a blowsy style (pointlessly picturesque) or the fluency of another kind offered by a philosophical or scientific vocabulary to formulate certain thoughts (thus put in a glass case), whereas to make a strict rule for oneself to express them in natural language leads one to delve into them and thereby discover ramifications one had not suspected;

to hold one's tongue enough so that the little (or relatively little) that one allows to come out on paper may have all the strength of a substance not diluted, an infinitesimal strength on the scale of the forces that control us but one capable of provoking a change in some hearts and some minds;

avoiding deception, sophistication, and carelessness in their various guises, to write like someone who knows *what speaking means*, and not to make use of language—a means of human commerce and a mechanism without which humankind would not even exist as it is—except with the greatest rigor and loyalty, in order that there may be some chance of communicating authentically to others what one says to oneself.

These principles, whose meaning always implies rejection, and each of which is a *no* rather than a *yes*, I believed for a long time to be very firm and dependable. More modest than positive prescriptions, since they were only very general prohibitions or warnings bearing on a few transgressions not to be committed, they seemed less vulnerable because of the very fact that their aspirations appeared more moderate. This was an illusion which would probably soon have been dissipated had I immediately submitted them to an examination instead of conserving them, treating them as a definite acquisition, within a general outline, and one that I would not study until later, when the time came to reach my conclusion.

Not to lie. However, unless, by chance, it is enough to say nothing at all, one must necessarily lie in a case where there is only harm to be expected from the confession of a truth: to cast into despair an ill person who is doomed and was not anxious to know it, to hurt a respected person who finds himself in difficulty, to cause the failure of an act that was just but could not be carried out openly, to throw oneself stupidly in the maw of police repression. In one's private life, it also happens that lying and not lying may both be forms of betrayal: of course one owes the whole truth to the woman with whom one lives, but is it praiseworthy to act as her informer, betraying another woman to whom one is connected by the secrecy of a collusion? This is a pernicious dilemma for someone who wishes neither to destroy that precious complicity by a disclosure (should the person in whom one confided feel that *knowing* was enough for her, and no formal legal demand would result from the revelation) nor adapt himself to duplicity... I cannot fail to recognize, either, that many writers and poets whom I admire were arrant liars: Defoe, as much a hypocrite as his name in French would signify [*de faux*, "false"], since he was a double agent, a hired pamphleteer, and the author of apocryphal Memoirs; Chateaubriand, whose autobiography is not a document one can always trust, even though the far side of the grave may be its guarantee; Nerval himself, who despite his purity did not fail to arrange his childhood memories as it suited him, as well as the tales of his travels to the East, and those of his incursions into the underbrush of dream and madness; Apollinaire, for whom lying was part of the enchanter's apparatus.

Not to promise anything that one is not certain one will abide by: a good excuse for refusing every commitment! Isn't it better to accept the possibility that one may not honor a promise than to behave so prudently that one will never even put oneself in a position to lose one's nerve? And in the case of many literary texts, what would be left of them if every impulse that had risked being excessive had been deliberately strangled in the cradle and if a correct manner of expressing oneself had not been supplemented by a surplus which was in fact beauty itself?

To proscribe ornamentation, so that words might be treated as something other than mere inconstant and empty wind. That rule—how could I reconcile it with my love of the baroque and of profusion, which needs above all to avoid being necessary? And could I (even in my own case) distinguish between what is accessory and what is essential, knowing that all sorts of ingenious ways of padding, even while using the most concise style, have been creative resources for someone like Raymond Roussel and that blatantly obvious filler words have served him as climbing pitons to reach the highest summits?

Not to speak lightly. But what, in the realm of sociability, would a conversation be without any portion of lightness? Hardly anyone but a pedant would forbid himself any lack of restraint in a casual conversation, and it is often through the most unexamined remarks, even the most trivial or inopportune, that real communication takes place between the speakers. In the same way, an art totally sure of itself and never refreshed by the uncertainty of a whim or a gamble could not be anything but a dead art.

No sacrilegious assault on the thoughts of another person? Yet of how many posthumous jewels, brought out into the light despite their authors' expressed desire for burial, would literature be deprived, if this order had always been followed! What is more, elementary discretion would bid us keep silent about private journals and bodies of correspondence, which in many cases would be not only a serious loss but the source of errors concerning the exact signification of literary works.

To avoid, equally, both a language too affected and also a language tainted with those locutions whose only purpose is to show that one is up to date on things and thus denote the worst vulgarity: the least contestable (it would seem) of all these precepts, because, being in the realm of taste rather than morality, it displays an ambition more limited than the others.

To be sparing of one's words and to keep, if necessary, a heroic silence. The Spartan child who did not unclench his teeth while the fox gnawed at his chest. The Christian martyrs who suffered and died without retracting, and sometimes without flinching, or proffering only prayers. *The death of the wolf.* Michel Strogoff, from whom the reddened blade held up before his eyes does not wrest his secret. The great exemplary figures of verbal economy: Sparta and laconicism; the historian Tacitus; William the Taciturn, whose motto I was taught by the *Breviary of a Pantheist*, by Jean Lahor (pseudonym of a friend of the not very prolix Mallarmé, Doctor Cazalis): "One need not have hope in order to act, nor success in order to persevere," which appears to express all the silent obstinacy evoked by the word "taciturn," which tinges with darkness and mystery the harmless first name of the defender of the Low Countries; the monk—Spanish, it seems to me, and perhaps a famous saint—of whom it is told how he stopped a fire by commanding the flames, thus breaking the silence which it had been his strict rule to observe for many years. There, no doubt, my system is revealed for what it is. It is a symbolic link (and verges almost on a pun) that I am establishing between ways of *holding one's tongue*, of which some are a matter of morality, others of rhetoric, still others of tactics: stoically to keep one's mouth shut against the whole world and say only what one wants to say, to rarefy one's words in order to increase the power of the few one writes or utters, to be silent as long as necessary in order to bring to a successful conclusion an action to which one has dedicated oneself. Based on feeling, as it is, this link would not be based on reason unless, speech being not merely an instrument of exchange, but truly the sacred mediator I would like it to be, all the various ways of compromising it were subject—like so many profanations—to one and the same unconditional reprobation. Yet things being what they are, and since my mystique of language reflects pious desires rather than the reality, my system, which, moreover, ought to be reinforced by numerous supporting reasons and a whole casuistry, looks to me like a bastard assemblage of rules for writing and rules for conduct, more circumstantial than it had seemed to me, since they are aimed—most of them—either at errors that, in order to express myself, here, in such a way as to be understood, I must not make, or at errors alien to literature but of which I ought to know I am incapable, in order not to have the impression of being a fraud as I write these pages, which continually claim total authenticity.

These rules, which, I might have believed, would, except for their number, be my Ten Commandments, have thus not stood this test: their transcription into commandments distinct enough to appear on Tables of the Law. But wasn't my folly the fact that I tried to fix into articles of catechism the bubbles of thought that issued from this desire which mounts into my head like an exhalation from all my fibers: not to do anything that would amount to taking licenses with one's own speech or with the speech of someone else, an insult (in both cases) to the quasi-divine nature that I attribute to language?

"Quasi-divine nature": a phrase that is timid, mitigated, because it results from a conflict between feeling and reason. To have the desire to write "divinity" (out of a need to valorize what the writer wields and, thus, to validate the choice I have made of this profession), not to give in to that desire (for, unless one believes in the Word as creator, it would be too absurd to deify language), to remove the difficulty by opting for a compromise: admitting as an adjective what one rejects as substantive, and, in addition, distancing oneself by means of the slight reservation of the *quasi*, with the notion of divinity that nevertheless—subject to this twofold precaution—one will not fail to suggest. What is more, it is in a sentence written in the first person and in the tone of a confession that this phrase appears, so that, in thus proposing something which, it is understood, concerns only me (as I am, with my tastes, my weaknesses, my idiosyncrasies), I commit myself less than by an assertion to which I would assign—whether explicitly or not—a general influence. No doubt this is an ill-disguised form of running with the hare and hunting with the hounds. If I were to dismiss it, I would leave behind me an equivocation awkward in itself and capable, besides, of becoming larger and more serious. Better, therefore, that instead of avoiding it I immediately clarify.

In the rigorous exercise of my profession—and in no other domain—I can attain my goal, which is, in sum, to believe in what I love and to love what I believe in: an old reflection that I can take up again today without changing anything essential about it, but that seems too general for me not to have to be more specific about it.

To love without illusions, to militate without joy—these things are commonplace, and one must conclude from this that it is far from being true that to love and to believe always go hand in hand. Only if one lives in accordance with one's vocation (exercising an activity that captivates one and seems valid), can these terms—whose duality affects the person who recognizes it like a division—be joined together indefinitely, at least within the limits of this activity. To say this seems like beating down an open door. Still, the very manner in which I noted this truism shows how very premature was any *Eureka!* To refer to the "rigorous" exercise of my profession is a restriction that would prove, in itself alone, that the thing is less simple than it seems here: there is no need to demand rigor if I must be overjoyed simply to follow this path I have chosen for myself. Yet that is still only a theoretical objection, and the real obstacle appears as soon as I try to see what my rigor will consist of. Will I practice this rigorousness in the domain of pure technique or will I extend it to what one may believe to be the duties of the writer, as a person whose works are the object of commerce, whether he wants that or not, and may possibly win him enough of an audience so that he has to take part openly in public affairs, he who does not disdain to offer himself to all and sundry through the channel of publication, when it is a matter of broadcasting his personal lucubrations? To limit oneself to technical rigor amounts to practicing art for art's sake, but the other rigor leads to social commitments that quickly take precedence over strictly literary concerns. Fleeing this twofold danger, I have tried to construct for myself a poetics and an ethics which overlap and are capable, without divergence, of guiding me in all areas. My aberration was that, into a system which, in order to satisfy me, had to plunge its roots into the heart of my elected activity but would have failed in its function had it not also covered with its branches a much vaster area, I introduced rules whose only logical relationship to literature was that they concerned situations in which the agent of literature is challenged. I was proceeding, in short, like a painter who forbids himself to be an exhibitionist or a voyeur with the pretext that his art has to do with sight and that one must not offend the latter either in another person or in oneself. No other way of justifying myself but the following: to postulate speech as an absolute against which no species of assault would be tolerated. Thus I would have needed more rigor than I possess, in order to thrust away my old demon and not indulge in hypostatizing language. Often, an unfortunate circumstance is enough to make one return to a vice of which one imagined one had long since been cured, and it is thus that I have come back—or very nearly—to the ideas of a period very early in my youth, when I believed I would find in nominalism the proof that the word is the ultimate reality, a decisive argument for a defense of poetry.

If I, a lost rambler trying to get out of his difficulty by reconstructing his route, review what was dictated to me by the idea of forging for myself a code at once literary and moral, I see that, as soon as it seemed to me that my construction was not holding together, I adopted these fallback positions: lacking a more direct connection between my writing taboos and my behavior taboos, to recognize that the latter respond in an interior way to a requirement of writing, since their observance must permit me to work without too bad a conscience; as the system failed to work smoothly even in its details, to make it more flexible by presenting it as the expression of a personal inclination, basically legitimate (I implied) but that I made the mistake of proposing as a sort of catechism. In both cases, in short, it was to myself that I referred, recognizing implicitly that what matters is the man, with the use he makes of language, and possibly what he thinks of it, and not the language itself. Thus, without realizing it, I effected the conversion that may permit me to emerge from the impasse.

Already, one point at least is gained: I had built up my system of prohibitions on a misuse of language, it has to be said. That writer's morality with which I wanted to equip myself, it seemed to me to go without saying, had to be based, since it was a morality of language, on the refusal to degrade the latter in any way at all. But it was in that that I was mistaken: how to deduce from language a specifically "professional" morality, since it is a thing belonging to everyone, and since in fact it is only an intermediary useful for all tasks, the worst as well as the best? Instead of trying to accommodate, I must therefore make a radical change in my point of view and seek within myself—I who make a profession not of merely using it, but of using it for special ends—what language refused me when I relied on it, as though, instrument of my profession, it should all on its own yield me my golden rule. It is from my own past that I have always wanted to isolate a lesson, applicable (if it comes in time) to the future that I hope to have available to me still. Thus a frank return to myself—who am the alpha and omega of the investigation—is better than this middle term: to theorize by referring, when I see that I have theorized badly, to particularities of this self, sometimes in order to legitimize myself, sometimes to make my mea culpa.

A journey back more than fifty years, in the direction of the North Sea—such is the immediate form that this return will take.

About ten years old, I am at Heist, not very far from Zeebrugge (for us, at that time, a simple dike closing a horizon, but which the shelling of the First World

War would extract from its geometry and its dark gray color), also not far from Blankenberge (whose name I liked in black and white) and from Knokke (that same Knokke-le-Zoute which is now so popular, the site, every year, of an international conference which, with the nobly disinterested tone of the talks that are held there, seems to me a sad poetry festival), small beaches both connected to ours by a light tramway running behind the line of dunes that half hid the sea. Either because of bad weather or because of an end-of-season plan (at the time when everyone was buckling their suitcases, getting together with other summer people, whom in principle one would see again or gratify with news, but whom in truth one would never meet again), we have gathered, my parents, my two brothers, perhaps my sister and her husband, in a parlor or bedroom in company with three other inhabitants of the hotel who are, it seems, Russians, but whom nothing, in their clothing any more than in their physiques, would lead one to regard as belonging to the Slavic world: the man, rather corpulent and generally wearing a cap (I do not know why, but we wondered afterward, in my family, whether he was not a spy or some other sort of suspicious personage with whom we had innocently compromised ourselves); the woman, also chubby, and who must have worn (unless this is an invention due to my too keen desire to restore substance to this trio so that it may help me to relive the whole of the episode in which it was involved) a woolen cap, perceptibly cylindrical and topped by a fat pompom; the little boy, probably so anodyne that I cannot recall—even imagine recalling—the least of his features, except for a sickly air ill-matched to the solid appearance of his father and mother. No doubt we have all had tea together and have now come to that great recourse of people who haven't much to say to one another: parlor games. Card tricks, I am almost sure, for it is a trick of this sort—probably one element of a series—that is the subject of the memory on account of which the afternoon in question retains for me, despite the gaps and the doubts about certain details, the same definition as, for example, the outings with heroic gallops that my brothers and I took on rented ponies or donkeys along the beach, largely exposed during the hours of low tide. Though I did not know any tricks and could only gape at those with which one or two of the grown-ups must already have regaled us, this was what I accomplished: they invited me to leave the room, where a deck of cards was spread out on a table, and, in my absence, someone touched one of those cards; after which they summoned me, I came back, and I indicated on which card a finger had been thus put, going perhaps even so far as to name the author of the gesture that had been hidden from me by the opacity of the wall. Hesitating a little, but without ever having to correct myself, I guessed right every time. As much as the success itself, what enchanted me was the power of intuition to which it testified, and, even though I was only an instrument in the hands of the game's organizer, I was proud of this talent, as though what had been involved was a marvelous mediumistic faculty possessed only by a few elite beings. If they had taught me to perform one of those tricks that astonish the shrewdest as well as the most naïve, I would certainly have been less happy than to reveal myself capable, without the slightest fakery, of an act that had to do with what I would call, in my vocabulary of today, double vision or magic. Mine was a proud euphoria, comparable to what is experienced by the gambler on a winning streak or the man in love discovering that each of his remarks, from moment to moment, renders more attentive and closer the erstwhile stranger: to feel oneself inhabited by luck. Thus I was horribly disappointed when someone told me, a little later, that it was only a farce, all of them having agreed not to touch any card and to declare, when I pointed to one, that it was truly that one which had been touched.

I have often thought of that little story, whose setting was a country which does not in the least number among those with which I am infatuated but is one to which I am attached, not only by the memory of my Aunt Claire but also by the fact that it is one of the first I visited and because I was still a small child when I went there. I have already said how it was to Belgium that I looked back in my mental aberration, as I emerged from the inhuman state into which the mastication of a gross quantity of poison had temporarily plunged me. Musing on what I had experienced at Heist-sur-Mer when I thought I possessed a gift that would have situated me singularly outside of the ordinary, I have long wondered to what extent a buoyancy of the same nature as that childish pride did not animate me when, having become a young man and not knowing very well what to make of my person, I wished *to be a poet*. I wanted this, of course, from a love of poetry and for the joy that I would derive from writing it, but—once past the phase of schoolboy poems in which I scarcely sought more than to turn to music my overflow of feelings—what I wanted most was to raise myself to the rank that I assigned to the person who uses language like a sort of Pythia proffering her oracles, a role as visionary which, to his benefit as well as his detriment, removes him from vulgar existence and makes him a sort of demigod (or quarter-god) living on a level to which ordinary mortals, prisoners of their norms, cannot have access. Certainly, my presumption was great, for it was, in fact, to the prerogatives of the genius that I aspired, and to a destiny quite exceptional which my own life hardly resembles, extremely comfortable and regular despite the dissatisfaction of which I complain. And it is perhaps just because I sensed how far this life was from being incandescent that I applied myself to exercising my craft as writer in a worthy way, imposing rules on myself as though, since no flame was devouring me, it was necessary that in my course of action, so lacking in magic, I should at least be someone who was correct, and, if possible, above all reproach. To treat language with as much deference as though it were in essence divine (something that, despite the nobility of the formulation, amounted to substituting for the sacred fire of the poet a strict professional conscientiousness), to situate myself politically "to the left" (last and pale avatar of my belief in the impossibility of being at once a poet and a respecter of the established order)—such were essentially those rules of which even the one having to do with politics remains quite platonic, since, without disobeying them, it was possible for me not to engage in any strictly militant activity and to confine myself to honest adoptions of positions (if necessary merely by apposing my signature to the bottom of manifestos or petitions). With that rule, a rule of *substance*, whereas my taboos were aimed rather at mistakes of *form*, I avoided the negativity of the latter only through a semblance of commitment. Not to move more than a stylite, using the excuse of purity—isn't that a consistent trait in me? And even if, from time to time, an action interrupts my inertia, isn't it to this that I always revert: to withdraw into oneself, to make it a point of honor not to allow oneself to be breached, to seek one's Good in a refusal of compromises, because in truth one loathes positive decisions and because one is too prudent to adopt the ostentatious economy which, to those errors accumulated in a debt [*passif*] that is possibly quite heavy, opposes a credit [*actif*] such that delinquencies and deviations will perhaps be no more than quaint errantry enlivening a graph that would otherwise be much too dry.

More defenseless than anyone if I write from another perspective, whatever the difficulties I may run up against in the composition of this book, I am inspired by my own desire to bring together, here, in a single compound what I love and what in myself I want others to love. Which is as much as to say that an incitement of a poetic order is held out to me here, and it is this that encourages me, rather than the austere desire to establish my beliefs once and for all. Certainly, by covering my eyes in the face of this reality I have complicated my task: whether a puritan reaction or a stroke of perversity which made me rebel against my true inclination, I have treated the love of poetry as merely one of my preferences, namely as one of the data of a problem that is different from that of poetry itself, the object of a choice that I made well before worrying about establishing its validity. A fundamental element, which poses many questions but cannot be *called into question*, and which there is no reason to bring up again except to find out what I mean when I speak of being a poet, an aspiration that has not ceased to be mine even when, from the point of view of literary genres recognized in schools, I have turned in an entirely different direction.

To write poems, to be a poet. A formulation of the same nature, though more general, *to write books, to be a writer* would be, in my opinion, only a pleonasm or a tautology and would lack the lively content of the terms that sum up my youthful ambition. The reason for this is that the writer is, for me, only the author of works in the domain of "belles lettres," whereas I have never believed that the poet could—like a builder of organs or pianos, characterized by the objects he makes artfully—be merely someone who makes pieces of poetry.

From an artisanal point of view, poetry may be regarded as nothing more than a genre, immediately defined by a certain mode of writing. Being "non-discursive" (in other words, giving precedence to a comprehension of the whole, or to creation, over analysis), it is situated far from aspects of the common good, and this remoteness is signaled from the outset by the fact that, instead of playing, here, the role of simple method of transcribing, language, here, seems strangely *distanced*: by the classical means that consists of subjection to a prosody and the employment of a select vocabulary, by the injection of images in strong doses (something of which the Romantics and their successors were past masters), by the invention of a rhetoric radically new, or, the reverse, by means of the extraordinary transparency that may be attained by someone who has faith in traditional rhetoric to the point of applying it with almost aberrant scruples (Raymond Roussel, for example, whose stylistic effort amounts to an almost maniacal concern for limpidity and for an impeccable use of the French language). But it seems impossible, unless it is a pitiful simulacrum, that such a distancing can be effected by someone who has not, himself, *been distanced* by some torment, some irony, or some other sign of profound disharmony, from everyday life, shaped by conventional ideas. To want to be a poet is thus not merely to want to find in language something other than what most people find in it, it is also to want that troubled and divided life that alone allows for poetry, which, unless one were fated to have such a life, one would exhaust oneself in vain trying to couch in writing. What is involved here, of course, is an impulsion that is unthinking, scarcely coherent, and not a choice based on solid foundations. Even at the time when I thought that unhappiness was my lot and my chosen sign, it was for salvation much more than for martyrdom that I was a candidate, since I reckoned that this unhappiness, once poured into the mold of lyricism, would lose a part, at least, of its harmfulness by being thus transfigured. And if, in order to reach my goals, I felt I was prepared to brave the setbacks of fate and desperate extremities, I did not know that such blows, when they come, do not have very much in common with the completely ideal image one may have formed of them. Experience and reflection, extended over many years, were necessary for me to discover, for example, that Rimbaud did not experience the adventure that excites us so: what he experienced *for himself* (and not according to the idea that others would later make of it for themselves), was quite simply a dog's life, as is shown by the complaints contained in his letters from Ethiopia. In the same way, what I may have believed about Nerval finding his solution in a sort of voluntary madness—a fusion of life and dream—seems puerile to me today: how great must have been his anguish, when, as a man who lived by his pen, he was prevented by his attacks from working, and, during the respites they left him, told their tale or exploited the material furnished by his delirium, at once in order to try to extricate himself from it and to produce the copy that was his livelihood!

To be a poet. If the person who is keen to be one, without false impersonation, must *live poetically* and reject the bourgeois mind—a slave to routine, and prosaic for that very reason—this break, more or less manifest and more or less radical, may assume many guises, of which the bohemian life, with its chaotic nature, is only one example among others and too neatly categorized, these days, not to be suspect, although, taken to an extreme, it may verge on heroism. To be a door open to dreams (little dramas the night has us perform in its own language) and to poetic events (those that, often very meager, have the special capacity of creating images even though they may not be the images of anything other than themselves); to have a life intense enough and singular enough so that it lends itself to legend (the profane form of myth); by taking the path of outright revolt or that of freedom of the passions, to commit oneself to the human direction in which poetry goes, as a means of freeing oneself from the rut—these are different but equally valid ways of "living poetically." Or rather *these would be*, for the great extent of this range of possibilities shows the inanity of a guiding principle so vague that there are scarcely any ways of being or acting at all removed from the norms that one cannot regard as responding to it, on one or another of these levels: of immediate feeling, of all-encompassing viewpoint, or of projection into the intellect. To put it another way: as living poetry, as possible themes for stories marked by a certain wonder, or as actions whose convergence with poetry will be recognized by means of a sort of calculation of trajectories. Or: in the present of lived experience, in the past of the story, or in the future of the great design of changing the present world into a world more liberated and open (a transmutation that, as such, is poetic despite the prosaicism of most of the acts necessary for this overthrow). Or, again: in the first person, that of the interested party, in the second person, that of his relations with others (including those who, later, will perhaps sympathize with the part he is playing), or in the third person, that of the assessment from which would emerge the ultimate meaning and effect of what he has done or written. Finally, counting by fours instead of by threes in order to widen the range: in the indicative of what is occurring, in the subjunctive of actions reverberating in a foreign memory, in the imperative of the control that one is so eager to exert (whether it is a matter of inspiring someone with love or of transforming something through political action), in the conditional of the last judgment which alone can say whether a certain life, as a whole, has really helped to loosen our fetters. Instructions, therefore, that one may understand in too many different ways for them not to have to be made more explicit (unless one admits that the true poet, a sort of complete athlete, must shine all in every sport). But in such a domain, isn't it absurd to search for what the guiding principle might be? To make plans to go hunting for poetry would be to deny its nature as an exceptional thing that would cease to be exceptional if its attainment, instead of occurring (beyond good or bad fortune) as an outstanding piece of luck, were an acquisition obtained through the application of a suitable strategy. To decide to live poetically (as one may choose to live as a debauchee or as a thrill-seeker rather than as the father of a family) is, in the end, nonsense and, in practice, almost inevitably leads to wretched affectations: to play the dreamer preserved from the daily course of things or Hamlet poised between reason and madness, to give the slight distortion that transforms into a miracle a relatively commonplace achievement, to nurture one's legend, to profess hatred or scorn for the bourgeois order even while one puts up with it, to flirt with revolution (while avoiding the total engagement that would lead one in fact to relegate poetry to the back burner), to misrepresent lukewarm or vulgar loves as passions lofty enough to be all-powerful, to behave like an absolute monster but to apply oneself most of all (it would seem) to being a damned nuisance to those close to one.

To write poems, to be a poet—this was in fact my youthful ambition. No question, at that time, of trying to determine what it was to *live poetically*. Everything was contained in my desire to write poems capable of being compared with those that I loved. Like the fabrication of gold for the alchemist philosopher (who saw it not so much as a laboratory success as the accomplishment of the work of perfection), to make such poems would have proved to me that, entrusted with a secret that was larger than any aesthetics or any morality, I was in the correct path, a state of grace as indefinable and, with greater reason, uncodifiable as that of saintliness. In surrealism, what attracted me immediately, and what I never renounced (even if I have rejected literarily the indulgence in automatism and even if I increasingly mistrust a wonder too easily manipulated), was the desire it manifested to find within poetry a total system: in a form suited to nourishing the imagination, the beautiful, the good, and the true, all muddled up together with the disrespect for conventional ideas and decoiffed of the capital letters that propose them as great fixed principles. A totality, of course, that I persist in pursuing, but going about it in the worst possible way. To try to explain clearly the poetic truth is to seek to circumscribe poetry by means of discourses, to enumerate its aspects with the excuse of better comprehending it, and, in fact, to allow it to escape, since its essence is of the order of all or nothing and cannot therefore obviously be retailed in small parts. Even if I were thus to succeed in having a poetics and a morality, I would not have won the game. I am aiming for a practical goal, and what I would need is—a thing alien to any theory—to feel I was firmly settled in the midst of poetry. On the level of intelligence and on the level of conduct, this implies (without its having to be demonstrated) that at least one is exempt, by nature and without even thinking of it, from such mundanities as stupid blunders and petty actions. Yet isn't it a stupid blunder that I turn myself into a speechifier and arguer in order to try to arrive at what poetry is, whereas this way of thinking, which bores me to death, even before anyone else, can only distance me from it? And isn't it a petty action to have chosen, instead of a dynamic method, a barrier of taboos behind which, negatively, I allow myself to take refuge: not to deceive in literature (a way of not having to invent anything and enabling me to answer criticism with the alibi of authenticity), not to lie where love is concerned (an argument for renouncing illicit loves), not to be a bourgeois conservative (a minimal law that permits one to fall back on "progressivism" if one knows one is not cut out to be a revolutionary).

That an unpromising system of prohibitions should have represented this morality that was supposed to be dictated to me by my profession—for this, I sought to justify myself by telling myself that, in attempting to establish a morality linked to poetry, one could proceed only through negation. Playing on this word, which enchanted me (not by its rather poor music but because of the almost mute irreducibility it evoked), I noted that negation goes hand in hand with the pursuit of poetry, since the latter aims to destroy—that is, to deny—limits. This was, of course, manipulating the language a good deal in order to give a positive value to what, in truth, did not escape its negative neutrality. But being a tool too abstract not to be good for all uses, this word, naked and null, which sucked me in like a void, lent itself in a parallel way to a less fraudulent plea: the fact is that to slap with a prohibition (to cross out or deny) a small number of things that the poetic process seems to exclude a priori amounts to subjecting it, by indicating what it *is not* instead of inserting it into a definition, to the slightest limit and, with that trifling restriction which protects it instead of hampering it, to giving it practically unlimited powers. Still, I did not understand that these prohibitions—severe, but apparently leaving open a wide field—sin by excess much more than by default, if one applies them without avoiding anything of what they entail: not to deceive (an order which, observed scrupulously by the author of confessions, would lead him to proscribe even the slenderest artifice of presentation or style), not to express oneself except in the most exact way, and as a consequence the flattest at the same time as the hardest to assimilate, to avoid diversions, to refrain from venturing over terrains about which one does not have a perfect knowledge, to abstain from all indiscreet intrusion, not to employ either terms that are too technical or locutions that are too clever, to reject all indulgence and all weakness—this is in practice to renounce the liberties, the impulses, and the leaps into the unknown which create the literary work, even to consign oneself to the negativity of absolute silence. Without denying some taboos that I believe are open to criticism in the letter but not in the spirit and that seem to me, at least, as strongly rooted in me as the very opposite inclination that attaches me to baroque eloquence, I am aware of how unreasonable it would be to erect them into a system and how loathsome—as is any sort of puritanism—to want to conform to them with a bigoted rigorousness. These taboos, or rules that appeared to me in the course of this work to be those from which I ought not to deviate lest I risk changing the meaning of the work—it seems to me that I appreciate them at their true value if I consider them, egotistically, to be the surest means, now, of adroitly extricating myself by fully exploiting my possibilities, and if I consider, from a broader point of view, that although they may fail to constitute the bases of an art of poetry, they represent, at least, something like the underlying structure of an *art of the autobiography*. But isn't it a fact that putting things back in their place in this way amounts to declaring that after so many years spent closely inspecting myself and describing myself, I have only managed at the very most to indicate the elementary rules that one must endeavor not to infringe when one devotes oneself to an enterprise of this sort? At the end of the enterprise, I discover the very rules that must preside over its conduct, and, far from having been broken, the circle thus remains closed. Except for a change which I can scarcely expect any longer, if my life may find its justification in the end, it will be in an area which, in the beginning, I did not consent to be mine, that of literature in the narrowest sense: after having wanted to be a poet (dreaming of living as a sort of mythological hero), I will have become the author of decent autobiographical essays that will perhaps play the role of defense and illustration of this literary genre. Unless I admit that (as I have often thought) the last word of any professional morality is *to do what I alone can do*, a principle as unexciting as that of the use of one's talents, the judicious implementation that I am effecting here is nothing but a declaration of defeat.

It was, anyway, laughable to make myself at once a rhetorician and a moralist, to wear myself out in endless subterfuges over vocabulary and grammar all while mustering myself to shape, with a few cuts of the scissors, the ethics that would fit me like a glove. Sterile pottering, from which I will have been deflected neither by my desire for clear-sightedness nor the program that was summed up in these few words, recorded, no doubt, when I began to understand that it would be better to climb down from my position: *To produce not a beautiful lie, but a truth that would be as beautiful as the most beautiful lie.* To try to achieve through writing something real that would be as fully satisfying as a marvelous fiction—I could have decided that this would be my rule, instead of persisting in my utopian quest. But even though the ambition might have remained lofty, to confine myself to this formula would have been to restrict my perspective too much, to content myself with authenticity (even simple anecdotal veracity) in the guise of truth, and, if my moral code was reduced to this demand alone, to toss the cargo overboard with the excuse of unballasting myself. Yet this note, a rapid indication of a possibility of finding my Good in literature itself, was a recall to order that should have prevented me from losing from sight the fact that in this art as in the other arts, whatever the goal pursued, nothing supreme could exist that was not made, I will not say "as though it were child's play" or even "as though it were play," but at least without boredom. Not that boredom, a state of lack from which a spark may leap and a frequent theme of poetic reverie, is too poor a terrain, but because a work (gentle or violent, serious or light) will be a very morose celebration if its organizer is bored to death when he is at work. However, in the complete failure that I am attempting to contain, leaving no stone unturned and searching among the reflections that I have accumulated for the one that would hold sufficiently firm upon examination to offer me a way out, the fact is that I am getting bored. And that is enough to show me how far, wandering in the labyrinth of too hesitant and laborious an account, I have strayed from beauty without managing, where truth is concerned, much more than this negative success: to reject several false ideas that I had thoughtlessly accepted as I went along.

A sulky pessimism, often mutating into the serenity of a comfortably ensconced disabusement, has replaced the harsher pessimism in which, formerly, it seemed to me I was endlessly struggling with myself. I believe, however, that I have not profited from the change, for that youthful pessimism, whose somber but rich colors endowed the composition of an entire imagery, enlivened me rather than paralyzing me. Inseparable from the desire to be a poet, it was (if one may put it this way) a lyrical pessimism or at least one that sought to be lyrical, whereas the pessimism of today, diluted in bourgeoisification and rendered insipid by the almost constant use of a tranquilizing drug, cannot be transfigured but is like an organic disease that one edulcorates with palliatives. Dilution, dissolution, dispersion such that my former pessimism, when I try to describe it, eludes my grasp as though I were wrapped in a fog even more difficult to pierce than the thickness of time, and as though my very wish to bring the past back to life rested on a foundation of mist. Nevertheless, within a sleep haunted by a whole evening's disappointing work, it seemed to me, during one of these past nights, that the contact was renewed. Momentarily cleared, the horizon has once again been obstructed, but the image by which I was obsessed for a part of that night survives my disillusionment, and I think that, despite its apparent lack of meaning, it speaks more clearly than the sentences I tried turn and turn about before the inglorious retirement to bed to which, abandoning any further resistance, I had resigned myself.

Young, both of them, a man and a woman appeared to me standing and seen from slightly below, which reminded me of the way in which characters are shown in the close-ups of one of the best-known works of the silent cinema, Dreyer's *Jeanne d'Arc*. Face to face, and so close together that they could have touched each other just by reaching out their arms a little, they seemed to me frozen in a pathetic immobility whereas, in truth, moved by an impetus outside themselves, they were turning rapidly on themselves, with a tendency to rise as though they were propelled by a helical movement from which, in the end, no flight resulted. The scene—or rather the tableau, since, except for this spinning, nothing happened—was so unlocalized that it is only when I endeavor to see it again without neglecting any detail that I situate these two beings either in a closed and empty place or in a conventionally limited space (the rectangle determined by the frame of a painting or, another rectangle, a cinematic screen). Concerning the man, as is logical, I have retained scarcely more than the indistinct whirl engendered by his rotation. But I can, on the other hand, draw an approximate portrait of the woman, certainly because it was at her that my interest was directed and because afterward the desire did not leave me to recapture that figure whose features, theoretically, should have been blurred by the rapidity of her gyration. Like the robe of a saint in a color-print with coloring derived from a simplistic symbolic system, she was wrapped in a long garment of a dull red, and I have no doubt that this reddish glow was a concrete manifestation of the "somber but rich colors" to which, in order to characterize my former pessimism, I alluded, reluctantly (for it enraged me not to be able to go beyond that too vague description). Her graceful, but not gracile, body was robust and fleshy. Her quite smooth black hair was gathered at the nape of her neck, and her face—a lovely, serious face, full and pale, presented in profile—

gazed upward. As I reconstruct it, reviving and combining brief snapshots made and remade in sleep or half-sleep, this figure, part tragic and part voluptuous, of martyr or lover, becomes that of a girl of the southern seas in loincloth or sari and, in order to complete my detailing, I would be tempted to summon up another image gleaned from the world at once perceptible and impalpable suggested by film: the great sunburnt islander played, I believe, by an Arab actress in the film *Outcast of the Islands*, taken from the novel by Conrad and shown in Paris shortly after the last world war.

The red note that dominated in this vision, where a tension independent of all intrigue expressed love and death, ought to invade me like wine. But what can I do? Already this tint, whose subdued luster only emphasized more fully the protruding bottom and arched spine that it enveloped, has cooled instead of intensifying, since, putting too much effort into bringing it out of its darkness to incorporate it in my interior landscape, I have set it beside other reds, sometimes deep, sometimes worn or washed out, that I keep in my memory: the color of lambrusco, a sparkling wine whose taste of dead leaves I love and which I cannot separate from the largest of the towns in which I have drunk it, the old and lively Bologna, where the struggles between factions have calmed down but whose faded red houses and arcaded streets, after the day's turmoil, become at night so muffled and silent that one would believe the only creature awake there is the hired assassin hidden in one of the cells which your footstep will expose; the tones, warm but fragmented and attenuated, of the ruins of baths or other constructions of the Roman era of bricks baked and baked again by the sun; the oxblood coating of the walls which, at the center of Peking, still surround the old Imperial City; the pompous decor of so many halls where, watching performances of operas, I crammed into myself a sad plenitude which my present-day pessimism, not even black but smoky gray, is no longer capable of attaining, except by chance and by forcing myself a little.

A ruby whose sparkle has dimmed, which does not exist even in the half-reality of a dream but only on the piece of paper where my writing contorts without managing to make itself anything other than writing—this is what I have obtained by confronting the red of the sari, the loincloth, or the robe with these tourist's or dilettante's memories. And I arrive at nothing more if I appeal, without changing the region of the specter, to other memories less tainted with aestheticism: the close view, to which will be added, dizzyingly, the touch, of the brown verging more or less on garnet offered by, in certain women, the two small and precious particles of the female body which are the nipples augmented by their aureoles; appearing at the distance of a promise or a regret, the palpitating flame, almost orange-colored and of a fruity succulence, which, in the vicinity of the great petroleum installations, I have often observed with a sharp sensation of greed and distress, as though the very image of life had suddenly been offered to me in a summary form that was immediately decipherable.

Still, this weakened color nonetheless has a meaning, which new terms of comparison will perhaps help to specify: the nuances of autumn and of sunsets, whose sumptuousness and melancholy are too well known for there to be any need to insist upon them; situated very far away in my youth and, it seems, at the point where the rue La Fontaine meets the avenue Mozart, the rather old and rather low corner house, neither private home nor "rental property" nor shop with living quarters above, and which, apparently abandoned, owed a part of its mystery to the slightly dirty or tired red verging almost on pink with which it was painted, as might have been, symbolically, a butcher's shop; in the domain of music, the rumblings of very deep and slightly raspy brasses which, since the Romantic era, can be heard sometimes in the orchestral subbasement of operas and which seem to express a heavy menace (something powerful that is still only brooding but will be unleashed); in that of geography, the volcanic regions and the torrid heat of countries from which one brings back "fevers."

When I accumulate these reference points, what is most important is not the desire to situate within the range of the senses the imaginary perception that I would like to secure. Close to crimson, the deep red of lambrusco corresponds fairly well to the shade that I have called "dull red" so as to contrast it to the harsh and vulgar reds, those of official honors and prize books, or the red, equally orpheonesque, of the traditional Mephisto. What need, therefore, to stray from the lambrusco to find other reds of which many (the refinery flame, for example, or ancient brick, even if illuminated by a recollection of Pompeian red) differ markedly from the one I am claiming to identify? No doubt their appearance counts less than what they are covering: the value of a certain past emotion, expressed by one of these varieties of red (or by an equivalent sound) but whose analogy with the color of the sari, itself inseparable from the tableau it highlighted, is a matter of feeling rather than a matter of palette. And how can I not see that I am establishing these comparisons in order to insert here and there certain words or pairs of words the way one secretly slips, into a conversation whose circuitous paths will put someone more or less off the scent, the phrase that one would not dare utter straight out but which, from the beginning of a conversation started precisely for this reason, one had resolved to pronounce?

"Sad plenitude" (a term echoed by "greed and distress," "sumptuousness and melancholy," which are no more than almost unchanged reminders of its ambiguity), "mystery," "heavy menace," and finally resolved into the plural "fever" of the tropics, these two words that I burned to write while describing the eminently sensitive peaks of the double dome of the female chest: "tender burn"— interpreted auspiciously as the fires of love and inauspiciously as that flame whose grasp could only reduce us to ashes—compose the message that I extract from my words, by treating them as the given text whose true content is revealed by a grid with exactly the right cutouts isolating some small fragments of them. But if, passing my vision through a sieve at the risk of ransacking everything, I had analyzed the whole of the scene instead of collecting from it only that equivocal red, I would have read almost the same message, without having to recompose it after dispersing it: the freighted destiny of two beings united but inexorably separated; the avidity and distress attested by their movement and its paradoxical fixity (the spinning of each around the immutable axis of which they were prisoner and the constant suppression of their rise along the two verticals); the mystery hovering over these tall, melancholy figures, the more visibly distracted of whom attained a plenary beauty; the ardor impelling the tender and unfortunate form who was connected by delicate ramifications to, on the one hand, the virgin warrior burning with hope and destined for the pyre, on the other that daughter of the Islands in whom were incarnated faraway places charged with sensuality, heat, and fever.

Inventorying a dream or paying particular attention to one of its details (that red, which, I noticed after a strange delay, is the same red as that of one of my pairs of pajamas, so that on the night when this color appeared to me I had, if not on my skin, at least in the piece of furniture in which my linen is kept the reference that I went so far to look for), I arrive at more or less similar terms, whether because the detail and the whole have, in fact, conveyed this same message, or because I attach such value to these notions that I contrive at every opportunity to bring them into play or that, in speaking of anything whatsoever which has rekindled the too often dormant fire I carry within me, I unfailingly end up coming to them, as though they represented the ultimate expressible truth regarding those emotions without which I feel I live at an animal level.

If, however, I cut short the reading of this dream and return in my thoughts to the period when I mistook for pessimism a spirit of refusal which, in fact, instead of restraining me, pushed me like a goad, I note—and I would really like to be able to laugh about it—that a simple word of two syllables had at that time allowed me to label this state and to say at least as much about it as I did with all the turns of phrase I used afterward each time I ventured to approach what is, for me, the central core: the word *fury*, exactly in harmony with the shade of red I have so laboriously tried to define. This word, in which, it seemed to me, there came together anger at having been born mingled with a rage (or furious desire) to live, a revolt against society (responsible for bringing me into the world, and the only circle in this world able to hear itself judging), a poetic delirium (or "fury" comparable to Orestes' at the hands of his Furies)—I had promoted its importance, playing somewhat fraudulently upon its semantic elasticity, as a term appropriate for designating what had to be regarded as the source of the surrealist spirit, one day when, in the Café des Deux Magots (in no way Chinese except for the discreet presiding of two large magots of wood or painted plaster installed on consoles), a few of my companions and I had come together in a sort of commission charged with specifying the relationship between this pillar of fire and that pillar of cloud which were guiding our march toward the Promised Land of surrealism and revolution.

But here my effort breaks off . . . What is this fury that marries horror and greed, resentment and effusion, unbridled lyricism and the desire to establish other customs? Even if it was more than an imaginary point taken abstractly as the center of the tumult of feelings and ideas that I wanted to connect to a single source, my noting the radical ambiguity of this fury—today quite tepid, and whose red has flaked off—will not be the means of my penetrating its core. It is a fact: there exist these moments which seem to me complete, and the latest of them was certainly the one in which, drunkenness having intensified my pain instead of attenuating it, I allowed my old sad fury to rise against me and experienced, in an astonishingly abbreviated form, what may infuse the ample aria sung by a soprano whose throat rhythmically swells, racked by sobs of melody. I loved (since I was capable of dying of it); I rebelled (rejecting, along with my life, a system that had too many impediments); I thumbed my nose at the various degradations caused by aging; deciding on my destiny and thus gaining height, I rose with one leap all the way up to that level from which all things appear gathered in a vast panorama, moving as is, always—in the picture book of common reality—a great urban or seaport setting reduced by distance to the size of a beehive or anthill: New York, which I passed through so quickly that I wanted at the very least to embrace it with a single glance and was taken, at my request, to one of its principal skyscrapers by the beautiful Valkyrie who was piloting me that morning; Barcelona, viewed from the top of Mount Tibidabo (*To thee I will give . . .* , the Tempter had said to the Son of God, showing him all the wealth of the world spread out before them); Algiers, which one can see deployed in a fan facing the sea; Genoa, built like an amphitheater and of which one will recall (contemplating it from the esplanade to which the funicular leads) the tangle of stairways and streets overlapping other streets, tunnels, elevators, modern office buildings, churches and palaces (in Baroque style or in Monte Carlo style, as in the Via del XX Settembre, with grandiose arcades), and, at the very lowest point, the, in fact, lowest income neighborhoods, where the disturbing notice *off limits*, affixed here and there during the American occupation, alternated with the sculpted stone Madonnas sanctifying street corners; the port of Copenhagen when one eats on the top floor of the Kodan Hotel (as I did, one evening, during the last stopover on my return from China); more recently, Tokyo, of which I will not forget the view, very partial but immense, that I had of it from our room, whence one's gaze, ignoring the tall buildings at the edge of the landscape on the left side, fell upon a public garden formerly included in the Imperial City, then, after shifting to the right and crossing a broad rectilinear avenue that ran all the way to the Tokyo Tower (thinner than the Eiffel Tower, and higher, though this is difficult to imagine, by some ten meters), a spacious avenue whose intense traffic seemed to us strangely silent because of the isolation created by the double window of the air-conditioned room where the norm was that one lived as though in an airtight chamber, upon one of the guard buildings of the palace (whose roof had four ridges raised at their extremities) overlooking the wall of dry stones arranged according to what in Greek architecture would be called, I think, the "Pelasgic system," that assemblage of blackish blocks carefully squared and adjusted, itself overhanging the great moat where swans navigated before our eyes as though to accentuate the impression of overflowing activity conducted in a spectral silence.

This fury, which I mistook for the original motivation, thus escapes my grasp and I am, as I confront it, like a theologian reduced to preparing a statement about the divine mysteries without trying to penetrate them, or—closer to my professional area—like a critic before a work that is valuable to the extent that, in fact, it eludes criteria: he may note that it contains something not seen or heard before, may indicate the *how* and if need be the *why*, but to analyze it like a schoolchild's exercise that must be marked could only deflect him from what is most important. What matters, however, is not so much to know whether I was clarifying or only qualifying when I invoked this fury as the source of all that which, in various forms, seemed to me to be poetry. What counts above all else is the determination that moved me—and that still moves me—to be authentically that particular type of writer evoked by the name (too much compromised) of "poet," the unconditional desire implying that beyond ethical or aesthetic imperatives the crucial act is, for me, this: to project myself into the *off limits* area where written language will be my thought reified and myself wrested from the vicissitudes of life by a death that gives me the highest intelligence of it, a bridge thrown across the void that encloses me as though within an island, the place, also, in which my own time is abolished (all partitions being struck down between the time I am writing about, the time in which I write, and the time of the person who reads me). It is, without any doubt, a very obscure directive that I may find in this! I will nevertheless retain the idea that to use language thus, a legacy of men of an older time that allows me to be understood by men of today and perhaps also those of later on, is an activity in which I am not the only actor, so that it obliges me to take into account another person. To admit this is both not much and a great deal: in theory a great deal, since it is to recognize that my vocation itself forbids me to behave as though I were the only one who existed; in practice almost nothing, for it indicates to me neither how I ought to act toward others, nor how many of them I must take into consideration (all, or only those with whom I am joined by the community of language). But if the act that is for me also "crucial" because in it I wear myself to a shadow and tear myself apart has the sense of an excess and of a recourse to the invisible presence of those others without whom I would not be able to speak and would not even have to speak, the result of this is that I would be betraying myself just as much by limiting the field of that movement as by not doing anything so that the other person (no matter which other person) might be treated as my equal. Drawn from words that are not mine, and addressed to whatever person will accept them, doesn't poetry—fundamentally, a blind expansion beyond my frontiers—tie me to the indiscriminate partner who is an *other* in relation to me, but my kind at the level of the species?

IV

And so, showing that by the practice of poetry one postulates the other as one's equal, I return to the truth that I had derived in the beginning: to learn that one does not say . . . *reusement* but *heureusement* is to learn that language has two faces, one turned toward the inside, the other toward the outside, and when—discovering altruism at the end of two or three volumes devoted to my own person—I declare that a poet cannot dissociate himself from the fate of his fellow man, it is from this twofold nature that I am drawing my argument, as if the most important element had already been included in my old discovery.

And so, here I am, clearly back at my starting point. The circle being a symbol of perfection, I could be proud of having thus looped the loop. But I note with scorn, lassitude, and disgust that after many years spent looking for a way out, I am managing only to deduce the consequences, purely logical and almost without effect, of what I have known from the beginning. For not one of these problems has been resolved: do I emerge from myself if I address, in fact, a tiny fraction who are already more or less persuaded? Opening my mouth to make myself heard, am I not obligated to substitute such words as *heureusement* for my too singular or abrupt words such as . . . *reusement*? Am I justified in saying that I write in order to "communicate," whereas (laziness, difficulty in expressing myself, horror of taking up the pen if I have nothing precise to express) I sometimes do not answer letters even when they seem to indicate that I have obtained my objective? Am I doing a great deal or almost nothing for others when, talking about myself as though about someone who could be another, I help those less sure of themselves to know themselves a little better? Does all free and sincere poetry, even the most detached, contribute to the advent of an age of freedom and truth? If the very nature of poetry requires me to strive to see that everyone should be unanimously recognized, shouldn't this choice that I am making be my primary theme? Another eloquent speaker, doesn't the popular advocate go farther than the poet and the Don Juan, since his role is to move, not in order to arouse in another a completely inner flame, but in order to urge those whom he has touched toward a goal with a broad scope? If justice must be done, and if revolution is the sole means to it, can I invoke it without uttering a firmly established opinion concerning the quarrels that divide the revolutionary camp? Fearing violence against myself, do I have a right to accept the fact that revolution uses violence against others, and often without moderation since it goes so far as to strike out against its first architects?

And so, disappointed, dismayed to see that I still have so much on my plate and stuffed too full to run under that impetus that would lead me to get lost in the maze of demonstrations, I confine myself to the little I have gained, this slender certainty at which I have arrived and which remains just as diaphanous when I situate it in relation to a few of the illustrated reference points that I have placed here and there, but to which I do not have the heart to return, except by taking them up again from memory: my furious attachment to the magic that sometimes seems to effect a fusion of the *over-there* and the *right-here* does not permit me to reject the arid Peking way, even though misfortunes like that of the bird fallen from the nest may be thorns that no horticulture can eliminate and even though I am spontaneously inclined toward the shadows, the lights, and the baroque folds of the Kumasi way, which is colored by an intimate flush and not a sharp red.

And so I am giving in, with the relief of avoiding the enormous consumption I would have to make, still, of sapless words, if I tackled problems that, scarcely broached, allowed other problems to appear behind them: the "therefore," "yet," "besides," "but," "nevertheless" that are instruments of connection, the "if," "because," "since," or "given that" with which one articulates an argument, the "however," "almost," "quasi," "hardly," "at least," and other convenient means of arranging for oneself a little margin in order not to lay oneself too open.

And so there is no question of my resuming on any new bases my search for a golden rule. Rather than elaborating an art of poetry and a morality, isn't the important thing to be, to the entire extent that one can, with the means at one's disposal, that hybrid of sage and madman, of truth-sayer and trickster that is called a poet, and, as for one's attitude toward others, to conduct oneself with as little narrowness and pettiness as one is equipped to do? No doubt I will even have to succeed, one day, in entirely persuading myself of it: in the game I am playing, even though one ends by winning or losing, there is no rule, and I will win or lose without any martingale permitting me to force chance and without my even knowing whether I am winning or not.

And so, after having given myself the luxury of describing, about halfway through these pages, how I committed suicide (an episode that was perfectly romantic), then having returned to the subject, and having finally decided to stop musing about it, there is nothing more for me to do but to take my bows. This histrion's gesture: it was when—back in harness—I calculated how odd it would be calmly to put a final period to the work that had been interrupted by that interlude, that I had the idea of it; this, the kind of gesture that ought to be able to accompany the exit that I would make, a half-posthumous exit calling for a slightly spectral feature of the sort that concludes the comedy of the German Romantic Grabbe, at the end of which Grabbe himself, having arisen from the depths of a forest, knocks at the door of the room where his characters are and *enters with a lighted lantern*. As for me, I have just extinguished rather than lit my lantern, at the end of a long soliloquy and not of a comedy for several characters. This is why, if hamletism is called for here, the fall of the curtain cannot be other than this one: splitting the page in order to bow, the author appears, his glasses on his nose and his Parker in his hand.

And so, let's say I am fictively performing this enactment of the scene and that it is taking the place of a final period. It remains true — irony of ironies — that I can certainly, after a failed suicide, brave the ridicule of another false exit and, having taken my leave, resume speaking in order to give a significant detail about what my state of mind was even when I was not yet all the way back from China. To review so many things before talking about a stroll that was marked not by any notable event, but by a simple impression, will have been useful for the following: to allow the ripening and ramification of the anecdote whose effect I had not immediately evaluated, but that explains, through a motive much more radical than those whose involvement I alleged, my ambivalent feelings about a country which, I had thought when I was still there, could, if the necessity arose, become mine.

I had arrived in Copenhagen in the afternoon, on a Finnish airplane, and I was going to visit the city with two of my friends from the delegation, a man and a woman. The first was a painter older than I by a few years, who has undertaken to restore its proper qualities to the profession of tapestry making, which has become an art of copying; the second was a literary woman whose husband, a writer I had met several times before the last war, was killed in a unit of the maquis, as though his humanist faith in democracy and the very high importance he attached to the athletic disciplines had led him quite naturally to heroism. The goal of the excursion was to see, in a hotel whose name he had forgotten, a tapestry that was the work of my friend, the only one of us who knew the Danish capital, whose charm lies in what is modern as well as what is old and quaint about this marine city, in which there live together without discord (as I would discover later) the life-size statue of the Little Mermaid from the Andersen tale, placed directly on a bank of rocks, sailors' clubs and fishermen's bars, shops rich in imported articles, grand royal buildings, and the model of industrial architecture which is the Tuborg brewery. Our destination, in fact, was scarcely more than a pretext, for hardly had we gone out before we stopped in a bar to drink some aquavit. I am certain that one would not really be able to have any insight into any city or region whatsoever if one did not taste the drink special to it. For instance, in Rome, Frascati wine, which one can describe as easy, as one will say of a tenor that he has an easy voice, and in Guadeloupe punch (vanilla punch especially), whose aroma, at once sweet, spicy, and alcoholic, expresses, it would seem, the complexity of the Antilles, a spot in the world where such diverse races and cultures have mingled. It is no different with aquavit, of which a subsequent trip to Scandinavia finally demonstrated to me its character, in my opinion, eminently "Nordic" (a fragrant dryness comparable to the light in these countries, often very fine at the same time as very hard, and the scale of colors, delicate and neat in general effect, that their landscapes may present). In this quite nice-looking bar, which aimed to captivate the lover of exoticism with its wall decorative mural portraying a comic-opera Mexico, seated on the classic high stools and having before us the little glasses filled with alcohol so transparent as to be almost invisible, we immediately felt very good. The clientele was exclusively male, and—to judge from its behavior, perhaps deceptive, it is true—it did not in the least deplore the fact that besides my friend from the delegation there were no other female human beings except two physically unattractive middle-aged persons installed in a corner; dressed like governesses or schoolteachers for families of the most bourgeois and puritan sort, they were playing, one on the piano, the other on the double bass, tunes from the era of *Le Boeuf sur le Toit* and singing, now and then, through a megaphone. Delighted by this unexpected reminder of our beautiful 1920s, we continued on our way in the highest of spirits, walking somewhat at random through the shopping streets and looking at the display windows. After two or three stops, each watered by an aquavit (a liqueur so colorless and so light that it seems that, even if one were to drink it in receptacles much larger than the actual thimbles in which it is customary to serve it, it would not affect the organism at all and would only give rise to a cheerful lucidity), we ended by finding the hotel with the tapestry. We exchanged a few friendly words with the correct, smiling, and rather stout gentleman who was its manager, and, of course, we consumed a final small glass. Happy about this expedition, which had been truly relaxing after the exciting but busy weeks we had spent in China, we went back to rejoin our comrades. Then, as it was time for dinner, our small group set off in quest of another hotel known to one of my two companions of that afternoon; he recalled that there was, on one of its highest stories, a restaurant where we could eat excellent fish while enjoying the spectacle of the ships at the quay. After a meal that was very pleasant (even though one dish of especially succulent fish was not available that evening), I returned on foot with one of the other diners for a last stroll. In my daily notebook, I carefully noted the name of the hotel so opportunely situated: Kodan, which I presume is a contraction of "Kopenhagen" and "Danmarck." This story, which is not even a story, would be too pointless to be worth reporting, if it were not precisely from that pointlessness that it derives its meaning.

A bar with a clientele as prosaically sophisticated as its decor. An outmoded music: fashionable in its time (that of my youth) but with quite a bit of time having accumulated since that time; neither popular enough to seem ageless, nor imposing enough to withstand aging; light music, corresponding to a quickly forgotten phase of a city-life luxury which, had it been less changeable, would not really have been that. Shops in one of which were displayed travel lap robes whose lovely checked patterns made one dream of trips to be taken as an indolent tourist. A restaurant exactly appropriate to people who are making a stopover: seafood and the spectacle of a quay active from morning to night. Ships that were very clean, illuminated, and no doubt about to depart. For a touch of the picturesque, girlie music halls (along with one or two tattoo parlors pointed out by my companion of the afternoon, and which are in the same street, but which I did not find this time). In other words, a bar that was a caricature but also a reminder of places that, for a long time, I had not been able to leave without wishing to return to them, and which, places where people were just passing through and home ports in which strangers and regular customers stood side by side, must be numbered—whether diurnal or nocturnal, made for drinking or for dancing, or filling all functions at once—among the great symbols of our civilization of solitary people who rub elbows; a city more cramped than Algiers, Barcelona, Genoa, London, and others where I am enchanted to feel a little lost, but a city whose Hanseatic appearance was enough to illustrate that word with its smell of merchandise that has come from far off and in which there echoes in a quiet way a universal sound, *emporium,* that comes to me when, instead of agglomerations so large that their pattern vanishes, I remember the very real Kumasi of the Ashanti country, encircling a marketplace in which there thronged a crowd of Africans of very diverse origins, drawn as much by the brilliance of the fabrics sold on that esplanade as by the more secret joys of the satellite neighborhoods. In Copenhagen, with capitalism in its commercial aspects (internal traffic and long-range commerce that engenders a cosmopolitanism expressed as much by fashions in clothing as by the disposition of places intended for leisure), I had rediscovered my folklore, composed in large part of all that luxury, which I love without believing in it and which I love perhaps all the more because I know how fragile and frivolous it is (whence my multifaceted pleasure in contact with false luxuries more fragile and frivolous even than true luxuries, since being only junk, they do not have even the semblance of seriousness of a successful thing in a completely vain area). Having just barely left Peking (and almost in tears, exchanging goodbyes with those Chinese friends who would still think of me from time to time, I was sure, without saying to myself at that moment what I would say to myself later, namely, that if they did, it would certainly be as one member, among others, of a delegation and not deliberately of me in particular), I was quite happy to plunge once again into the questionably iridescent waters that I recognized as my nourishing milieu.

Certainly, I had faith in the new China and I was awestruck by the old China, or rather—for to express myself thus gives the impression that there existed for me two Chinas—I saw in China a country that was not only, because of its past, a rich theme for reverie, but also, because of its present, allowed for a confident hope. About Black Africa I had built a myth even before going there, and I had remained attached to that sentimental construction to such a degree that, on the day on which, in the rail car that was taking me back to Le Havre, I was overcome by such great anguish, it was when I thought that even this myth would henceforth be powerless to excite me that I believed I had reached my lowest point. With China, nothing like that: throughout my entire stay, I had been able to restrain my imagination even as I was waxing enthusiastic, and I was observing, not in order to rediscover what I had already invested in the object I was contemplating, but simply in order to try to judge; thus the bond that I thought I had formed with at least some people from there seemed to me a concrete bond of comradeship, a bond that was actively valid, in relation to an immense work in progress, and not as the seal of a unilaterally imagined fraternization. Now, in Copenhagen, direct experience had shown me that if I was at home somewhere, it could be only in a city belonging to the capitalist world and in the presence of what such cities offer that is least useful to communities. That this sparkling foam appears on the surface of an indefensible state of things I was convinced, and communist China remained for me a definite value. But the fact was evident: I loved that foam. Between feeling and idea a shocking divergence appeared, so that I was soon prevented from acting, since I could hardly tolerate such a contradiction, not wanting hypocritically to make light of it, and not knowing—I who am incapable of writing on the basis of ideas that are only ideas—how to discuss this China, too exciting for me not to be compelled to speak of it at length and about which, after a discovery relating to myself alone, I did not have to change my judgment, but which I had realized was situated outside my chosen sphere. Not without employing some ruses, I passed beyond this difficulty, but I never did mend what had come apart in Denmark, when China suddenly slipped to the periphery, however strongly it might still continue to occupy me.

Invitations to go on trips (from the ships to the travel lap robes); places for people without roots or who are not at home except outside their homes; melodies which — inciting one to pleasure, to love, or explicitly expressing a Negro yearning — filled me in earlier days with diffuse desires, and which, in the ridiculous form in which I heard them again, led me to smile at the same time that they imbued me with homesickness for the period in which they had stoked these desires in me. What I had perceived during this stopover, which was still unforeseen even that morning and had no preestablished program (for we had at first expected to return by way of Sweden), was of course certain aspects of the modern West, but aspects that struck me as ironic allusions to the vanity of things: whether you are here or there, and in whatever way you occupy yourself killing time, time which laughs at you while waiting to kill you, you will always play the fool. If they affected me so, it is because they gratified in me, the casual stroller, a taste for futility too obvious to deceive and acted like a sort of homeopathic drug, palliating what seems to be my uneasiness as a man, and not only as a Westerner, by making my awareness of it most acute.

When one gives, one does not take back. But: "Drive away one's natural disposition, and it will come galloping back!" [What's bred in the bone will come out in the flesh.] Thus one can never be sure of anything: the left hand will take back what the right hand has given, one burns what one has adored, one adores what one has burned, after the rain comes the fair weather, one who laughs on Friday will weep on Sunday. A seesaw motion, governing my flights up and my tumbles down, my marches out and marches back, my false departures and false exits: I, the other; inside, outside; poetry, morality; preferences and obsessions, opinions and duties. A pendular movement, to which is added another back-and-forth motion, so routine that I barely think of talking about it: from my office in the Musée de l'Homme to my long table of bare wood at 53 *bis* quai des Grands-Augustins; from a work on ethnography (the history, not yet finished, of the plastic arts in Black Africa) to this volume 3 of the book in which I am trying to express what touches me the most intimately, so that I have to go — a change of task connected to the change of locale — from a kind of writing whose aim is to give an objective account of a mass of facts especially difficult to organize because they concern me very distantly, to an opposite kind which in truth I am not managing to prevent completely from being contaminated by the first, this style constantly hampered by my fear of being caught in the act of omitting or mistaking something; from a work carried out under contract and as part of my official job as researcher, as it is also part of my earlier commitment to those who once were colonized peoples, to a freer work in which what I seek to bring together—a decision I can revoke at any moment—is myself and my own attitude toward what is around me. This is the most troubling division just at present, but not the only one, for my life is subject to many other acts of balancing, on all sorts of levels and conforming to various different rhythms: hours of work and hours of relaxation (reading to the little extent that I can, meeting a few people I like very much, sometimes going to the theater); waking and sleeping, with, between the two, the gray area of dream, though only when I am lucky; mornings often mired (at least at the start) in bad ruminations and evenings generally more unconstrained; working days and country weekends during which, not always for my own good, I have ample leisure to think only about my personal research; the hectic time of my life in Paris and the time, in principle more open, of vacations and trips; beyond all this, the ascendant phases and the depressive phases which (without my being immediately warned) have their correlations in what I write here, and, certainly, explain in part the alternation of my feelings of ardor and my feelings of remorse. Segments of years, months, weeks, or simply days, stretches of time which, most of them, are also stretches of mood affecting my very being and consigning it to instability, whence my fear of being an erratic instrument for weighing almost equal to the scales from whose beam a pleasant Antillean woman helped me to suspend a heteroclite heap of objects, during a dream of which the beginning had as its setting the mountain and the end a house flanked by a garden. But, if *the best is the enemy of the good*, isn't nitpicking, which is what I am doing, the thing that prevents me most surely from achieving a fair weight?

> *De vos jardins fleuris fermez les portes,*
> *Les myrtes sont flétris, les roses mortes!*

> Of your flow'ring gardens, the gates now close,
> The myrtle is withered, and dead the rose!

I had sung this song at the farewell dinner we gave our Peking friends, and, if I sang this one, it was for several reasons. First of all, the limited repertory I have available to me is of the most undependable kind, and limiting myself to this quotation—which does not need a context—seemed preferable to embarking on something longer, which a gap in my memory would perhaps have forced me to leave in suspense. Furthermore, it is a song that Max Jacob showed me sometime in the past, so that, thus associated with the image of the writer who was my first guide, it bears a specific sentimental value and seems to me richer in poetry than if I had discovered it another way. Finally, I was quite sure that those two lines would be understood by my listeners as an allusion to the departure which, the next day, would close off the flowering days I had lived in China. No choice, therefore, could be better: a pretty song to which I am particularly attached, very French, and completely suited to the occasion—what friendlier homage could I pay to our Chinese hosts and hostesses? What I had not foreseen, despite certain misgivings, was that the period during which I took this trip—that in which Mao Tse-tung's maxim *Let a hundred flowers bloom and let the new emerge from the old* set the general tone—would soon be followed by a less liberal period; tolerance, then, would no longer be in season and, seeing the "Hundred Flowers" fade behind gates, henceforth closed, I would say to myself that by singing that song—whose sad and tender simplicity I was taught to love by a man who remained present through his works and through the equal beauty of his legend—I was uttering, without knowing it, prophetic words. Certainly, in the China of today (the China of industrialized communes, which has just now in its turn reached the age of unreason in which the people are manufacturing their atomic bomb), I would be less at ease than in the China of almost ten years ago. Certainly, also, if I went back there I would experience upon my return, with even more acuity than in 1955, the impression of having returned to the fold. But it is no less certain that, even while knowing how much it would cost me to give up certain forms of civilization governed by the law of supply and demand, I am decidedly not close to separating myself from China: it seems to me impossible that it should have, today, lost everything of what I saw there. In any case, how could I turn away from this country when it represents, more than ever, *the red spot of hope* for the Asiatic and African nations that are no longer officially subjugated, but that people are endeavoring to put back under the yoke in other ways?

Among various questions that have remained in suspense, this one at least has been clearly stated: even though indelibly European, I remain faithful to China as to all the countries whose exoticism had, in the beginning, attracted me. But it is no less clear that this statement, the final polishing of an idea that does not follow from any decision, is just as conventional as the information given in an epilogue by authors of earlier times, for whom a novel could not close without the reader being informed about the fate of all the characters who had wriggled about in it like shadows. Even though I had decided not to conclude, didn't I believe that it was impossible for me to be done, here, with an essay begun some twenty-five years ago without saying what had happened, not to puppets that I had imagined, but to the various elements that I have been mixing up along a path followed with a perseverance at which I am the first to be surprised? As for the Chinese idea, I have just pointed out that it now lives tranquilly in its hole, like the honest person of whom one learns that after his multiple tribulations he is at last spinning out peaceful days in his little house in the country. Must I report that a certain other idea, in just recompense for its merits, is having a brilliant career, even explain—in the way one recounts that a wicked man has been converted to good or vice versa—how yet another (what would be revealed, perhaps, by a close examination) has been transformed into its opposite, undergoing the metamorphosis that affects so many thoughts when one takes them as far as they can go? To draw up a report of this kind would oblige me to reread everything and would lead to my getting bogged down again. Thus, thrusting away all systematic research, I will confine myself to a few of the addenda that would be called for by the practice of narratives of earlier times.

Even though still eager for walks, the bitch Dine is no longer as alert as at the time when I saw her in a dream rushing headlong from the top of a cliff. In human years, she would now be at least seventy-five, and, for quite a long time, I have thought that instead of having in one's home a creature whose life is merely an abridged version of our own, it would be better—because this would be less depressing—to have one (an elephant, for example) superior enough to us in longevity so that its decline would not be perceptible to us.

In several temples of Kyoto and Nara, there were statues that reminded me of other statues of an exacerbated baroque style which I had seen in China. But not one of them touched me as much as the strangely leaping figure of the Taoist chapel of the environs of Kunming, even though they were of a higher quality and manifestly older. The paintbrush this one was carrying I found again on one of those Japanese sculptures, so that it cannot be a question of a purely circumstantial attribute, as we had been given to understand by our very uncertain guide of the Mountain of the West as he told us the dramatic story of the author of the gilded statue.

Sinanthropus Pekinensis, whose cave I had visited at Zhoukoudian like that of an Adam or a Prometheus, saw his record for antiquity beaten, and by far, by *Zinjanthropus Boisei* first, then by *Homo habilis*, both of whom left behind, in the region of Tanganyika (today joined with Zanzibar to form Tanzania), remains because of which Africa has assumed the rank of the continent where there came into being, among other curious examples of the animal kingdom, the first adumbrations of humanity (in other words of a species capable of fabricating tools and endowed with enough cerebral substance to be supposed to be capable of speaking, if not already of discoursing).

For a long time I preserved in my bedroom (above my bed, on one of the boards of a set of bookshelves) the prettily imitated bird that a little Chinese girl had given me. Yet it simply disappeared one day and this flight seemed to me bizarre. But an electrician had come to install an outlet there and I said to myself that as he was working he had knocked down the bird—very light and rather poorly balanced on its feet—and that this pleasing simulacrum, dropped in a corner and reduced to scarcely more than a formless little heap, had then been carried off and thrown out inadvertently when, the worker having left, the housecleaning had been done.

Stranger, certainly, was the disappearance, in the course of subsequent works, of the provision of barbiturates that I had reconstituted during a trip to Berne, where I had procured some for myself at two pharmacies without the least formality except that in the second of these shops, I had to assure the young saleswoman that I was a foreigner and just passing through, as though only the natives or inhabitants of Switzerland were worth protecting against the possible damages of a toxic product. No one in my home could have filched this provision, concealed with care, and I wondered if, without my remembering it, I had not hidden it again, this time with such cunning that it was no longer possible for me to know where. My investigations coming to nothing, I ended by imagining that after all it was not out of the question that I had myself done away with it in a fit of somnambulism or in a state bordering on it. But that is a hypothesis of last resort and, as far as I know, of such improbability that the enigma remains intact.

If there are vanished objects which one would tend almost to doubt really existed, so inexplicable does their absence remain, there are, on the other hand, some that one believed to be mythical and whose real existence one suddenly discovers. This is the case of the "drum-trumpet," the toy that I had ardently coveted when I was a child and which, later, I admitted belonged to the domain of reverie. Yet since I told that story, I have had the surprise of finding such a toy in the hands of a little Algerian boy whose mother placed him in our care for a few days while the father, who was fighting for independence, was imprisoned in Fresnes. One blows into the trumpet while maneuvering a pull-knob, which activates the little stick that strikes the very flat body of the drum incorporated into the instrument. But little Malik, dreaming perhaps as much as I had done at his age of a wonder that he did not possess, preferred to use it as if it were a camera.

The fact that from a distance we may no longer be able to decide whether the thing that inflamed us with a mad longing existed as a thing that was the object of a desire or, on the other hand, as the pure expression of that desire—such an uncertainty may trouble us, but not, by far, to the same degree as being induced, by testimony that does not accord with our own, to doubt the reality of a fact that one has considered certain. At a dinner party in the home of mutual friends, someone rather young and likable tells me that the gymnasium at 5 rue Pierre-Guérin—situated for me in a time almost as remote as that of the "drum-trumpet"—still exists and that it still matches the portrait I drew of it; but this conscientious reader adds that he found nothing there resembling the stairwell cage I spoke of, that cage into which (dashing out of his house like a whirlwind because his wife, giving birth and bleeding abundantly, needed immediate help) the director of the gymnasium had leaped in a single bound. For several days, I was very disturbed by this statement, which undeniably contradicted what I had written. I felt I had been caught in the act, if not of lying, at the very least of making a mistake, and this mistake seemed to me not only the sort of mistake that could render my entire work suspect but, in my own eyes, a sign of a disquieting capacity to drift. Thus it was with real pleasure that, after reflecting at length on the possible causes of my false report, I recalled that the director in fact lived in a building in the rue des Perchamps, quite close to the rue Pierre-Guérin, whence the fusion of the two places that had been effected in my memory, an error, finally, venial enough so that the authenticity of my tale was only slightly damaged by it.

No doubt, the fragile edifice I have raised with materials that are often old needs more than one replastering of this kind. But the few instances of poor workmanship by which it remains certainly affected hardly count, compared to a defect more serious than an inexactness, here and there, of detail: this book (which ought to be my own truth, and about which I have occasionally gone so far as to think that, writing it being enough to justify me, it perhaps authorized me to lie concerning what was not part of it) keeps escaping me, for it is traversed by certain themes of which—since I am seized by them rather than they seized by me—I am not managing to unearth the secret, probably because they extend down to a level as deep as the unformulated taboo that would perhaps have obscurely restrained me, had my mother still been here, from paying the most deadly insult to the life she gave me by trying to rid myself of it.

If I announce that I have at last written the article on Césaire but that the overview of the African arts remains incomplete (because of an excess and no longer because of a deficiency, for, too prolix, my coauthor and I are being obliged to do some major reworking), these eleventh-hour pieces of information have only an anecdotal value. What one ought to do is not to satisfy one's professional conscience according to protocol, with clarifications and revelations that have no more weight than standard formulae inserted into a contract, but to be able to say, for example, why this ambiguous female image has retained so much charm for me ever since my adolescence: the moving spirit of Alexander's Ragtime Band, a group of probably English minstrels that appeared in the old Alhambra in the rue de Malte, when each attraction there was still a "number," announced on either side of the stage by illuminated numerals corresponding to the position it occupied in the program. A blond figure whose delicacy and vivacity contrasted with the deliberately loutish looks of the musicians in full plantation dress, she first appeared decked out as a young boy. Then, after a procession in silhouette and the flight by leaps of all the members of the troupe (including her), no doubt jumping over the source of light by which the silhouettes were formed, one saw her in an elaborate evening gown at the front of a stage box isolated by one projector, and each instrumentalist went from the wings to the hall to address his serenade to her. Led by this pretty creature in a new guise, dressed, I believe, in a sort of sailor's costume of pink material (the garb of a chorus girl and almost of a little child that seems to me now to have been the tunic of a kindly Hermes Psychopomp guiding the souls with songs and dances), the finale had as its setting a backdrop reproducing a page of music: the famous song *I want to be down home in Dixie*, which belongs to the music-hall repertory of some fifty years ago, unless it is one of those American "coon songs" of which, at about the same period, I possessed a collection; each of the notes legible on the great white page opened like a porthole to frame the face of an instrumentalist, daubed with an intense black except for the periphery of the mouth, which, very pale, simulated thick gluttonous lips.

One disturbing thing is that perhaps especially when—out of private embarrassment, an incapacity to explain, or repugnance at involving myself in a long analysis—I note something, without claiming to give the key to it, that, although I myself am blind, I show myself truly openly. It may therefore be that others, more detached, immediately see the signification of this trait, one of those that would be all the more eloquent if I said nothing about them: my insistence on describing—like a Don Juan cataloguing his conquests—the forms of women or girls who, most of them, were to me only figures and who all, in their equal imponderability now, appear to me as nymphs who arose at various moments of that twofold odyssey, the wandering of my life, though it was not very adventurous, and that of its projection on paper in a succession of overlapping insights. In New York, a beautiful, armorless Valkyrie had piloted me, holding me by the hand each time, at least, that we had to cross a street or an avenue, and, in China (where the studious Cloud-the-color-of-pearl had been our hostess and the most attentive of our guides and interpreters), the hand of a schoolgirl had never left mine during the entire walk we took through the rooms of a social center for children. In a dream, a pleasant Antillean woman, whose fingers became active at the same time as mine, helped me to gather in a drawer my scattered belongings and to suspend the whole thing from a sort of beam of a scales. At the Claude-Bernard Hospital, a friend whom I falsely recognized—an angel who appeared suddenly and quickly disappeared—kept watch one morning standing by my bedside, then a charming physical therapist (brown-haired and as chubby as the girl who, on the boulevard Beaumarchais, talked to me about Taormina) taught me the motion appropriate for relieving a certain discomfort caused by my wounded throat and, shortly afterward, pointed out to me which way I ought to go if I wanted to take advantage of the airy tranquility of the garden. In this same hospital, the memory of my Aunt Claire began to haunt me in the guise of other phantasms, before appearing expressly as a muse whose immaterial presence encourages one or (a comparison less strained) like a figurehead presiding over a difficult return to the life of which my resuscitation was merely the preliminary phase. In the parenthesis in which she was situated, not only by exoticism and social distances, but by the particular circumstances of the "phony war," hadn't Khadidja, too, been an image, with whom I had chanced to have an ephemeral but close love relationship and a relationship of simple physical familiarity, like the afternoon on which that girl whose dark look later made me regard her as an angel of death had washed me as a nanny or a nurse might have done? Lastly, for some three years now, isn't it still a female guide descended from some planet or other to whom I turn now and then, when I dream of the other Algerian (this one a "pied noir," a native of Sidi-bel-Abbès), an expert caretaker, pretty, gay, and comforting, who, in the clinic where I was staying, was the main one to occupy herself with me when I underwent the operation that, for many men of our climates, marks the definitive entry into old age, just as in Black Africa circumcision marks the passage from the state of little boy to that of young man?

Aging tends to incline one to religiosity . . . And what, after all, are these nymphs, these Venuses or diorama saints if not pious images with which, confronting a future more and more constricted, I surround myself for reassurance? Not that I—a Louis XI with wrinkled face under his hat superstitiously garnished with a circle of blessed medals—expect from this a guard or some help in my salvation, but because it is always consoling to think (even if it is not at all useful) that at several points in our life we have encountered something that resembled a miracle. It is religiosity nevertheless, for to seek support from these images which are merely memories, and of which one, even, is the image of an image, since the original appeared to me only in a dream, is to call, not upon living beings but upon beings as unreal as the gods invented by men because they lacked the daring to recognize that they were entirely dependent upon themselves. No more alive than these gods, and, after all, absolutely safe: icons on my walls, portraits amassed little by little in a family album, or flowers commemoratively slipped between two pages, whereas there are gods of commerce no less difficult than the god of the harshest and most demanding human creatures. If I reject easy solutions, how can I fail to mistrust these images, objects of soft daydreams that probably humor what is least avowable in me and distance me from naked reality without leading me to the diamond of poetic reality!

Without leading me to the diamond . . . A complaint I make against my egerias, as though, even when I want to begin prospecting the virgin lands of poetry again, I wish to be held by the hand and guided like a child. This child that persists in me despite chronology and which, today as yesterday, invents fairy godmothers for itself in lieu of the other, inexorably terrestrial fairies with which a man must come face to face; this perpetually anachronistic child, who has occasionally believed he was behaving like an adult but has always needed someone to show him the way: those trips, especially, from which I would have retreated if I had had to make them under my own direction (Egypt, where I knew a friend would pilot me, and where, using as a pretext in my own eyes a completely surrealist repugnance for touristic activities, I refrained from visiting the glorious Valley of the Kings because I would have had to go there alone; Black Africa, which I traversed profiting from that sort of organized trip which is a mission of which one is not the leader; China, which was served up as though on a platter but for which the wait, all the more enervating because I did not know if everything would not be ruined by the presence of a spoilsport in our delegation, had put me into such a fine state that one day I made as though to break my head against the walls, so unlikely did my imminent departure seem); those great decisions under the aegises of people or countries considered to be models (Nerval, for example, or, now, China, about which I have trouble accepting the fact that it may not be above all reproach); lastly, this very quest itself, over which preside—faceless mothers, such as were shown not long ago in so-called metaphysical Italian painting—those notions in which I put my trust, almost blindly, for reasons less of the mind than of the heart: authenticity, communication.

"Authenticity," which is my great watchword but has no meaning except when contrasting a true object with an unmistakable forgery, so that one can make it a touchstone neither for approving or condemning works which there are no grounds to reject as apocrypha, plagiarisms, or mendacious accounts, nor for distinguishing in ourselves what we ought to treat as our most precious possession.

"Communication," less imbued with religiosity than "communion," but just as nebulous as soon as one uses it in a loftier sense than that of the communicating door, telephone communication, or communication to a scholarly society. Recalling me to undisguised reality, my crisis of several years ago and its aftereffects, now cleared up, have led me, finally, to mistrust this term, which, usable on the level of strictly verbal communication as well as on the level of channels and communications more subtle than roads and railways, communicates too easily to the least precise idea its appearance of dry precision. Whether misapprehension or dishonest simplification, I embraced under its heading two things in truth most unclear, and which cannot be reduced to their merely social aspect, as that heading slyly invited me to do: aesthetic communication (to move the other by causing him to share what one has thought or felt) and amorous communication (to be moved by each other). Not only did I think thus to possess the idea that, when the time came, would help me to put clearly into perspective the essential part of what I had defined, but, playing the saint, I gave a moral turn to my two great aspirations, since, in both cases, what was involved was, when taken to an extreme, merging with others. However, naïve or not, the operation was especially inconclusive because love and poetry—I neglected this point—are far from representing the whole of human communication, the latter being capable of occurring, beyond all effusion, in a piece of work or any other act undertaken together with another person. What is more, it was defective in that I would not be able to claim, without deceit as to my deeper motives, that in life as in art my great aim is to "communicate" with another: can I, in effect, posit that to achieve a tacit agreement is what matters most to me, whereas through poetry—that poetry which I would like to seize hold of again and which makes this book a search for the lost ring or an indirect attempt at a return to the fold—I want to contrive to enter into close contact with the world, in the same way that I expect the act of love to bring me into close contact with nature itself and not just with another person? What is more, if love and poetry were merely particular instances of commerce with our fellow human beings, how could they so madly elate us and transport us so far outside ourselves?

However, the fact that love and poetry both present themselves as marvelous excesses is only an analogy, which in no way authorizes one to mingle literary life and sentimental life in the foolish way I did (to the point of making a complete mess), when, driven in theory by my thirst for a full and entire communication, I embarked upon what were in practice only the commonplace affairs of a pen-pusher in seventh heaven because he had met some female admirers. One of these, the most knowledgeable and perhaps the most sincere, was for me not physically attractive, but so powerful was my longing for a woman's approval that something nevertheless was initiated between us. As for the other, who captivated me enough so that despite the more than seven years that have elapsed I can recall, not without some rancor, that—a bad lover, without any doubt—I never managed to elicit from her throat the word *tu*, which would have been the sign that between her and me, even if momentarily, all distance had been abolished, certainly in every respect we communicated so little that I had wept, one day, even less over the quarrel that was separating us than over the philistinism evinced by her remarks. With one as with the other, I had at first played the role of the man in high office to whom novices come to ask advice, and my weakness had been, in both cases, to throw myself, a dog seizing a bone, on what was offered to me: the attention of a woman who had appeared from outside and, theoretically, was avid, as I still am, to discover, in literary terms, her formula. To carry on a dialogue with one, and to try, with the other, to experience what would be for me the last avatar of love (in the manner in which China had appeared to me as the incarnation of the distant voyage that would be followed by no other) was quite natural. But I am ashamed of having yielded to the ridiculous author vanity that was slumbering in me, and of having allowed it to bite the bait so voraciously. Not to mention the fact that to indulge in this double affair, not even cynically but out of an incapacity to control events, and to conduct myself (a schoolboy with muddled emotions) toward each of my two accomplices as if the virtues of the other had perfected her own, was to put up with a strange vaudeville in order to satisfy my appetite for total illumination through one flesh and one mind.

Further specifics that are, in the end, necessary: what I retain especially about communication is the moment when it seems to establish itself, an instant that is dazzling but limited, like all those moments in which one could believe time had been shattered but which do not cause it to fly asunder except illusorily, since they are followed by an indeterminate series of other, similar instants. To communicate, to merge with the other—is this what one so often seeks, in love or in poetry, through those vertiginous instants for which one feels prepared to sacrifice either a solid understanding between two beings between whom everything is transparent, or the intimacy which crystal-clear words spoken without passion or agitation may establish between us and the things (or the people) who surround us? Isn't it rather because we love this vertigo in itself, as it is, beyond all reason, and are simply anxious that, shared, it be true not merely for us alone, as are both the dream and the sort of provoked hallucination framing what is euphemistically called solitary pleasure? If even in vertigo I demand this sharing, it is not for itself: in almost all that I do, even if I do it on a whim, I need someone to play opposite me, for otherwise it would seem to me that it is only half-done, whence the high value I attach not only to a reciprocal love, but to friendship, to a common passion, to a certain kind of literary recognition, and hence, equally, despite my penchant, repressed only with difficulty, for bouts of drunkenness, the repugnance that I have always had to becoming intoxicated all by myself.

"Communication," "authenticity," what rotten planks such words are! As though they spoke volumes, I rarely use them without a slight inner tremor, although the indecisiveness of their boundaries could fairly draw down upon me, from my interlocutor, the following remark, accompanied by a grimace of scorn: *You don't know what you're saying!* It was by thus attributing to me an incoherence close to the mental chaos in which a baby is plunged that in the old days my brothers would tease me, and I was frightfully vexed to hear my older brothers intimate to me that my talk, like everything that I had in my head, was merely infantile verbiage. To know, to say: to have knowledge, to express through speech. In fact, isn't it common that, even in maturity, one does not know what one is saying, since, as one uses words one often distends them or causes them to slide from one acceptation to another, to the point of making impossible, for oneself as for anyone else, any valid knowledge of what it was their mission to express in the moment in which one used them? This is the case for these terms, loaded, for me, with the magic of key words, whereas it is because of their elasticity, their very uncertainty, that they can be endowed with a content so rich.

But also, what is the matter with me, that I have chosen to theorize instead of attempting, if I wanted to justify myself and convince others, to do it in an exclusively practical way: speaking my own language and stopping up my ears with wax in order not to be seduced by the accents of some siren (including the joy of awakening echoes), as I follow my own sinuous trajectory, obeying only my own inclinations and leaving to the reader the burden of determining where my journey was leading, if in fact it was leading to some definable place. Age, besides, augments the confusion, not only because the senses and faculties become dull, but because one often tends (with a seriousness that is comic if it is not hypocritical) to treat as questions that are still being asked those which, one forgets, have long since resolved themselves on their own: love, for example, even though I would not be able to respond to it except more poorly than ever, if I happened to inspire it, and even though, on the other hand, I know I am joined to a companion by bonds such that life without her seems inconceivable to me (for I can say, without bragging, but in full awareness of the lost-child side of me that has always prevented me from doing without a firm support, that only my cowardice before the imminence of the mortal act could induce me to survive her if the future were to sever, by her death, an undivided couple like the one I incarnated, by myself alone and for myself alone, before changing into the old actress fêted so long ago); poetry, which has become a necessity for me because it is my only recourse, now that the die has been cast and I cannot dream of transfiguring my life either by love or by a great journey (which today I envisage from the perspective of a diversion or my professional occupation, nothing more), nor by revolutionary activity (knowing too well the limits of my dedication and what a distance there is between approving of the goals of the revolution and acting as a revolutionary).

When obliteration by death or senility is no longer seen as a fate but expected as an evil that is preparing to strike one, it happens—and this is my case—that one loses even the desire to undertake anything at all: one evaluates the little time one has available still, a time that is constricted, with no relation to that of the periods of one's life when it was out of the question to think that an enterprise might lack the time it needed to develop freely, and this cuts short all motivation. In the same way, even if one has long been accustomed to it, as I have, it is a hard thing to be aware, each day, that the night—henceforth obstructed by fatigue or sleep—will no longer be that infinitely open period during which a man whom nothing has weakened can love and spend himself without counting. Whether I am more lucid, more vulnerable than another man, or more greedily occupied with my own person, it seems to me that someone whose existence has thus gone from unlimited to limited lives in a sort of asphyxia. How can this be remedied except through an expedient by means of which, in a place where on all sides I run up against implacable limits, a breath of the limitless could still flow? As last resources, art and poetry offer themselves as means of loosening the grip . . . But isn't it a pity to diminish them to the point of treating them as replacement products allowing one to palliate the distressing penury of old age! An ignoble role, I will not deny it . . . However, this poor function—tempering final defeat with a shred of victory—is not the only wretchedness that art and poetry conceal under their mantle of grandeur, and, pursuing this farther, oughtn't one to regard it as the least fragile of their justifications?

Now more than ever, they in fact respond to an immediate need, and, if they are capable of holding fast when the other reasons for living have crumbled away, this is a proof of their strength. I am talking here, of course, about an art or a poetry that cannot be reduced to art for art's sake or to a pure classicism: art and poetry cannot be made, as my torment demands that they do, bearers of the limitless unless they are animated by that immeasurable ambition—to measure oneself (whatever form may be taken by this challenge) against the incommensurate. The cloud on the horizon is that one would have to be sure, for the trick to work, that the crushing defeat spared that particular faculty, and this would be to ignore the terrible pressure of physiological contingencies and to gamble on a miracle.

Aside from this, the proximity of my annihilation (the destiny of all living beings), what, then, do I have a right especially to complain of? Materially, and in my love life, I have suffered, up to the present, only damages whose sum does not exceed the norm; my regular job is one of the least tiresome conceivable and, what is more, I have become a writer, in other words a variety of artist, namely what I dreamed of being when I was very young, while fretting and fuming at the idea that I would never succeed in this, at least with a more glittering title than that of stubborn amateur. The hitch is that I have not become in any way the artist (or the poet) that I imagined: someone who has stepped through the looking glass. But here again, it is not a matter of a particular curse of which I have been the victim. I now know enough great artists, and I believe I know them well enough, to perceive that I was the dupe of an illusion: even if he is a genius, the artist, within himself, does not live as a legend or a cartoon; despite his occasional getaways, he remains mired down in our congenital swamp just as much as those who, contemplating him from outside, may suppose that his art transforms everything for him. A great disappointment, certainly, considering what my childish naïveté allowed me to anticipate in case I were to take my place, even if in a modest rank, in the phalanx of the elect. Nevertheless, the fact is that my capacity for enthusiasm with respect to the beauty that issues from a human brain has not been diminished by this to the degree that, ordinarily, I tend to think it has. Stumbling in my own work, I have often despaired of literature in general and not only of mine. However, there are books that I read, theater performances that I attend, pictures that I look at, or pieces of music that I listen to with a profound joy. There is no longer any question, in these minutes of spontaneous reconciliation with art, of thinking that literature has no meaning or is a perpetual misinterpretation. What I vilify when I see it from the inside retains all its value when I see it from the outside. If the writings that cost me so much pain and irritation were equal to those which, when they come to me from others, procure me this joy, and if I could know it, I would then have some reason for believing that by conducting myself, in my area of specialization, in somewhat the same way as those shock workers honored by the countries of the East, I am a thousand leagues from having obtained what I originally desired, but have not entirely wasted the time that was allotted to me. In which direction the future will decide this, I can hardly imagine; but I foresee that in any case its response will not be that which, if I could know it, might satisfy me. Pointless as it may be to grill myself about this, to pose such a question is nevertheless not absolutely negative, for it proves to me that the flood of my pessimism allows there to emerge the rock of at least one article of faith: to ask myself if some Last Judgment will or will not classify me among those who have not wasted their time is to admit in effect that the game is not so incoherent that there may not be winners or losers.

Inside, outside. My life as, in detail, it unfolds within me and as, broadly, it appears to others. In becoming a writer, I opted for a certain representation of the world or rather for a particular way of representing it (reading it through a grid more sensitive than the grids of rationality). I opted at the same time for a certain morality (the rejection of calculations too stingily reasonable), and, even though I decided not to raise it to the level of a system, it continues to direct my actions. The same was true of becoming an ethnographer, a profession which, much more than from the scientific angle, had attracted me as a means of coming into contact with living realities, and which in the end became an auxiliary of the first profession, by accustoming me to observe and by helping me to broaden as well as to humanize my conceptions. From this inner morality that governs me without, or almost without, my knowledge, though it has not spared me from lowering myself to several vile actions (which I would perhaps not cover with this shamed half-silence if they had been more boldly criminal) and also has not stopped me from stewing ridiculously about trifles in my daily routine, what has resulted, outwardly? A conduct whose positive aspects oscillate between a somewhat boy-scoutish doing-good and a somewhat lady-patronness good behavior: obeying the main commands of the union to which I belong; participating from time to time, without great energy, in a street demonstration; signing statements, petitions, and protests whose purpose is to defend sometimes the rights of individuals, sometimes the freedom of nations; subscribing the support of a few progressive or antiracist organizations; contributing my legal testimony to people fighting against repression; in private life, opening myself to confidences and giving comfort, by taking care to establish (with arguments that scarcely have an impact on me) that life is worth living and by affirming, if necessary, that to kill oneself would only be an avowal of defeat; when the opportunity presents itself, showing myself to be financially helpful or obliging; without being able to flatter myself, in this case, that I am giving assistance to someone who deserves it, but moved solely by the fear of being taxed with niggardliness, giving generally large tips and, when it appeals to me, or sometimes also moved by superstition ("the good Lord will repay you"), dropping a coin into the wooden bowl or palm of a beggar. So, a lot of fuss about nothing. I have sweated blood and water, and hurled fire and flame, to end up, in my daily practice, being a man like any number of other bourgeoisie who claim to be progressive, an author accepted into the anthologies and in whom perhaps his effort at sincerity will be praised, his exactness of expression, even his ingenious junctions and interconnections, in the absence of that mysterious thing which (in the work of certain people) fulgurates in even the least phrase and which I believe to be the most important thing.

A poor gift which fate has presented to me, I am left, however, with the scar inscribed on my neck that I have compared to an initiatory mark: a sort of "tree of life," as was, in its ambiguity, the black equilateral triangle that my half-sleep had shown me, resting successively on one of its sides and on one of its points. If there is no great poetry except that which is *total* (conjoining life and death), how could one make life and poetry truly coincide without putting, at least, the tip of one of his shoes on the threshold of death?

Must I, who will have as posthumous viaticum neither hanged-man's rope nor revolver bullet, any more than a Harar or cut ear—because I would be making up my mind too late, now, for it to have any meaning other than the suicide of a ruined man or a doomed invalid—view this scar, since I lack an attribute of the sort included in the figures of saints displayed in churches and museums, as something analogous to the cross of the brave or the Tonkin medal, which in other times and places one buried with the old dotard parent to whom it belonged? Empty boasting aside, it seems to me to constitute in any case the fibula (the jewel, whether clasp or brooch, with which one may close a garment by bringing together its two edges, otherwise separated like the two lips presented by my throat, which had been split over several centimeters), the fibula with which everything that I have on my mind is summed up, gathered by means of a sign drawn on my very flesh that will excuse me—but this is not to say I know what the future will actually bring—from committing myself to the tedious composition of the *Fibulae* that I was planning to write in order to attach firmly, and dominate at last, my scattered perceptions.

This mark, whose curiously clawed form calls to mind an insect with six legs that has incrusted itself under my Adam's apple, remains for me the object not of a retrospective horror, but of a pride out of proportion to an act only half accomplished (a failure without which, in truth, there would certainly be a *he* whose image a few people would preserve, but not the shadow of an *I* to talk about my pride or my horror). Like those veterans who dwell on their war because they have not known any other great adventure, and who, should the occasion arise, like to display the traces of their wounds, I refer back to my failed suicide as to the great, adventurous moment that represents, in the course of my life, so nearly free of difficulties as it has been, the only major risk I have ever dared to take. And it also seems to me it was at that moment, as I married life and death, drunkenness and sharpness of vision, fervor and negation, that I embraced most closely that fascinating thing, always to be pursued because never altogether grasped, which one might think was deliberately designated by a feminine noun: poetry.

MICHEL LEIRIS (1901–1990), born in Paris, was an early surrealist, an ethnographer, and a prominent and influential writer of poetry, essays, a novel, and, most important, the four-volume, thirty-five-year project of autobiographical and linguistic self-reflection *The Rules of the Game*, of which *Fibrils* is the third volume to appear in English.

LYDIA DAVIS, recipient of the 2013 Man Booker International Prize for her fiction, is the author of, most recently, *Can't and Won't* (2014) and *The Collected Stories* (2009). She has translated many works from French and other languages, including Proust's *Swann's Way* (2003) and Flaubert's *Madame Bovary* (2010).